HERCULES
The RAF Workhorse

By

Andy Muniandy

This is Copy No. *608* in a limited edition
of 5,000 copies

the author,

Andy Muniandy

Associate Member RAeS   MBE, RAF

First Published in 1993 by A Muniandy,
15 Downs View Road, Swindon, Wilts SN3 1NS

© A Muniandy 1993

ISBN 0 9522608 0 8

Designed and edited by Jeremy Flack of Aviation Photographs International - Swindon 0793 497179
Cover design by Paul Ridgwell at Disctech Ltd. Fax No: 0249 817017
Proofreading by J.A. Osborough
Typeset by Stables Studio - Swindon. Fax No 0793 766324

Printed by Sanon Corporation Sdn. Bhd., Kuala Lumpur, Malaysia. Fax No: 603 - 2421639

Colour Separation by Colour Match Sdn. Bhd. Kuala Lumpur, Malaysia. Fax No: 603 - 2453560

HERCULES

THE RAF WORKHORSE

By

Andy Muniandy

THE ROYAL AIR FORCE BENEVOLENT FUND

The "Herc" has been serving the Royal Air Force for more than a quarter of a century, but the RAF Benevolent Fund has served the RAF for three times as long! Since 1919, in fact, when Lord Trenchard first set it up. The Fund has come a long way since then, when the welfare expenditure for its first year was £919. In the years that have followed, the Royal Air Force has not only won its spurs, it has forged proud traditions - but at terrible cost. Those years have seen dramatic changes. Aircraft technology has developed at an almost unimaginable rate, while conditions of service, pensions and social security have all improved dramatically. But some things, like the spirit and dedication of the men and women who serve or who have served, have not changed. Another, sadly, is the need for some of these people to be helped over difficult times, since no Government can institute and maintain a system that copes adequately with all eventualities. During those intervening years the remit of the Fund was extended to what it is today, relieving distress or need among past and present members, irrespective of rank or sex, of the Royal Air Force, the Womens' Services, the Royal Auxiliary Air Force and the Reserve Forces, including their widows, children and other dependants. Since 1988, welfare expenditure has exceeded £7 million each year, while the Fund's total expenditure over its lifetime has reached more than £110 million, spent helping some 800,000 people. We need an average of £20,000 a day for our work. Any help you can give will be most gratefully accepted by the Director Appeals at 67 Portland Place, London - and by all those who will benefit from your generosity.

Foreword

Hercules, the legendary figure of Greek mythology, was the personification of physical strength whose primary role was the protection of man. In times of need, men depend upon the strength of Hercules. Similarly, during the past 26 years, the Lockheed C-130 aircraft most aptly named Hercules in service with the Royal Air Force has built up a splendid reputation for strength and reliability.

Every year since 1967, operating from military airfields, major civil airports and rough, unprepared landing strips alike, at all hours of the day and night in all sorts of weather from the poles to the equator, RAF Hercules crews have logged many thousands of flying hours on training tasks, air transport and transport support operations, and mercy missions in many different parts of the world. All in all, the RAF Hercules force has flown well over one million flying hours with a record of safety and achievement which bears tribute not only to the Lockheed Aircraft Company, but also to the aircrews and ground staff of the Royal Air Force.

The Hercules was not built for speed, but for the job she was designed to do she is well nigh unbeatable. The aircraft is capable of lifting a substantial payload over thousands of miles, and is well suited to operations in the field where knocks are the norm and the crews are often called upon to operate the aircraft to its limits. The Hercules has always proved itself to be very strong and reliable; she always delivers the goods, and she inspires love in those who fly her. In some parts of the world amongst starving people the arrival of a Hercules has meant salvation.

However, the story of the RAF Hercules is not just a success story about an aircraft and aircrews, it is the story of an RAF station. The Hercules entered service at RAF Lyneham in 1967 and, since the mid-1970s Lyneham has been the home of all RAF Hercules. The whole station is tuned to the needs of the Hercules and every member of the team plays an essential part to ensure that, whenever the call comes, Hercules is ready. In truth the Hercules is only as strong as Royal Air Force Lyneham is strong.

For my part it has been an enormous privilege to serve as a member of a team from time to time and I treasure many wonderful memories of the Hercules and the people who served with me at Royal Air Force Lyneham. I am delighted to note that the proceeds from this book will go in part to the Royal Air Force Benevolent Fund. Some men look to the Hercules for help in times of need, others turn to the RAF Benevolent Fund; either way they are not left wanting.

Air Commodore J Hardstaff MBE
Station Commander
RAF Lyneham
(Sept'79-Nov'81)

This book is not an official RAF publication, it is the result of much hardwork by one individual. With little or no financial or practical support, but with a great deal of initiative and determination, Master Engineer Andy Muniandy has successfully completed this ambitious project. I know that he persuaded numerous colleagues to order copies and I am sure that they will not be disappointed

The text and the photographs tell the story of the RAF Hercules and its many achievements during the past 26 years. The book is full of fascinating facts and figures about this famous aircraft and I am sure that it will appeal to a wide audience.

Group Captain D N Adams BSc, MRAeS, RAF
Station Commander
RAF Lyneham
(1991-1993)

CONTENTS

CHAPTER 1

The Royal Air Force Hercules

Following intensive discussions with the Ministry of Defence, the then Labour Government, headed by the Prime Minister Mr Harold Wilson, ordered a total of sixty-six of the Lockheed Hercules aircraft.

The Handley Page Hastings C.1

The Lockheed Hercules C.1

This Hercules fleet was to replace the ageing Hastings and Beverleys which had provided the Royal Air Force with its long range transport capacity for many years.

The older of the two types that the Hercules was planned to replace was the Handley Page Hastings, the prototype of which made its maiden flight on 7th May 1946 at Wittering. The production version - the C.1 - flew on 25th April 1947 and No 47 Squadron was the first to be equipped with this new long range transport aircraft. The Hastings had a crew of five and carried either 50 troops or 30 paratroopers. It was an all-metal stressed skin construction and powered by four Bristol Hercules 106 piston engines, each producing 1,675hp which gave it a maximum speed of 348 mph at 2,200ft and a normal range of 1,690 miles.

No 70 Squadron was the first overseas unit in the Middle East to be re-equipped, followed by number 48 at Changi, Singapore. Other Hastings equipped

squadrons were Nos 36, 47, 53, 59, 70, 99, 114, 116, 202, 242 and 297. The Hastings was used extensively during "Operation Plain Fare" - the Berlin Airlift - although the rapid loading and unloading of freight using the side doors was a disadvantage. Its decline in global use commenced in 1959 with the introduction of the comfort provided by the Bristol Britannia. From then on the Hastings was used solely as a tactical aircraft. Following fatigue problems, the Hastings bade its farewell at RAF Colerne on 6th January 1968 with a four ship formation. A total of 146 production Hastings were built for the RAF.

Following its introduction into RAF service, the Hastings had subsequently been joined by the Blackburn Beverley which first entered service in March 1956 with No 47 Squadron at Abingdon. Other squadrons to be similarly equipped were Nos 30 and 53, with No 84 in the Middle East and No 34 in the Far East.

The Beverley was a high wing monoplane powered by four 2,850hp Bristol Centaurus 273 piston engines. It had a crew of four and could lift a total of 45,000lb of freight in its large hold. Alternatively a total of 70 paratroops or 94 troops could be carried. With a wing span of 162ft, it was not only the largest aircraft in the RAF but the first aircraft designed for aerial delivery of heavy army equipment. Freight could be easily loaded and unloaded from the aft through large "clam shell rear-loading doors" which were removable for air drops. Passengers could be

The Blackburn Beverley C.1

accommodated on the second deck in the tail boom. Despite a maximum range of 1,300 miles the Beverley suffered from a short range of only 230 miles when flying at maximum payload. Besides its low speed it also suffered from lack of pressurisation.

The Beverley was used extensively for para drops, casualty evacuation, and supply drops as well as being used during a number of relief operations to civilian populations. It also saw action in Aden, Yemen, Kuwait, Borneo and in many other parts of the British Empire. The Beverley was finally retired from RAF service on 6th December 1969. A total of 47 Beverleys were delivered to the RAF.

The Hawker Siddeley HS.681 Vertical Short Take Off and Landing (V/STOL) transport was planned to be the replacement for the Hastings, Beverley and Argosy but this was cancelled by the Labour Government in February 1965.

In June 1965 an order was placed for twenty-four Hercules. The model chosen was basically the Hercules C-130H. Initial discussions required the fitting of Rolls Royce Tyne engines but this was rejected on the grounds of cost effectiveness. However, a compromise was reached in that certain British-manufactured components were to be installed. These included the fitting of British Navigation Aids (Navaids), radios, autopilot and roller conveyers for palletised loads. This variant of the Hercules was designated the C-130K by

Lockheed. A further twenty-four Hercules were ordered in October 1965 plus a final batch of eighteen aircraft in March 1966 making a total of sixty-six aircraft.

Marshall of Cambridge (Engineering) (MCE) - recently renamed Marshall Aerospace - was chosen as the "Designated Centre" and was initially contracted to prepare the aircraft prior to the Ministry trials as well as being co-ordinators for all future engineering development.

By the time that the first aircraft was completed some 80% of the electronics equipment for the RAF Hercules was to be supplied by British firms. In 1965 the Ministry of Aviation awarded a contract to Miles Electronics of Shoreham for the design and constructions of a flight simulator. To support British firms further, Lockheed of Georgia placed a contract with Scottish Aviation at Prestwick to manufacture centre fuselage sections and another with Elliott Automation for the manufacture of fuel gauges under licence from Honeywell Inc of the USA. A third contract was awarded to Marsten-Excelsior for the supply of moulded nose radomes. These manufactured components were shipped to Marietta where they were installed in the Hercules prior to delivery to the UK.

For once, the Government of the day made a positive decision and announced that the Hercules was to replace all the Hastings and Beverley squadrons and that in 1970 it would also replace the Argosy. In other words the RAF was to use the Hercules not only in the tactical role but also as long range transport for global use.

So, what was so special about this machine? By May 1992 two thousand Hercules had been completed with this particular airframe being delivered to the Kentucky Air National Guard of the USAF. The chosen name of "Hercules" is a fitting one as it is capable of moving great and bulky loads to combat troops with ease from a range of surfaces from paved runways to unprepared surface strips. It was also designed to move combat troops from the main base and to land at the forward base strip which would be as close as practical to the battle front. However, this "Military" aircraft has since been used in peacetime to alleviate the sufferings of human beings - victims of famine, flood, earthquake and civil war - by the dropping of food supplies and medical aid. It has performed so many virtually impossible missions that it would not be possible to record all of them in one book. However, details of some of these missions together with those of the continuous engineering, avionics, modifications and technical details are given in later chapters.

The means of transporting troops to the forward bases and battle areas have changed tremendously in the last 60 years. Instead of moving them to these areas by ships or land transport they are now being ferried by tactical and strategic transport aircraft as speed has become a major factor . Prior to World War II the German Air Force had utilised transport aircraft and gliders - small and large - in their involvement of the Spanish Civil War. The experience gained there enabled them to walk over Europe during their early invasion during 1939 to 1941.

The American aircraft industry had its development of air transport innovations in the early '30s. The Douglas Aircraft Corporation had built the 20 seat Dakota DC-2 followed by the DC-3 for commercial use. This faithful and reliable aircraft was ordered and used in great numbers from 1940 by the United States Army Air Corps. The DC-3 was commonly

The Douglas Dakota in RAF Service

known as the the "C-47" or "Dakota" in military use. The Royal Air Force started using the Dakota from 1943 for transporting troops, and for towing the Horsa and Hamilcar gliders in World War II.

The Fairchild Aircraft Division commenced design of its C-82A Packet for tactical use in 1941 but its service entry in late 1945 meant that it was not tested militarily in World War II. Its design was

unusual with twin booms supporting the tail surfaces. This provided a rear loading access greatly expediting the loading of freight and vehicles. It also had a side door for dispatching paratroopers. The C-82A subsequently evolved into the more powerful and successful C-119 Packet.

The Korean War proved that larger and faster aircraft were needed to move troops than the faithful C-82 and C-119. A policy decision was taken by the USAF in 1951 decided to replace all the piston engined transport with large turbo-prop powered aircraft. The General Operational Requirement (GOR) was sent out in February 1951 to Fairchild, Douglas, Boeing and Lockheed.

The request was for the design of a utility aircraft that could carry logistics without any facilities, take-off from prepared or unprepared surfaces and airland or airdrop close to the area of conflict. In layman's terms what they wanted was the speed of a jeep, the ability to lift large loads like a truck and fly like an aeroplane. One of the requests by the GOR was for a payload of 25,000lb to be delivered to a bridgehead at a radius of 1,000nm at high speed. In its passenger carrying capability it has to be able to carry 64 fully equipped paratroops or 92 troops.

Lockheed won this contract and an order was placed to build two prototypes. The advanced design department at Lockheed produced the Model 206 which subsequently became known as the YC-130 Hercules and whose basic design has since changed very little except in the nose area.

The second prototype Hercules was actually the first to fly. The maiden flight of the YC-130, serial numbered 53-3397, occurred on 23rd August 1954

The Lockheed YC-130 Hercules maiden flight

from the Lockheed plant at Burbank, California. After two long runs along the runway, the most memorable moment came on the take-off as its wheels left the ground after reaching only 855ft of the long runway. Powered by four 3,750shp Allison T56-A-1A turboprops, the pilot initiated a 30° climb and the Hercules then climbed to 10,000ft. A few

16th December 1966. The then Deputy Chief of the Air Staff, Air Marshal Sir Reginald Emson, received XV177 on behalf of the RAF. It was flown by the RAF crew consisting of Pilot (Captain) Wing

1st RAF Hercules in production in Marietta

tests were completed and after an uneventful flight lasting 61 minutes it landed at Edwards Air Force Base in the Mojave Desert. This short flight was the first of many milestones for the "Mighty Hercules".

Following completion of the two prototypes, the production of the Hercules was shifted to the Lockheed plant at Marietta, Georgia, where on 10th March 1955 the first production model C-130A was rolled out. The trials on these initial aircraft were carried out over many months until every imperfection of design and performance was rectified. The Curtis-Wright electric propeller was replaced by a hydraulically-operated one. This was fitted to the C-130A model. Subsequent models were fitted with the Hamilton-Standard four-bladed propeller. The "Roman" nose was replaced with a radome which housed the weather radar scanner.

The first Hercules destined for the Royal Air Force was given the Construction Number 382-4169 and the serial number XV176, it first flew at Marietta on 19th October 1966. The second aircraft built was XV177 and it was this one that became the first RAF example when it was handed over at a brief ceremony held outside the B4 Hangar at Marietta on

Commander Mel Bennett, Co-pilot Squadron Leader David Wright, Navigator Squadron Leader Cyril Loughheed, Flight Engineer Squadron Leader Fred Pennycott and Air Quartermaster Flight Lieutenant John Sutton. On their flight to the UK the aircraft suffered a near total electrics failure over the

Handover of the 1st RAF Hercules at Marietta

Atlantic. At this point the crew could hardly have imagined at that stage that they were witnessing the start of one of the most successful eras in the history of the RAF. This bare metal transport aircraft sporting RAF roundels touched down at Marshall's Engineering Works in Cambridge after its eventful flight from the Lockheed plant on 19th December 1966.

It was at Marshall's of Cambridge Engineering (MCE) where the two tone brown and black camouflaged paint was applied. In addition the communications, Navaids and autopilot were installed. As the ferrying of these aircraft from

The first Hercules C.Mk1 (or C.1 as it was more commonly known) to be delivered to RAF Lyneham was on 1st August 1967 and the initial deliveries were to No 36 Squadron. The second unit was No 48 Squadron which took delivery of its aircraft and flew

XV177 at Cambridge Airport awaiting delivery to the A&AEE for trials following modification and painting by Marshall's of Cambridge

Lockheed to MCE progressed, XV177 and XV178 were delivered to the Aircraft and Armament Experimental Establishment (A&AEE) at Boscombe Down during February and March 1967, respectively, to begin trials and evaluation and acceptance tests.

The first RAF unit to receive the Hercules C.Mk1 , as it was officially designated, was No 242 Operational Conversion Unit (OCU) at RAF Thorney Island on 3rd May 1967. The six Hercules based there were for training Hercules crews. Prior to this all crews were trained in the USA and after the end of their course they ferried a Hercules aircraft to MCE.

them to its base at Changi, Singapore as part of the Far East Air Force. The third unit to re-equip was No 24 Squadron at Lyneham followed by Nos 30 and 47 Squadrons based at RAF Fairford. The last was No 70 Squadron at Akrotiri, Cyprus in November 1970 and was part of the Near East Air Force. XV294 became the 999th Hercules in the production line and was delivered to the UK on 29th February 1968. The 66th and last RAF Hercules, XV307 was the 1015th built by Lockheed and was delivered on 31st May 1968.

CHAPTER 2

RAF Lyneham

A Brief History

A quick glance at any area of the station will tell you that Lyneham is not a standard RAF base. None of the buildings conform to the usual pre-war design,

centre for the training of airmen aircrew engaged on ferry duties to overseas destinations and for the preparation and dispatch of aircraft being recovered from storage for service overseas.

Hercules over RAF Lyneham

nor is the Station laid out in the classical pattern. The architecture, to say the least, is mixed.

Lyneham came into being in May 1940 with the establishment of No 33 Maintenance Unit which stored aircraft that were not in regular Service use. Flying activity intensified in August '41 with the arrival of No 14 Flying Training School with its Oxford training aircraft. However, only six months later, the FTS moved on and Lyneham became the

Since those early days as part of Ferry Command, Lyneham has always been a terminal airfield for international flights, including a period between 1943 and 1945 when BOAC operated civil schedules from the base. Following the formation of RAF Transport Command in 1943, Avro Yorks and subsequently the Handley Page Hastings of No 216 Squadron, re-equipped even later with the VIP-variant of the de Havilland Comet 2 jet airliner, formed at Lyneham in 1955. The Comet 2, an example of which stands as Lyneham's gate guardian, were supplemented in 1962 by five of the Comet 4C. In December 1959, with the Hastings force concentrated at nearby Colerne, Lyneham became the home for two new squadrons, No 99 and No 511 Squadrons, flying Britannias. In Transport

Lyneham's de Havilland Comet 2 gate guard

Command, Lyneham was the hub of the RAF's long-range freighting, trooping and VIP operations.

The first RAF Hercules destined for squadron service was delivered to Lyneham on 1st August 1967 to begin the re-equipping of No 36 Squadron. Crews of No 48 Sqn, which were to be based at Changi, Singapore, took delivery of their aircraft at Lyneham and deployed to the Far East in October of that year. No 24 Sqn, the second of the two Hercules squadrons to be formed at Lyneham, re-equipped in 1968.

A major rationalisation of RAF air transport location policy began in 1970 with the move of the Britannia to nearby RAF Brize Norton. In 1971, the two Hercules squadrons that were based at RAF Fairford (Nos 30 and 47 Sqns) moved to Lyneham, to be joined later that year by No 48 Sqn on its withdrawal from the Far East. Thus Lyneham became home to five of the six Hercules squadrons in existence in the early `70s - the other being No 70 Sqn in Cyprus - plus the VIP Comets of No 216 Sqn. Further rationalisation took place in 1975 following the 1974 Defence Review: No 242 Operational Conversion Unit (OCU) moved up from RAF Thorney Island, the Engineering deep servicing organisation moved in from Colerne, No 70 Sqn returned from Cyprus and three Squadrons, Nos 36 and 48 Sqns flying Hercules and No 216 Sqn flying the Comets, were disbanded.

Lyneham is now home to the entire Hercules Force - four squadrons, plus the OCU together with the support needed. This includes first and second-line servicing, the training of the ground servicing personnel, radio and radar servicing support, role equipment support, together with all the supply and administration to operate the 60-strong Hercules Force.

The Station Organisation

In addition to the Squadrons, Lyneham has a conventional four-wing organisation comprising Operations, Engineering, Administration and Supply Wings. UK Mobile Air Movements Sqn (UKMAMS) is a resident part of Lyneham with a function which is a vital and integral part of the air transport operations. Equally important is the part played by the the lodger units, No 4626 (County of Wiltshire) Aeromedical Squadron, Royal Auxiliary Air Force, to assist in the medevac role and No 47 (Air Dispatch) Sqn, Royal Logistics Corps, who prepare, load and dispatch air-dropped stores.

1. The Operational Squadrons. With engineering at Lyneham being fully centralised, the four squadrons (Nos 24, 30, 47 and 70 Sqns) are made up of aircrew and admin staff only. Currently there are 22 or 23 five-man crews on each squadron. All of these squadrons are employed in the basic Air Transport (AT) role - the carriage of freight and passengers around the world - but each has another role. Nos 24 and 30 Sqns specialise in Airborne Tanking, whereas Nos 47 and 70 Sqns are trained in the Tactical Support Role - the air-dropping of paratroops and supplies. Three crews from 24 and 30 Sqns are detached to the Falkland Islands for a period of four months for operational duties.

2. The Operational Conversion Unit. With a staff of more than 130 on its books, No 57(R)Sqn - which was previously known as No 242 OCU - is the largest Conversion Unit in the RAF. It comprises:-

Ground School
Hercules Conversion Sqn
Hercules Training Sqn

Initial training is given to some 28 crews per year plus annual refresher training for about 90 crews per year as well as short Co-pilot-to-Capt courses.

Simulator Sqn - Recently re-equipped with three new simulators this facility provides conversion and refresher training. It is also hired by foreign air forces.

The Link Miles Hercules Simulator

Support Training Sqn - Trains tactical crews for No 47 and 70 Sqns
Tanker Training Flt - Trains crews in Air-to-Air Refuelling (AAR) techniques.

3. Operations Wing. Lyneham is a 24 hours/365 days per year station because the Air Transport (AT) movements could not be restrained by "normal" working hours. The function of Operations Wing is to exercise overall control and co-ordination of all aspects of the Station flying task. This includes provision of all airfield facilities and services for both Lyneham's aircraft and the many civil and military visitors, both British and foreign, that pass through Lyneham. The Operations Squadron, located in the Station Operations Room in the terminal building, is the hub not only of the Wing but also of the Station. It co-ordinates all the immediate supporting requirements for the smooth departure and arrival of each flight. Such services include route weather forecasts, in-flight catering, refuelling and turnaround servicing, crew and

Station Operations

passenger transport, customs, aircraft parking and loading and unloading for some fifteen thousand flights per year.

The Air Plans department is responsible for task planning, contingency planning and intelligence support. The Task Planning section makes the necessary advance arrangements for most of the station's own flying effort, and allocates individual tasks to the operational squadrons and the OCU. It raises all the necessary documentation to provide a complete record of each route flight, for the use of crews and operations room staff. The contingency Plans section is responsible for maintaining

Lyneham Fire Section located in the centre of the airfield next to Air Traffic Control tower

operational contingency plans and plans for Lyneham's transition to war. These plans are regularly exercised during TACtical EVALuations (TACEVALs). The Intelligence Section of Air Plans provides continuous intelligence support and documentation for worldwide Hercules operations in peace and in war. Similarly, under the direction of the Station Navigation Officer, flight planning, navigational and communications information is held and continually updated for all parts of the world, and each flight is provided with a comprehensive flight back-up to support its particular itinerary. The Wing includes a large Air Traffic Control Squadron which provides direct aircraft control for the airfield and its surrounding Special Rules Zone 24 hours a day. Lyneham's position in a region of high intensity flying with many surrounding airfields and military exercise areas, together with the civilian airways for transatlantic traffic to and from London passing directly overhead, makes ATC Squadron's job a busy one.

Other sections of Operations Wing include the Flight Safety organisation and a selected Hercules crew whose job it is to flight test each aircraft after its return from deep servicing by Aircraft Engineering Squadron. The large airfield Fire Service, the Meteorological Section, both manned 24 hours a day by civilian personnel, come under the control of the Wing and it is also the point of contact with HM Customs.

4. Engineering Wing. Comprising some 1,700 personnel, this is by far Lyneham's largest section. All servicing is centralised, and Lyneham carries out first and second-line servicing on all 60 resident aircraft, plus second-line servicing of the Met Research Hercules which is normally based at DRA

Three Hercules undergoing servicing by AES

Farnborough. The timescale for aircraft servicing has traditionally been calendar-based but is now based on flying hours - the change has reduced the servicing cycle and provided some relief on the limited hangarage at Lyneham.

The Engineering Wing is one of the largest in the Royal Air Force. The size of the Hercules fleet, the layout of Lyneham's airfield and the need to provide

Hercules on jacks during servicing by AES

24 hour, year-round shift coverage has necessitated the establishment of two entirely separate line servicing squadrons. Each of the squadrons is responsible for the first line servicing, associated rectification and primary scheduled servicing of its own allocation of aircraft.

Second line coverage is provided by the Aircraft Engineering Squadron (AES) which maintains the aircraft "Minor" and "Minor Star" scheduled servicing teams. The Aircraft Support Flight provides aircraft component servicing and painting and surface finishing facilities. Surface finishing at Lyneham has become "green". Gone are the unpleasant paint strippers and in are hi-tech nylon bead blasters.

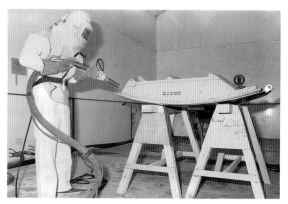

PMS in use to strip paint from a crew door

Additionally the Hercules Servicing School, which undertakes all pre-employment and advanced Hercules engineering training, forms part of AES.

The co-ordination of first-line servicing and the allocation of aircraft to the daily flying programme is the responsibility of personnel of the Engineering Operations (Eng Ops) and Plans Squadron who maintain a very close liaison with Operations Wing and UKMAMS. Eng Ops and Plans Sqn are also tasked with the planning of Primary and Minor servicings, the maintenance of Aircraft and Engineering Records, Aircraft Washing and the handling of Visiting Aircraft.

Lyneham's Mechanical Engineering Squadron (MES) is a very large organisation and the personnel of its three flights are responsible for providing a wide range of support facilities both to aircraft and to the station. The General Engineering Flight, located on the main site, provides Lyneham with

First visit by a Ukranian AF Antonov An.12 "Cub" to Lyneham

As with all other engineering squadrons at Lyneham, the Electrical Engineering Squadron (EES) is somewhat larger than its counterparts on most other stations. EES comprises three flights: an Avionics Flight, responsible for second line maintenance of Hercules electrical and avionic equipment and for ground photographic services; a Ground Radio Flight, responsible for the maintenance of all ground

Servicing propellors in the Propulsion Bay

Ground Support Equipment Servicing, a Station Workshop and a Station Armament Section. The Propulsion Repair Flight, on "D" Site near the ATC Tower, are tasked with the servicing, repair and modification of the Allison T56 engines, the Hamilton propellers and the AiResearch gas turbine compressors. The original propellers fitted were Hamilton Standard but all subsequent servicings are by British Dowty Rotol. The Role Equipment element of the Role and Survival Equipment Flight (RSEF) is responsible for the supply, maintenance and repairs. The Hercules can be operated in any of twenty main role equipment configurations and the Flight is responsible for the fitting of the huge number of components involved. Finally, the Survival Equipment Section of the RSEF, maintains all items of Flying Clothing and Survival Equipment.

navigation and communication aids at Lyneham, including the PABX and Commcen, and a Simulator Servicing Flight to carry out the servicing of Lyneham's three Hercules flight simulators. With the exception of some of the Ground Radio Flight employed in the ATC tower, all EES personnel work on the main site.

Last, but not least, Lyneham has a large MT Squadron which is dispersed over four sites on the station and runs well over 300 vehicles. The MT Maintenance Flight is located on "A" Site near Bradenstoke village. The MT Control and Coach Pool is on "C" Site while the heavy specialist vehicles such as refuellers and cranes operate from "D" Site. The Trade Training and Licensing Section is also located at "C" Site.

Reassembling an Allison T56 engine and gearbox

A "quick fix" for a "broken" Hercules on the line is provided by a crew from ALSS

The two Line Servicing Squadrons (LSS) are named "A" Line (ALSS) and "B" Line (BLSS) and between them employ some 460 engineers. Each squadron is commanded by a Squadron Leader Engineer and is composed of five separate flights each commanded by a Junior Engineering Officer. Four Line Servicing Flights on each squadron work on a shift pattern that enables both squadrons to remain open 24 hours a day, 365 days a year. The fifth flight, called Support Flight, works a normal 5 day week.

The fleet of 60 Hercules aircraft is divided roughly evenly between the two Line Servicing Squadrons. ALSS looks after fourteen C.1P Hercules and fifteen C.3 Hercules aircraft. BLSS looks after twelve Hercules C.1P, fourteen C.3 and five Hercules C.1K tanker aircraft. BLSS also provides maintenance support for the Farnborough based meteorological research Hercules W.2 aircraft. It has an atmospheric sampling probe and as a result the aircraft is known as Snoopy. Sharing the aircraft out in this manner allows each LSS to act independently under the co-ordination of the central Engineering Operations and Plans Squadron.

Although BLSS maintains more aircraft than ALSS, each LSS has an equal share of the flying task: two of the tanker aircraft are always deployed to the Falkland Islands and the tankers remaining at Lyneham fly less frequently than the freighter aircraft.

The task of the line servicing flights is to carry out the front line engineering that ensures the aircraft

Aircraft towing by one of the LSS. Notice that due to the tail height the of the Hercules the hangar doors all required modification

remain airworthy and always ready to fly. Their task includes aircraft handling (marshalling, towing, re-fuelling etc), rectification of minor faults and flight

servicing (the preparation of an aircraft for flight and checking of its condition when it returns from its particular flying task). The Support Flight of each LSS comprises a Primary Team, a heavy Rectification team and a group of four SNCOs known as the Day Trade Managers. The Primary Teams carry out Primary and Primary Star servicings on each of their LSS aircraft at 250 and 500 flying hour intervals respectively. These servicings involve the lubrication of major components and an examination of those areas which cannot be examined on a daily basis. These servicings take between three and four days to complete.

LSS groundcrew refuel the aircraft with AVTUR

Each Heavy Rectification Team comprises six technicians who carry out the more complex repair tasks that require continuity of manning, such as fuel tank repairs. The Day Trade Managers are all very experienced SNCOs who provide a focal point for the dissemination of information to each of the Line Servicing Flights and investigate unusual faults.

As the front line engineers, personnel from the Line Servicing Squadrons are often required to deploy to other operating bases all around the world. This happens when large numbers of Hercules movements are planned to occur at a base other than Lyneham. Many NATO exercises fall into this category. Deployment of LSS personnel also regularly occurs to recover aircraft that have broken down away from base.

The biggest recent deployment of engineers from the lines was, of course, the Gulf conflict. Approximately 150 airmen and officers (including WRAF) deployed into the conflict area in support of the massive air transport effort. Many more personnel were detached for short durations around the fighter bases in Britain and Germany to help them to deploy their personnel and equipment by Hercules to the Gulf. To cope with the loss of manpower at home, engineers from throughout the RAF were detached to Lyneham.

LSS groundcrew undertake repairs in the Gulf

These people were integrated into all elements of the LSS and Aircraft Engineering Squadron. This assistance enabled both the LSS to continue with the full range of daily and scheduled maintenance despite record flying hours which, in some months, were twice the normal rate. One major consequence of these high flying rates was that the Primary Teams had to work shifts and were completing their servicings in 24 hours instead of three days.

Out of the conflict area, massive demands were placed on the engineers who, like many others were using makeshift facilities and making the best use of any accommodation available in very crowded airfields. Accommodation for the Hercules aircraft themselves also caused problems as a great diversity of types and nationalities of aircraft were operating from the same bases. Despite these problems, the engineers from the LSS at Lyneham performed magnificently, undertaking everything that could be required of them and more.

They even took on extra tasks such as assisting with the handling of visiting aircraft that had no ground crew of their own. But things were not all bad for the personnel deployed to the Gulf. Those stationed in Riyadh agreed that the food prepared by the field kitchen in a tent was "better than you get at home".

5. Administrative Wing. A conventional Administrative Wing provides service support for a uniformed and civilian strength of over 3,200, a "population" including dependants of around 10,000, and an estate covering some 2,500 acres on which stand some 690 working buildings and almost 1,000 married quarters.

Administrative Wing is responsible for a wide range of activities. As a result the Wing consists of five Squadrons; Personnel Services Squadron, Accounts Squadron, Station Services Squadron, Education and Training Squadron and Catering Squadron. In addition, the Medical and Dental Centres, the Chaplain's Centre and RAF Police Flight are part of Administrative Wing.

6. Supply Squadron. The function of Supply Squadron is to assist in the efficient operation of the Station by satisfying the equipment requirements of the complex web of squadron, flights and sections that make up Lyneham. This formidable task not only includes the provision of technical equipment to support the Hercules, but also of clothing and barrack stores to meet the needs of the Station's most important resource, its people. They believe that by efficiently satisfying personal and domestic requirements they are helping to create the right sort of atmosphere in which people can perform at their best. Much of the squadron's work involves the receipt, storage and issue of equipment to support Engineering Wing.

These tasks are carried out by the Electronic Storage Group (ESG) which is located in the Electronics Centre and by the Technical Storage Group which holds equipment both in the Supply Squadron headquarters building opposite J1 Hangar and in a large hangar on B Site. Items supplied range from washers to wings, from resistors to radars and from tappets to tail fins. Delivery is carried out by the Squadron's own fleet of vehicles and to assist the larger customers they run a series of Forward Stores out at the engineering work place. Petrol, Oil and Lubricants (POL) is another important part of the service that they provide.

Most of the section's facilities are located in a purpose built complex on "C" Site, but other storage facilities are spread throughout the Station. Petrol and diesel fuels are dispersed on a self-service basis, using an electronic key to record the vehicles involved, and is available 24 hours a day. However, they do not give Green Shield Stamps!

To support their aircraft when they are down route, the Mobility Supply Flight (MSF) provides a series of packs of spares.

7. United Kingdom Mobile Air Movements Squadron. UKMAMS comprises two fairly distinct elements: the Base Movements Flight, which is responsible for processing all passengers and freight through Lyneham, and the Mobile teams which may be deployed at short notice anywhere in the world to load or unload any of the RAF's transport aircraft.

8. Royal Auxiliary Air Force. Lyneham is the home of No 4626 (County of Wiltshire) Squadron, RAuxAF, a unit comprising of a number of specialist and non-specialist volunteer personnel who undertake a range of medical activities and support to help meet RAF needs in the casualty recovery, treatment and evacuation roles.

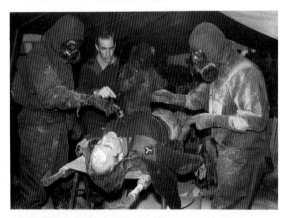

RAuxAF medics during final training before deploying to the Gulf

A unit of the RAuxAF Defence Force is based at Lyneham to provide airfield protection.

9. No 47 (Air Dispatch) Squadron, RLC. In a unique arrangement, an Army unit is responsible for the preparation, loading and dispatch of all stores air-dropped from RAF aircraft. Personnel of No 47(AD) Sqn fly as crew members when on dispatching duties.

Hercules Task
Transition to War (TTW).
Lyneham's principal TTW tasks would be in supporting and deploying the specialised task forces, Allied Command Europe Mobile Force (AMF) and United Kingdom Mobile Force (UKMF), to the flanks of NATO. Lyneham would also be involved in the recovery of any British Forces from overseas, such as the Falklands, and then become totally committed to the deployment of British Forces with their equipment from UK to the area of tension or conflict. During the Cold War period this would have been on behalf of Allied Command Europe to reinforce RAF in Germany and BAOR, and bring 1 (BR) Corps to a war footing. Reinforcement and re-supply tasks would probably continue beyond the outbreak of hostilities, with routes and tactics amended where possible to reduce the threat to the unarmed and poorly protected transports.

Out of Area (OOA).
In any emergency situation outside the NATO arena, the Hercules Force could be engaged in operations to deploy and support British forces almost anywhere in the world. Indeed, the two tactical Hercules Squadrons, Nos 47 and 70 Sqns, are tasked in peacetime to provide air mobility for the UK's OOA intervention force, 5 Airborne Brigade, should that force be deployed to conduct a Services Protected Evacuation of British nationals from foreign parts. However, not all non-NATO emergency situations require the seizure of an airhead and the intervention of an armed force; in many cases, a standard airlift will suffice. Nevertheless, the Hercules brings an impressive list of capabilities to any OOA operation.

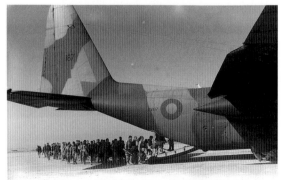

Troops being airlifted during the Gulf War

CHAPTER 3

The Hercules Technical Details and Roles

Airframe

The Hercules is a high wing, high aspect ratio (to give maximum lift) long range, land-based monoplane. Fowler flaps fitted to the wings provide further lift by extending the wing area by 50% for take off. Further extension (to 100%) provides drag which assists during the landing run. The high wing allows the installation of the Allison engine and the

are removable. The rugged utility interior resembles a large truck without any fanciful trimmings. Each wing is manufactured in two sections with the centre wing section being constructed as part of the fuselage. The empennage section consists of the fin, rudder and elevator sections. Because of the original short fuselage length of 99ft 6ins a large rudder is fitted to provide stability and control.

Hercules in flight showing the high wing position

Empennage showing the large fin and rudder

large 13ft 6ins diameter propellers. The fuselage is made up of extruded longerons and formers riveted together with skins to form sections which are then bolted together. The whole fuselage assembly resembles a long tube with a flat floor whose panels

Ailerons are fitted to each wing outboard of the flaps to give roll control. The movements from the pilot and co-pilot controls are transmitted mechanically via the flight station torque tubes and cable to the hydraulic booster unit. This merely opens a valve when the control column is moved, and ports hydraulic pressure which then moves the aileron control surfaces via the push rods. Trim tabs, operated electrically, are attached to the port aileron section which make small adjustments in aircraft attitude. The one trim tab fitted to the starboard wing is for ground adjustment only.

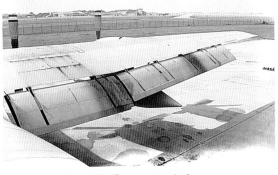

Hercules wing with flaps extended

Elevators are provided to give pitch control and are mounted and hinged at the trailing edge of the tailplane. Hydraulic power and control is similar to that to the aileron. Trim tabs are also attached to the trailing edge of the elevators.

The rudder provides directional control and is mounted and hinged at the rear of the fin. Power and control is also the same as for the ailerons. A trim tab is similarly, attached to rudder's trailing edge.

Engine, Propeller and GTC

The Hercules is fitted with a constant speed Allison T56-A-15 turbo-prop engine. This is a gas turbine power unit connected by a supporting structure and extension shafts to a reduction gear assembly to which the propeller assembly is fitted. The complete unit is termed as a Quick Engine Change (QEC) assembly designed for quick and easy removal and installation. The power section consists of the air inlet housing which directs the airflow through to a 14-stage axial compressor. This compressed air is directed to the combustion section via the diffuser. The combustion section itself comprises of a six can annular chamber configuration. Fuel is introduced to each chamber along with the compressed air where it is mixed and ignited. The resultant hot gas exits from the aft end of the combustion chamber and enters the turbine assembly. This hot gas drives the four stage turbine assembly which then rotates. This drives the compressor and via the extended shaft drives the reduction gear box assembly. The propeller is mounted on the forward face of the reduction gear box assembly. It is the propeller which provides the main source of propulsion, although a small amount of additional thrust is generated with the expulsion of the remaining hot gases from the exhaust assembly.

A Quick Engine Change assembly

The propeller assembly is a constant speed hydro-mechanically operated unit. Finer refinements of the

propeller control are provided electrically and electronically. A synchrophaser provides faster propeller response and helps to reduce vibration and noise variation (beat). The four bladed propeller fitted is the Hamilton standard 54H60, the base of each being mounted within a spinner and containing an integral oil control, de-icing heaters, a synchrophaser, a manual phase control and one de-icing timer.

In flight the engine runs at 13,820rpm while the propeller turns at 1,021rpm. When the throttles are moved forward more fuel is delivered and the Turbine Inlet Temperature (TIT) increases but as the engine speeds up the prop blades coarsen to absorb the extra power. Hydraulic fluid under pressure from the valve housing is ported to the forward or rear of the piston to coarsen or make finer the blade angle. Many safety features are built into the system such as the ability to feather the propeller when an engine is shut down in flight. Others include automatic mechanical pitch lock, automatic negative torque control and a mechanical low pitch stop. The final safety feature is the safety coupling which disconnects the engine from the propellor.

On the ground the "Beta" system controls fuel and flow as well as the blade angle for taxying and reversing. The gear housing, which is fixed, is located behind the propellers and contains the reservoir of propeller operating oil, oil pumps, valves, the governor and other associated mechanisms which direct oil to the pitch change piston and enables the constant speed operation, full feathering and reversing.

The engine is started by an air driven starter which requires a source of bleed air. This can be provided by a Gas Turbine Compressor, (GTC) mounted forward of the left hand undercarriage blister, or from an external source in the form of a Palouste. The GTC is also a basic gas turbine engine but uses a two stage centrifugal compressor instead of an axial compressor like the Allison. The GTC can only be used on the ground and the bleed air supplies can be used to power the Air Turbine Motor (ATM) which drives a generator and is also for air conditioning and pressurisation.

During a normal start an external AC power source is connected to the aircraft. After a series of checks by the crew, the GTC is electrically started by the Flight Engineer (FE) from the sub panel of the Engineers Overhead Panel (EOP). The air pressure is used to check the integrity of the bleed air ducts for leaks. The bleed air manifold is then pressurised. The Low Speed Ground Idle (LSGI) button is depressed which controls the RPM between 69-75.5% by limiting the fuel in the FCU.

The Flight Engineers overhead panel

The engine start is monitored by the whole crew.

1/ The FE selects the switch to open the number three Bleed Air Valve.

2/ With the throttles in the Ground Idle position, the Captain moves the number three condition lever to the "Run" position, arming the start circuit.

3/ Simultaneously, he pushes the number three engine starter button and holds it. The starter button's integral filament lights up and the starter valve opens. This supplies a regulated amount of air to turn the starter motor which rotates the engine and propeller via the reduction gear.

4/ Air now flows through the 14 stage axial compressor. To prevent compressor stall, valves at the 5th and 10th compressor stages remain open, this air being ducted overboard.

5/ The compressed air (high temperature and pressure) enters the diffusers. Most of this air flows through the six combustion chambers and some around them for cooling. Finally this exits through the four stage turbine unit and the jet pipe.

The Flight Engineer selects Bleed Air

The start is now controlled automatically by the micro-switches in the Speed Sensitive Control (SSC).

At 16% RPM the SSC actuates the following:-
a/ Fuel shut off valve opens and provides fuel to the burners.

b/ The ignition relay is energised providing high voltage to the igniters.

c/ The manifold drip valve is closed. It opens below 16% to drain away unburnt fuel.

d/ The parallel valve is closed. The two mechanical fuel pumps run in parallel. At low RPM it is inefficient to run in series.

The FE calls fuel flow, ignition, oil pressures, hydraulic pressure and parallel. The combination of the starter motor, FCU and the combustion products allows the engine to accelerate smoothly.

At 60% RPM the starter button is released. The closing of the starter valve is confirmed by the Navigator who is watching the bleed air valve manifold pressure gauge and when noted he calls "pressure rise". Further acceleration of the engine disengages the starter clutch which allows the engine to increase rpm free of the starter.

At 65% RPM the SSC actuates the following:-
a/ The power to the igniter is switched off.

b/ The manifold drip valve released. It is now held closed by fuel pressure.

c/ The parallel valve opens. The two pumps now run in series and the FE calls "Series".

At approximately 72% RPM the engine stabilises. After a few seconds the FE pulls the LSGI button and the engine accelerates to about 96.5% and stabilises. The FE checks the Voltage and Frequency meters and switches the generators on.

The Captain removes his hand from the condition lever.

Before 94% RPM the TD system limits the Turbine Inlet Temperature (TIT) to 830°C by reducing the fuel by up to 50%. Above 94% the TD system limits the TIT to 1077°C and also the compressor bleed valves close at the 5th and 10th stages.

Following a short series of checks the Number Four, Two and One engines are started.

Engine Specification

Engine: Allison T56-A-15, constant speed, turbo-prop, air starter. Sea-level, static, standard-day take off power rating at 100% RPM is 4,910 equivalent shaft horse power (eshp) comprising 4,591shp (shaft horse power) from the prop and 319eshp jet thrust.

Acceleration: The bleed valves at the 5th and 10th compressor stages prevent choking of the compressors at low RPM.

Fuel: Fuel topping when RPM reaches 105%

Air from the diffuser is taken to the bleed air manifold for anti-icing, nacelle pre-heating and air conditioning.

Engine Oil: Capacity 12 US galls per engine.
Oil Type: 0-156, OX 27.
Dry sump.

Propeller: Hamilton Standard type 54H60 four blade, constant speed fully-feathering, reversible pitch, with a 13ft 6in diameter.

Prop Oil System: Integral 5.24 imp gall.
Oil type: OM15

FUEL

In the basic C.1, there are six tanks in the wing and they are termed Nos 1, 2, left hand auxiliary, right hand auxiliary, 3 and 4 plus there are two externally mounted tanks located on pylons between the engines. These eight wing tanks can carry a total of 62,900lbs - this is the structural limitation. At Specific Gravity (SG) of 0.8, this represents about 7,862 gallons! Nos 1, 2, 3 and 4 tanks feed their own engines but a cross feed valve allows this fuel to join

the fuel manifold from where it can be fed to any engine. There is one fuel booster pump in each tank which provides fuel under pressure. In an emergency, fuel can be dumped from all the tanks through a dump manifold. There is one fuel dump pump in each tank with the exception of the auxiliary tanks which uses their fuel boost pump as the dump pump.

When fuel is supplied under pressure, for instance from No 1 tank to its engine, it passes through the following components - initially the Non Return Valve (NRV) from where it passes through the firewall shut-off valve, fuel heater and strainer, low pressure warning switch, engine-driven fuel pump, fuel control unit, fire shut-off valve, Temperature Datum (TD) valve and the flowmeter and finally to the six Duplex burners.

Ground refuelling and de-fuelling for all tanks is through the Single Point Refuelling (SPR) panel located rear of the starboard wheel well. However, apart from the auxiliary tanks all other tanks have a receptacle to receive fuel individually via a hose from the fuel bowser.

Groundcrew refuel from a bowser. One of the external fuel tanks is also visible

The fuel quantity gauges, fuel pressure gauge, warning lights, switches for the fuel boost and dump pumps and dump valve switches are located in the sub panel of the overhead panel. The fuel gauges are duplicated externally in the SPR panel.

During Operation Corporate it became necessary to extend the range of the Hercules. These resulting variants are covered in Chapter 4 under the Hercules modifications.

Air to air refuelling

Provision is made to receive fuel in flight through a

Groundcrew connects the hose at the Single Point Refuelling panel

probe mounted externally above the right side of the flight deck. A pipeline is routed aft of the mounting and runs parallel and through the starboard inner wing section to join the refuelling manifold. Two NRVs are fitted - one is to prevent fuel draining out should the probe nozzle break off during contacts with the tanker and the other is to prevent fuel entering the probe pipeline. The controls for the AAR are located in a panel above the Navigator's instrument panel. The C.1K is the tanker version and is additionally cleared to dispense fuel in flight to other aircraft via the Hose Drum Unit (HDU).

A Hercules C.1K tanker in the process of air to air refuelling a Hercules C.1P transport

Fuel Specifications

No 1, 2, 3 and 4 are all integral fuel tanks. The auxiliary tanks are three-cell bag type located each side of the wing section. The external tanks are mounted beneath each wing between the engines.

Tank	Capacity*	Capacity	Usable fuel[+]
1 and 4 (each)	1,124 galls	8,992 lbs	8,928 lbs
2 and 3 (each)	1,033 galls	8,264 lbs	8,192 lbs
Aux tanks (each)	758 galls	6,064 lbs	6,064 lbs
Ext tanks (each)	1,166 galls	9,328 lbs	9,064 lbs
	8,162 galls	**65,296 lbs[+]**	**64,496 lbs**

* In Imperial Gallons.
[+]Due to structural limits the maximum fuel load is 63,700lbs of which 800lbs is unusable therefore the maximum useable fuel is 62,900lbs.

Fuel boost pump pressure:	15-24psi
Aux and Ext pump pressure:	28-40psi
Dump pump pressure:	28-40psi

Approved Fuel: AVTUR/FSII or alternative AVTUR AVTAG/FSII or alternative AVCAT AVCAT/FSII

AC electrical power to drive all fuel pumps.
DC electrical power to control fuel and cross-feed valves and for refuelling.

Hydraulics

Hydraulic power is used for the following:-
Flying Controls, undercarriage, brakes, nose-wheel steering, operation of the cargo ramp and door plus the flaps.

There are three hydraulic systems used in the Hercules. The booster system which is mounted forward of the right hand undercarriage blister. Underneath its reservoir of hydraulic fluid is the electric suction boost pump which provides a head of fluid to the main Engine Driven Pump (EDP) which pressurises fluid to each hydraulic powered control unit. No 3 and 4 engines reduction gear box drives the EDPs and this system powers half the flying controls. The utility system, which is slightly bigger but similar to the booster, is driven by 1 and 2 engines and drives half the flying control units. It also controls the movement of services as the normal supply source for the wheel brakes, nose-wheel steering, landing gear, and flap operation.

The auxiliary system differs from the other two in that it has only one pump which is driven electrically. It has a larger reservoir and provides

The utility system and resevoir. From here the hydraulic power is supplied to the flying controls and undercarriage via a maze of pipes

hydraulic power for normal operation of the cargo ramp and door, for emergency brakes, and the emergency lowering of the nose gear. On the ground it has one other function in that it can be connected, via a changeover valve, to the utility system for its functional checks to be carried out without running the Nos 1 or 2 engines.

Groundcrew check the main wheels for damage

The main tandem wheels are mounted within a blister externally at the side of the fuselage to give maximum space in the cargo compartment. In the limited wheel-well space there are two large wheels, which are connected to two oleo legs which in turn are mounted to two screwjacks. These provide straight up and down movement. The multi-disc

brakes similar to the ones fitted to most cars are mounted inside each wheel and tubeless tyres are fitted to the wheels. For safe braking, an anti-skid control is incorporated to operate in conjunction with the normal brake system. The tandem wheel arrangement with large footprint tyres enables the Hercules to land virtually anywhere - on prepared and unprepared surfaces. The twin nosewheel provides steering on the ground. The hydraulic system switches, instruments and warning lights of the hydraulic system are mounted to the lower portion of the co-pilots instrument panel.

Hydraulics Specification

Booster System: Mechanical driven pumps mounted on the rear of the reduction gear in Nos 3 and 4 engines.

Operating pressure: 2,900 - 3,200psi
Reservoir capacity: 1.6 imp galls

Utility System: Similar to Booster System (pressures and pumps) but mounted on Nos 1 and 2 engines.

Reservoir capacity: 2.6imp galls

Auxiliary System: Electric pump or hand pump

Operating pressure: 2,900 - 3,300psi
Reservoir capacity: 2.8imp galls

Hydraulic fluid: OM 15

Landing Gear

  Nose: Steerable twin wheels
  Main: Tandem main wheels
  Track: 14ft

Operation: Mainwheel - utility system hydraulic pressure. Manual (emergency extension only)
Brakes: Utility system (normal with anti-skid)
                Auxiliary system (emergency no anti-skid)
Nosewheel steering: Utility system

Flaps

Normal: Utility system
Emergency: Manual

Anti-icing and De-icing

Ice protection is provided by hot air tapped from the diffuser and electrically from the bus bars.

The wing and tail section are heated by hot air to remove the ice (de-ice). The radome and engine are also protected by hot air either automatically or manually, the probes for the automatic icing system being located in Nos 2 and 3 engines, and the amber warning light is located below the fire emergency "T" handle in the overhead panel.

Electrical heating is utilised for heating the nine windows and pitot heads. Electrical heating for the propeller spinners and blades is automatic but the ice detection system can be initiated manually.

The main wing leading edge has been removed during servicing to expose the bleed air duct and electrical cables

The ice protection panel, switches warning lights ammeters and gauges are located in the sub panel off the engineer's overhead panel. The radome control switches are at the navigator's station.

During freezing conditions the aircraft will require spraying with a de-icing agent prior to engine start. The aircraft surface area is too large and requires too much energy to de-ice unaided

Air Conditioning and Pressurisation
There are two air conditioning units which use the bleed air from the aircraft bleed air manifold, one for the flight deck, and the other for cargo compartment.

Ram air is ducted in via the auxiliary vent valve to ventilate the aircraft when it is required unpressurised. For pressurisation, the flight deck conditioner provides 30lbs/min of air in flight and the cargo compartment conditioner provides 70lbs/min of air. One flow regulator for each conditioner allows the hot bleed air from the manifold to enter the refrigeration units. On reaching the flight deck conditioner, which is located under the flight deck floor, the cooled air is split. Part is further reduced to an icy cold temperature and is then joined with the turbine by-pass hot air and mixed, they pass through the water separator before passing through the flight deck outlets and the pilot's and navigator's footwarmers. Some of this air is also used as the windscreen de-misting.

The larger cargo compartment air conditioner provides similar cool air with the exception of two items - one allows under-floor heating to be selected and the other is that not all the cooled air goes through the water separator.

Pressurisation is maintained by a pressure controller, manual control switch, outflow and safety valve. This is basically is to control the discharge of the air in the aircraft to the atmosphere. In an emergency the aircraft can be de-pressurised electrically or manually. Normal pressurisation is by the use of the rotary switch to "Auto pressurisation" but it can be controlled manually.

The controls for the air-conditioning, under-floor heating, temperature selector, pressurisation, pressure controller differential gauge and the rate indicator are all located in the sub panel in the engineer's overhead panel.

Oxygen
The aircraft oxygen system consists of a re-chargeable 25-litre liquid oxygen converter located in the nose wheel well. After passing through the heat exchangers, it supplies gaseous oxygen at 300psi to the six pressure oxygen regulators in the flight deck and four in the cargo compartment. The liquid oxygen quantity indicator and the warning light is located in the Co-pilot's instrument panel. Two portable MA-4 oxygen bottles are situated beside its charging point on the flight deck and a further two in the cargo compartment.

Air Conditioning and Oxygen Specification
Air Supply: Conditioned bleed air
                Ram air
                Flight deck supplies 30lbs/min in*
                Cargo compartment 70lbs/min in *
*In flight

Pressurisation: Max diff 14 to 15ins Hg
        Max diff 14.6 to 15.9 ins Hg (Safety Valve)
        Max Neg diff 0.76in Hg (Safety Valve)

Oxygen: 25 litre liquid oxygen at 300psi.

Portable Oxygen: Four MA-4 portable bottles
                One Mk.9 unit

Topping up the liquid oxygen system

Electrical System

There are four Primary AC electrical bus bars in the aircraft which power various components. Each of the four engine-driven generators powers a bus bar but any two generators can power all four bus bars. The bus bars are termed Left Hand, Essential, Main and Right hand. The Air Turbine Motor (ATM) driven by bleed air drives the fifth generator and this always provides power to the Essential AC bus bar but only when it is switched on. The engine must be running "on speed" around the 100% RPM mark for the generator to be brought on line but various safety features are built including Voltage regulators, frequency sensing elements and a generator control which ensures the bus bars are powered between 92.5% (low range at the flight idle gate) or 106% (high range when full reverse is selected). If there is an earth fault or over-voltage in the generator the sensing element trips this generator off line and another generator assumes the extra load by taking over the bus bar.

The secondary AC system consists of two bus bars. The Co-pilots instrument bus bar which powers the aircraft flight systems such as the Altitude Director Indicator (ADI) and the Horizontal Situation Indicator (HSI) is powered by the Essential Bus Bar or by the Isolated DC bus via an invertor. The AC, Instrument and engine fuel control bus which powers the engine, hydraulic, and fuel quantity instruments is also driven by the Essential AC bus or by the Essential DC bus via an invertor.

DC power is provided by four Transformer Rectifier Units (TRU). Two are driven by the Essential AC

An Electrician changes a circuit breaker

bus and the other two by the Main AC bus, and the converted DC powers the Essential and Main DC respectively. There is a 24v battery located forward of the crew entrance door which is wired to the Battery bus - when it is switched on, it connects to the Isolated bus. On the ground, current flows from the battery to the Isolated, Essential and Main or vice versa but in flight it is from Main to Battery.

Aft of the battery compartment is a receptacle where external AC or DC an be plugged in and this powers the aircraft on the ground. The five AC, four DC loadmeters, warning lights, voltage and frequency meters, selector and generator disconnect switches are located in a sub panel in the Engineers overhead panel.

Electrical Specification

The generator is mounted on the reduction gear and the output is controlled by various components located at the Main AC distribution panel at FS 245 - the point which divides the flight deck and the cargo compartment, and under the flight deck floor. The generator in No 1 engine feeds the Left Hand (LH) bus bar, No 2 the Essential (ESS) No 3 the Main and No 4 the Right Hand (RH). Any generator can power any bus bar and the transfer is provided by relays and fuses. For instance when the first engine (No 3) is started on the ground it will feed its own bus bar and the ESS. However if No 4 is started it will not feed its own RH bus but only the ESS and the Main.

Engine Generators – Qty 4:
>   Type: 200/115V, 3 Phase, 400HZ
>   Load: 40 KVA (Air), 25 KVA (Ground)

ATM Gen. – Qty 1:
>   Type: 200/115V, 3 Phase, 400 HZ
>   Load: 30 KVA (with fan) 25 KVA (no fan)

Secondary AC:
>   Co-pilots instrument bus 115V, 3 Phase, 400 HZ, 250 VA
>
>   Aircraft Instruments & Engine fuel control bus 115V, Single Phase, 400 HZ, 2.5 KVA

Inst Transformer – Qty 2 each of:
>   Type: 26V, 1 Phase, 400 HZ
>   (C-12 compasses)
>
>   Type: 26V, 1 Phase, 400 HZ (instruments)

Battery – Qty 1:
>   Type: 24v 36 Ampere Hour (AH)

TRU – Qty 4:   28v 200 amps

EXT AC: 200/115V, 3 Phase 400 HZ 40 KVA

EXT DC: 28V 400 amps

Hercules Roles

Aeromed Role
The ramp and doors of the Hercules make it an ideal "mobile hospital" for evacuation of patients from devastated areas speedily. The equipment to re-role the aircraft to aeromed role is carried in the aircraft permanently. There are enough stanchions, tracks and brackets to allow up to 64 stretchers on a C.1 and 97 on a C.3 to be carried. There are 9 DC

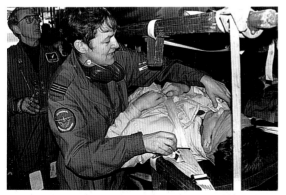
A member of No 4626 R Aux AF medical team attends to a Medevac patient

electrical power outlets throughout the aircraft plus 2 outlets for the "iron lung" to be connected. Another type of stretcher which may be carried is the Comet frame which fits into the existing 20 inch grid floor tie-down points. It swivels on its frame, allowing patients to be inverted whilst still strapped into the stretcher.

A medic attends to a baby prior to departure

The Aeromed Section at RAF Wroughton co-ordinates all aeromed tasks. It supplies any specially required equipment such as incubators, and allocates escorts. There are basically three classes of patients; psychiatry, stretcher and walking. There are various degrees of these basic three categories; these are also of various priorities from life or death need to travel, to its being merely a convenience that they return to the UK. These flights do not necessarily terminate in the UK.

Air-to-Air Refuelling. The Hercules is capable of tanking, receiving or both depending the Mark.

Search and Rescue. The Hercules has 10 hours endurance without refuelling. Air Sea Rescue (ASR) equipment can be carried and dropped to survivors.

Maritime Radar Reconnaissance. Using the

A technician checks a pair of NVG

Hercules lengthy endurance, it is capable of providing a visual watch of shipping - predominantly in the South Atlantic

Tactical Support. The Hercules is equipped for medium level transit using Station Keeping Equipment (SKE) to maintain formation, low-level approach to drop-zone or airhead, airdrop troops or equipment, and airland. It can also be used for Special Forces Operations, Night Vision Goggles (NVG) operations, including airfield assault.

Members of 5AB board the Hercules at Lyneham

5 Airborne Brigade

The Fifth Airborne Brigade is based at Aldershot. Their main task is to travel "light" and react rapidly to a given situation and surprise the enemy by striking deep into his territory.

Hence air transport is needed to fulfil two options. One is to airland the troops using the Tactical AirLand Operation (TALO) and the other is by parachute. As a result the fifth Airborne Brigade and Lyneham work close together. Using different parachute techniques, the troops can be despatched from a high or low level altitude. The low level despatch is done from a height of 250ft using the Low Level Parachute (LLP).

Tension mounts as the aircraft is three minutes from the DZ

The moment arrives when the Hercules passes over the DZ, hopefully with an element of surprise to the enemy. This time it was just an exercise but who knows next time

A Gurkha amongst a group of paras relaxes while the aircraft is in transit to the DZ

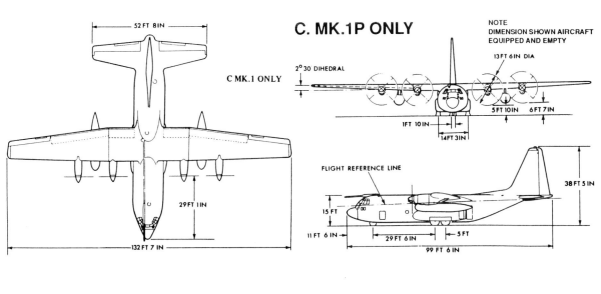

C. MK.1P ONLY

C MK.1 ONLY

52 FT 8 IN

29 FT 1 IN

132 FT 7 IN

2° 30 DIHEDRAL

NOTE
DIMENSION SHOWN AIRCRAFT
EQUIPPED AND EMPTY

13 FT 6 IN DIA

5 FT 10 IN   6 FT 7 IN

1 FT 10 IN

14 FT 3 IN

38 FT 5 IN

FLIGHT REFERENCE LINE

15 FT

11 FT 6 IN

29 FT 6 IN   5 FT

99 FT 6 IN

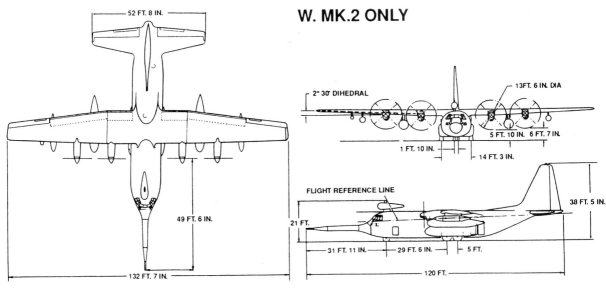

W. MK.2 ONLY

52 FT. 8 IN.

49 FT. 6 IN.

132 FT. 7 IN.

2° 30' DIHEDRAL

13 FT. 6 IN. DIA

5 FT. 10 IN.   6 FT. 7 IN.

1 FT. 10 IN.

14 FT. 3 IN.

38 FT. 5 IN.

FLIGHT REFERENCE LINE

21 FT.

31 FT. 11 IN.   29 FT. 6 IN.   5 FT.

120 FT.

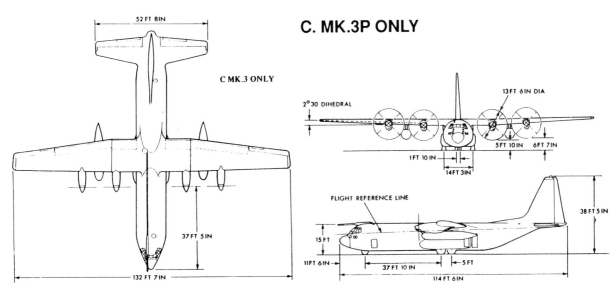

C. MK.3P ONLY

C MK.3 ONLY

52 FT 8 IN

37 FT 5 IN

132 FT 7 IN

2° 30 DIHEDRAL

13 FT 6 IN DIA

5 FT 10 IN   6 FT 7 IN

1 FT 10 IN

14 FT 3 IN

38 FT 5 IN

FLIGHT REFERENCE LINE

15 FT

11 FT 6 IN

37 FT 10 IN   5 FT

114 FT 6 IN

	C.1P	**C.3P**
Powerplant:	4 x Allison T56A-15 turboprops giving 4910eshp	4 x Allison T56A-15 turboprops giving 4910eshp
Basic Weight:	78,000lbs (approx)	83,000lbs (approx)
Max Take off Weight:	155,000lbs	160,000lbs
Max Fuel Capacity:	62,900lbs	62,900lbs
Max Payload:	44,000lbs	42,000lbs
Still Air Range with 3,000lbs payload:	2,950nm	3,000nm
Cruising TAS:	315kts	315kts
Typical Max Loads:	92 Passengers	126 Passengers
or	64 Paratroops	90 Paratroops
or	74 Stretchers	97 Stretchers
or	5 Pallets	7 Pallets
or	1 Puma Helicopter	1 Puma Helicopter

Dimensions

	C.1P	C.3P
Wing Span:	132ft 7ins	132ft 7ins
Length:	99ft 6ins	114ft 6ins
Height (Fin):	38ft 5ins	38ft 5ins

Cargo Compartment

	C.1P	C.3P
Length:	41ft	56ft
Width:	10ft	10ft
Height:	9ft	9ft
Capacity:	4,300cu ft	5,860cu ft

Number of C-130K built: **66**

Serial Range: XV176 - XV223 (48)   *C/ns:* 382-4169/4182/4188/4195/4196/4198-4201/4203-·4207/4210-4214/4216-4220/4223/4224/4225-4228/4230-4233/4235-4238/4240-4247,4251-4253

XV290-XV307 (18)   *C/ns:* 382-4254/4256-4259/4261-4264/4266-4268/4270/4272-4275/4277

Conversions:
C.Mk1K   XV192*, XV201, XV203, XV204, XV213, XV296
W.Mk2   XV208
C.Mk3   XV176, XV177, XV183, XV184, XV188, XV189, XV190, XV193, XV197, XV199, XV202, XV207, XV209, XV212, XV214, XV217, XV219/223, XV290, XV294, XV299, XV301/305, XV307

* XV192 re-converted to C.Mk1P

CHAPTER 4

Hercules Modifications

A Selection of Marshall's Main Tasks on RAF Hercules (fitting out, painting and modifications).

Starting Dates;

1966 Delivery programme including fitting out and painting of the RAF fleet.

1969 Fuel contamination and tank corrosion rectification programme.

1972 Conversion of a C.1 to W.2 (Meteorological Research aircraft).

1975 Major maintenance.

1975 Replacement of all centre wings.

1976 Major rebuild of XV181 following a landing accident.

1977 Refurbishment of all outer wings.

1979 Conversion of 30 C.1 aircraft to C.3 (15 feet stretch).

1982 Fatigue testing of refurbished outer wing

1982 Provision of in-flight refuelling probes for Falklands crisis.

1982 Conversion of six aircraft to tankers.

1983 Fitting of Station Keeping Equipment (SKE) and OMEGA navigational system.

1987 Fitting of Infra-Red Counter Measures (IRCM)

1990 Gulf Crisis support including introduction of enhanced navigation, communications and defensive systems.

Two and a half decades of Hercules Operations

1. Initial Procurement. The RAF's Hercules, ordered in 1966, was based on the Lockheed C-130E model with the advanced T56-A15 engine and fitted with British navaids, radios, autopilot and roller conveyer and some British-made airframe components. Marshall of Cambridge (Engineering) (MCE) (now renamed Marshall Aerospace) were appointed Design Authority and were responsible for embodying the initial modifications.

For MCE, the Secretary of State's announcement presented an opportunity to build on its success with earlier projects for the Royal Air Force, including support of the Valiants of the nuclear deterrent force. The Company accordingly made a successful bid to the Ministry of Aviation for the RAF Hercules fleet to be supported at Cambridge. Contracts were subsequently signed appointing MCE as the United Kingdom Designated Firm for the Hercules as well as Lockheed Marietta. It was also to provide technical liaison between the two companies. This was the start of a long and happy association.

Fitting Out 1966

The first Royal Air Force Hercules to arrive in the United Kingdom, XV177, landed at Cambridge on 19th December 1966 after flying directly from Marietta. An extensive programme of fitting out, external painting and flight testing by Marshall preceded the delivery of all sixty six aircraft to the Royal Air Force from 1967 onwards. The RAF's variant of the C-130E was defined by Lockheed as the C-130K although its official UK designation became the Hercules C.Mk1. Also in 1966, MCE was appointed by Lockheed as the first Authorised Maintenance and Service Centre for Hercules aircraft, and work has subsequently been attracted from over 50 operators world-wide, ranging from routine servicing and maintenance to large modification and repair programmes.

Centre Wing Fatigue Test Rig

In the mid-1960s structural fatigue was discovered in the wings of some of the USAF Hercules which had already been in service for over ten years. After further extensive testing by Lockheed, the USAF decided to replace the wing centre sections of their aircraft. The results of these tests were made available to MCE, and the Ministry of Defence Procurement Executive decided that a specimen Hercules centre wing should be fatigue tested to reflect the different operating patterns of the RAF aircraft. Accordingly, MCE designed and built a test rig and commenced an intensive test programme which continued until January 1975.

Wing Tank Fungal Corrosion 1969

In November 1969, an emergency maintenance problem presented itself without warning. A spot of moisture was detected on the under-surface of the mainplane of a Hercules undergoing pre-flight inspection at Cambridge. The inspector wiped off the moisture but another spot appeared. The inspector then detected a pin-point hole in the paint so he applied a thin piece of wire which passed easily through the tank plank.

An inspection of the tank interior revealed signs of severe fungal corrosion of the lower wing planks. Other aircraft were checked immediately, with similar results, and it was decided that the entire fleet should undergo a detailed investigation without delay.

MCE was given the responsibility for this investigation and dispatched inspection teams to all RAF Hercules locations, including those in the Far East. It was discovered that the entire fleet showed signs of contamination to a greater or lesser extent.

Following fuel draining and tank purging, washing and scrubbing, the aircraft were inspected and categorised under four headings, ranging from fungal contamination but with no corrosion to very severe corrosion requiring wing removal and rebuilding. There were eleven aircraft in the latter category.

To assist in rebuilding the wings, MCE designed jigs to allow the wing structure to be turned for access to the lower planks and to locate accurately the wing root and corner fittings, as well as the front and rear spar caps, to ensure no movement of the wing structure whilst planks were removed and replaced. Another problem was the time required to cure the sealant between coats. The Company therefore designed and produced special equipment to reduce the curing time from 72 to 18 hours.

The urgency and magnitude of the programme is illustrated by the fact that in March 1970 there were nineteen RAF Hercules at Cambridge, seventeen of which were in work on tank corrosion. Lockheed responded magnificently with accelerated supplies of replacement wing planks manufactured at their Marietta plant and the whole programme was completed by Marshall in just 14 months.

It was thought that the fungal corrosion might have resulted from contaminated fuel picked up between the UK and the Far East. As a result, enhanced fuel management systems, both on the ground and in the aircraft, and improved quality control procedures were therefore introduced concurrently with the wing rebuilding programme and have subsequently prevented any recurrence of this problem. These measures included the introduction of strontium chromate cartridges into the fuel tanks of all the RAF Hercules and the provision of fuel containing the additive FSII (Fuel System Icing Inhibitor) which contains an anti-corrosive as well as anti-icing inhibitors.

The Meteorological Research Hercules W.2

In 1972 it was decided to add another aircraft to the Meteorological Research Flight based at the Royal Aircraft Establishment, Farnborough. The Hercules was the chosen aircraft and in due course XV208 was withdrawn from normal RAF service and delivered to Cambridge for conversion to its new role.

The Marshall Aircraft Design Office was responsible for the design of the substantial modifications for this unique aircraft which was designated the Hercules W.Mk2. The most significant visible changes to the general external appearance, apart from the white and grey finish,

XV208 during conversion to W.2 at Cambridge

were the large weather radar pod mounted over the cockpit and long instrumented, nose probe. Much detailed attention was applied to reducing resonance to an acceptable level under all flying conditions. Internal provision was made for the fitting of television cameras together with an impressive array of complex weather recording equipment, the stowage and ejection from the pressurised aircraft of radio sondes (parachute deployed atmospheric measuring devices) and a removable recorder van installed in the cargo compartment. The van was designed for quick installation and removal and provided a self-contained, air-conditioned centre for the control, reception and recording of meteorological information. The design eliminated both static and impulse electrical interference between the aircraft and recorder van systems. Acoustic baffling was incorporated in the van to reduce noise to acceptable levels. The first flight of the modified aircraft, affectionately known within the RAF as "Snoopy", took place on 31st March 1972. XV208 operates worldwide from its base at Farnborough on its task of weather reconnaissance and research, but returns periodically to Cambridge for modifications and maintenance. This aircraft was flown to the Gulf at the end of the War to sample the pollution and atmospheric effects of the oil well fires in Kuwait.

Major Maintenance

The major servicing of the Hercules fleet was carried out by RAF Colerne tradesmen up until 1974. From then on MCE have undertaken the work which currently takes 90 days per airframe.

Centre Wing Replacement

Following the centre wing fatigue test programme, the RAF decided in 1975 to change the centre wings

on their aircraft to the latest Lockheed standard, thus extending the service life of RAF Hercules considerably beyond the ten years originally envisaged. Accordingly, Marshall manufactured special jigs and this work was carried out progressively at Cambridge.

Fitting the centre wing section to XV297

Outer Wing Refurbishment

Concurrently with the 1975 decision to replace the centre wings, the option of replacing the outer wings to the latest specification was considered by the Ministry of Defence. The alternative course was to refurbish the original outer wings, including the replacement of planks, and to incorporate fourteen wing fatigue modifications, one of which involved the fitting of new engine truss mounts. After consideration had been given to UK employment, costs and the availability of dollars, the Ministry decided to refurbish the wings at Cambridge. This programme of work commenced in 1977 using the jigs and the expertise acquired during the wing tank corrosion rectification.

Aircraft Recovery

While on a training exercise at Thorney Island in

Damage sustained to XV181 at Thorney Island

The same view of the nose wheel bay after repair

1976, XV181 was extensively damaged almost to the extent of being considered a write-off. This aircraft was recovered and rebuilt by MCE at Cambridge.

The Stretch Programme

A problem that the RAF regularly encountered was that the Hercules "bulked out". In other words the density of the loads resulted in the Hercules freight bay being full but the aircraft was capable of carrying still more weight.

C.3 conversion at Cambridge showing XV189 in a dismantled condition forground while XV217 at the rear has been re-assembled

In 1978, the Ministry of Defence Procurement Executive decided to adopt a Lockheed design to lengthen thirty of the RAF's standard C.1 aircraft by 15 feet by inserting two fuselage sections of 100 inches and 80 inches respectively at stations fore and aft of the main wing box. This variant was designated the Hercules C.3 and the conversion increased the troop carrying capacity from 92 to 128 and load carrying volume by 37%. The first Hercules selected for conversion was flown by the Royal Air Force to Marietta in 1979. A group of MCE technicians flew to Marietta in September of that year to observe and participate in the prototype

stretch which was completed by Lockheed. The remaining twenty nine aircraft were completed at Cambridge in a programme commencing in 1980. The first C.3 was handed over to the RAF in August of that year and the author was one of the crew to deliver it back to Lyneham.

Wing-tip to Wing-tip Fatigue Test Rig

The outer wing refurbishment programme produced a wing structure which was unique in many respects to the RAF aircraft but there was no test data available to confirm the fatigue life of these refurbished wings. Because the RAF wished to extend the life of its aircraft for at least another 20 years, it was decided that a fatigue test of the full RAF wing was necessary to establish the test data. Marshall was therefore tasked in late 1980 to build and operate a wing-tip to wing-tip fatigue test rig. Testing continues to this day keeping factory simulated flying hours well ahead of those of the lead aircraft.

The Wing-tip to Wing-tip fatigue test rig

Falklands Crisis - In-Flight Refuelling

The 1982 Falklands crisis brought new challenges for the RAF's air transport fleet. To support the expeditionary forces in what was code named "Operation Corporate" the RAF set up a massive airlift using Hercules transport aircraft flying from RAF Lyneham to Ascension Island. However, owing to the distances involved and the inability to refuel in South America, it was not possible for the

Hercules to reach the Falkland Islands and return without in-flight refuelling. On the evening of Thursday 15th April 1982 MCE received an emergency telephone call instructing the Company to proceed with all possible speed with the design, manufacture, installation and flight trials to provide the Hercules with an air refuelling receiver capability. A skeleton plan of the system layout, including a receiver probe mounted above the cockpit, and a fuel management plan were drawn up during the night - the first metal was cut on Saturday 17th April in advance of approved drawings.

Marshall engineers fitting the refuelling probe

Fitting the probe plumbing on top of the fuselage

The first aircraft was completed and cleared of MCE and Boscombe Down Flight trials, which included day and night wet couplings, and was ready to proceed to the Falklands on 5th May. Five further probe-equipped aircraft were delivered for immediate service on the 13th, 28th and 31st of May, and on the 5th and 6th of June.

This conversion enabled essential supplies to be dropped to our Forces - a factor which was crucial to the success of the military campaign. The aircraft were refuelled from Victor tankers using the

The finished probe which is off-set to the right

established tobogganing technique to enable the Hercules to fly fast enough behind the Victor.

The successful achievement of this vital conversion, and getting it right first time, was only possible as a result of the build-up of in-depth experience by MCE as the Technical/Maintenance Centre for the Hercules aircraft for over 16 years. The Falklands probe conversion, even though produced as a rapid response to an emergency situation requirement, proved to be so successful that it was fitted, virtually unchanged, to the rest of the RAF Hercules fleet and remains so to this day.

On 30th April MCE was given a second Falklands challenge with an instruction to proceed with all possible speed to provide four Hercules with an in-flight tanker capability. This involved mounting the Flight Refuelling Mk.17B Hose Drum Unit (HDU) on the aircraft's ramp floor and fitting strakes on the underside of the ramp to smooth out the air flow and stabilise the trailing of the refuelling hose and drogue. During the course of the programme a number of problems developed, particularly with the cooling of the HDU - this being the first time an HDU had been housed within an aircraft cabin. Having identified this cooling problem on a test flight which extended into the evening, the design team met during the night to define the remedial actions to be taken.

The first tanker completed MCE and Boscombe Down flight trials and was delivered within 76 days of the instruction to proceed. The remaining three

Fitting the Mk.17 HDU onto the ramp

aircraft were ordered and completed in early 1983. The Falklands Campaign clearly identified the need for a long range strategic tanker. Marshall's success in responding quickly for the Hercules paved the way to the Company winning the contract to convert another Lockheed aircraft - the Tristar.

Hercules C.1K tanker refuels a C.1P transport

Belly Re-skining
Following the intensive flying which involved frequent rough strip landings during "Operation

Bushell" in Ethiopia the total of sixteen Hercules involved suffered considerable stone damage on their underside. As a result extensive re-skinning was required.

Fitting of Infra-Red Counter Measures (IRCM)
A number of Hercules were fitted with an IRCM system to counter a possible treat from the air-to-air or Surface to Air Missile (SAM).

The Gulf Crisis
In late 1990 events in the Gulf brought Marshall challenges similar to those of the Falklands Campaign. Urgent Operational Requirements were met by the design and installation of additional navigation and defence equipment in less than the agreed programme timescales, and by carrying out additional servicing work, all under the UK code name "Operation Granby".

Continuing Support
In addition to being awarded successive contracts for the Major Maintenance of RAF Hercules since 1975, the Company has also helped to support Hercules aircraft for other civilian and military operators worldwide for many years. This has, in particular, included support and modifications for aircraft from Australia, New Zealand and several Asian and Gulf states as well as from many American, African and European countries.

This brief record of MCE collaboration with Lockheed on the Hercules is a testimony to the very close working relationship which developed between staff at Marshall and their opposite numbers at Lockheed-Marietta.

This relationship is well summarised in the following extract from a letter written by Mr Bob Ormsby, the then Group President of Lockheed Aeronautical Systems, to Sir Arthur Marshall following the handover of the last stretched aircraft in 1985.

"As the manufacturer of the Hercules, we always have a great interest in who modifies our aircraft and how well they do it. Even though such modification work is not ours, the airplane is known as a Lockheed product and our reputation is involved. We have never been concerned about this when

Marshall has performed the work. Because of the long and excellent relationship between our two companies, we know the work will be done as well as if we had done it ourselves. This program is but another example that our confidence is well placed."

Engineering Wing Modifications - Lyneham
Certain modifications which can be designed and manufactured locally are utilised in the aircraft. Below are some of them.

1. Underfloor Heating Re-circulating Fan. The Cargo Compartment Air Conditioner pushes the bulk of the 70lbs/min conditioned air through the overhead ducts. When the underfloor heating is selected, using the switch on the Flight Engineer's overhead panel, it diverts a maximum of 43lbs/min air through the louvres on the floor on both sides of the aircraft side/wall. A re-circulation fan is fitted to a point near the roof above one of the overhead ducts and it used to be one of the noisiest pieces of kit inside the cargo compartment. It was found that by fitting a silencer in the form of padded material the noise would be reduced. The suitable modification was designed and successfully fitted to the entire fleet.

2. De-mister for the Flight Deck Dome (CUPOLA). For Air-to-Air refuelling, fighter affiliation, and for formation flying, the glass dome in the flight deck is a very useful piece of kit, but it originally started to mist up after a few seconds. Station Workshops made an assembly to duct the conditioned air from the Flight Deck Air Conditioner and route it through a flexible pipe to the dome assembly. (All the air that comes to the

The cupola is not fitted to all Hercules

flight deck air conditioner is removed of any moisture by the water separator.)

3. Additional louvres in the flight deck. When operating out of hostile areas metal backplates are used on the back rest behind the seat. This causes less circulation of air for the shoulder area and it is unbearable if operating from a hot environment. To alleviate this, two sets of louvres are fitted to the flight deck air conditioning systems' pipes and these direct forced air towards the metal plate area, hence some "cool" comfort for the pilots.

Major airframe changes
1. **C.Mk1.** The standard first model following delivery from Lockheed and final fitting out by Marshall of Cambridge.

2. **C.Mk3**. The stretched version modified from the C.Mk1.

3. **W.Mk2.** The weather reconnaissance and research variant operated by the Royal Aircraft Establishment's Meteorological Research Flight at Farnborough modified from a C.Mk1.

4. **C.Mk1LR2.** The standard Hercules with two Andover long range fuel tanks fitted to the forward section of the Cargo Compartment.

5. **C.Mk1LR4.** Standard Hercules with four Andover long range fuel tanks fitted in the Cargo Compartment.

6. **C.Mk1PLR2.** Standard Hercules as C.Mk1LR2 but with a probe for Air-to-Air refuelling.

7. **C.Mk1PLR4.** Standard Hercules as C.Mk1LR4 but with a probe for Air-to-Air refuelling.

8. **C.Mk1P.** Standard Hercules as C.Mk1 but with a probe for Air-to-Air refuelling.

9. **C.Mk1K.** Hercules tanker with a probe modified from a C.Mk1
Variant descriptions

Hercules C.Mk1
The basic Hercules C.Mk1 has been fully described in Chapter 3

Hercules C.Mk3

The Hercules C.Mk1 conversion is described in the Stretch Programme above.

Hercules C.Mk1LR2

Two large Andover long range transit tanks are fitted to the forward section in the freight bay of the Hercules. These tanks are about 15ft long and 4ft in diameter and enclosed on to a frame. This is a single unit piece of equipment and is secured to the floor points in the aircraft. The rear section has a vertical sight glass with a "blob" on it and is housed in a visible cylindrical metal casing. When the fuel is pumped in the blob rises to the top and the graduated scale at the side of the casing shows the amount of fuel in imperial gallons. This has to be converted to pounds by the Air Load Master and the Flight Engineer after an adjustment is made of the contents, because of the angle of the aircraft in flight or on the ground, from a graph. The tank has a cap on the top nearside to the sight glass from where the fuel can be brought in with a long hose and attached to the fuel bowser through a coupling. This orifice also doubled up to determine the fuel physically by inserting the end of a broom handle that is part of the aircraft role equipment. At the lower portion of the tank a hose is fitted to a receptacle and connected to a collector box behind it which has three electric pumps. These pump the fuel to the aircraft fuel manifold through the fuel cocks and a non-return valve (NRV). The other tanks are also connected to the collector box. From the manifold the fuel enters any of the eight tanks.

Selection of fuel from these tanks to the wing tanks is from the Air-to-Air (AAR) refuelling panel above the Navigators instrument panel. These two tanks are termed the forward fuselage tanks 1 and 2 and each contains 7,000lbs of fuel. This fuel load gives a range of an extra 1,000 miles. The plumbing of these tanks started from drawings on the blackboard in the Aircraft Engineering Squadron (AES). After trials and errors the "team" successfully installed the necessary pipes, cocks and a non-return valve (NRV) which was subsequently refined by Marshall's of Cambridge. It took five days for AES to complete this modification and the aircraft was then re-designated Hercules C.Mk1LR2.

Hercules C.Mk1LR4

Same as C.Mk1LR2 but with two further Andover tanks installed rear of the collector box. These four tanks provide an additional fuel load of 28,000lbs which also reduced the payload by 28,000lbs plus the weight of these tanks.

Hercules C.1PLR2

Same as C.Mk1LR2 but with a probe fitted to the top of the flight deck slightly offset to the right of the centreline of the aircraft just above the co-pilot's head. The probe is fitted with a Mk.8 nozzle at the forward end and a NRV at the other end. From the probe NRV, the delivery pipeline is routed along the outside of the fuselage (faired in to minimise drag) to a position level with the trailing edge of the right wing. The pipeline is coupled with the ground refuelling line, via a NRV at a point between the off-load valve and the single-point refuelling connector. This allows a reasonable payload to be carried and air-to-air refuelling to be undertaken giving it a good range. This configuration was frequently used to ferry passengers and freight to the Falkland Islands and still had sufficient fuel to return to Ascension should a landing have proved impossible (in case of bad weather at Stanley).

Hercules C.Mk1PLR4

Same as C.Mk1LR4 but fitted with a probe for air-to-air refuelling.

Hercules C.Mk1P

The Standard C.Mk1 Hercules with a probe fitted and no fuselage tanks.

Hercules C.Mk1K

A C.Mk1 fitted with four Andover long range fuel tanks as in the fuselage as the C.Mk1LR4. A total of six were converted to tankers and all tankers have probes fitted as standard. This allowed the tanker to receive fuel in flight and dispense fuel. This mark was widely used and was operated from Ascension as the augmented tanker to refuel the daily Hercules schedule to Stanley. Two of these were detached to Stanley from September 1982 to refuel Phantom and Harrier aircraft. The system consists of the fuel transfer equipment of a Mk.17B hose drum unit (HDU) fitted in a frame mounted on the aircraft ramp. A drogue deployment box is located in the cargo compartment door. A secondary serving carriage is fitted aft of the HDU to feed the hose into the drogue deployment box, to enable the aircraft to be pressurised when not refuelling. A pressure door is fitted around the delivery hose where it passes into the drogue deployment box. The door is opened manually, after depressurising the aircraft, before operating the HDU.

An internal view of the C.1K with the four tanks

To assist in initial deployment of the drogue, a retractable air scoop is fitted on the underside of the drogue deployment box. When the refuelling hose is fully trailed it measures 80ft. Refuelling signal lights are fitted on each side of the drogue deployment box and floodlights inside the box illuminate the serving carriage. Hose floodlamps are fitted externally.

All the controls of the HDU are fitted beside the Navigators instrument panel. The supply of fuel for transfer is managed from the engineer's fuel panel.

The probe of the Hercules C.1P approaches the basket deployed from the C.1K

Watching the Weather with Snoopy by MEng Alan Kitson

Almost from the first time I knew I was to join the Meteorological Research Flight (MRF) at RAE Farnborough, I was aware that many Flight Engineers have a somewhat sketchy idea of the work of the "Flight".

We do not, as some people suspect, go flying off into the nearest cumulus-nimbus just to prove that it's there! I have been around for too many years to allow myself to be put into a situation that is even remotely dangerous.

So what on earth, you ask, do you do? As most of the equipment used in the back of Snoopy (as our W.2 Hercules is affectionately known) is far too technical for this humble engineer to explain in detail I will try to keep to basics and work on the KISS principle.

The MRF is currently a lodger unit at the Defence Research Agency (DRA), Farnborough and is a direct descendant of the RAF's high altitude flight. The RAF aircrew element of two pilots, two navigators and two flight engineers operate the Hercules as an airborne research laboratory for numerous meteorological project scientists, supported by technical and scientific staff. Scientists at Bracknell (Met Office HQ) and several universities very often make use of our facility for a variety of atmospheric studies. Unlike most posts filled by RAF aircrew, we work completely within a civilian environment. This obviously means that the Service aircrew, civilian scientists and technical staff must work in close co-operation and with a mutual understanding of each other's problems, if each sortie is to be a success.

Snoopy is an old friend of mine, XV208 being an ex-Far East Air Force (FEAF) C.1. Marshall of Cambridge were given the task of modifying the airframe to a shape which is almost as we see it today. The aircraft was diverted to MRF in 1973 after trials at Boscombe Down.

The major differences from the "fleet" Hercules are the 22 ft long "barber's pole" of the probe nose, the transfer of the CCWR in the nose to a zero drag fairing above the flight deck, (shades of basic aerodynamics!) and three extra wing pods - the two larger ones using the fittings of the "A" model Hercules external fuel tanks. There are also the many and various scoops, probes and vanes. The overall effect of the hangers-on is a reduction of target speed by about five knots and an increase of four knots in the minimum control speeds compared with the C.Mk1 and C.Mk3.

Snoopy showing the CCWR on top of the cockpit

Inside, the flight deck is visually similar except for the addition of extra circuit breaker panels - controlling power for the scientific equipment (MRF Power), an angle of attack and stall warning indicator and an inertial nav system. Behind the Captain's position an extra seat is fitted to facilitate the aircraft scientist who directs operations from there in conjunction with the aircraft Captain. Using a remote TV screen fitted to the rear of the captain's seat he relays any information from the scientists stationed in the depths of the freight bay. In the freight bay a team of scientists and observers work in two specially constructed caravans and at pieces of equipment internally secured around the aircraft.

From a scientific point of view the aircraft is used to study a variety of atmospheric phenomena ranging from the basics, such as the structure and dynamics of clouds and the evolution of weather fronts, to the effect of topographical features on wind structure and the more modern problems of transportation of pollutants and the amounts of trace gases in the atmosphere, a problem highlighted by the "green revolution".

Although other nations have meteorological research aircraft, with which we work closely at times, none are so comprehensively equipped. This allows us so much more flexibility in completing the many tasks allocated to the Flight. A typical day on the Flight

starts with an up-to-the-minute met briefing at 0830. Much use is made of Metosat pictures that are regularly updated. The Metosat being a satellite which has been placed in a geostationary orbit about the equator to provide weather information. Following the general met brief, the scientist concerned with the day's experiment will give a specific brief on what he or she requires from the aircraft, crew and met observers. The general area of operations is decided at this point, although precise locations and altitudes will be left until we approach the area. Flexibility is the name of the game and the plan could and often does change as the experiment is progressing. From the aircrew side, the pilots and navigators will make final arrangements with the various air traffic agencies and special tasks controllers. With the take-off due at 1030 the two Flight Engineers confirm any special requirements with the scientist. On occasion the cabin altitude pressure must be set at a particular height or it may be that a certain piece of equipment needs to be kept cooler than is usual. They then move out to Snoopy, the operating Engineer completes the paperwork and the number two to check the all important rations. Then the aircraft checks are completed with very little change from those on the standard Hercules.

Our typical experiment could take us out over the South-Western Approaches looking for cumulus clouds to study the effect they may have on solar and terrestrial radiation. Having reached the area and the aircraft scientist is happy with the cloud formation, a profile descent is then made. This would probably commence at FL250 at a constant speed of 180kts and descent at 1,000ft/min down to 50ft above the sea. During the descent, the aircraft will have been acting as a controllable sonde measuring temperature, pressure and humidity. Accurate flying is essential especially towards the bottom of the profile. To this end the Air Engineer will call out radar altimeter heights, also checking visually and on radar for possible obstructions - ships, rigs etc. Once down at low level we could be required to fly at anything between 75 and 200 ft over a leg length of up to 150km to take measurements of sea surface temperature. Similar runs would be made within and above selected clouds over the same geographical point or within the same air mass, requiring considerable navigational accuracy. Once the scientists are satisfied with the data collected (or airfield closing time approaches!) a final profile ascent will be made and the aircraft flown back to base. The scientific data is recorded on magnetic tapes for later evaluation and can also be taken from the in-flight computers on paper copy for up-to-the-minute assessment.

Met Research Flight has a requirement for worldwide operation to research into weather phenomena. Snoopy is sent off on detachment to all types of locations from the cold of Norway to evaluate satellite remote probing systems and based at Oulu in `Finland to study the properties of snow and ice surfaces and the effect that they may have on met satellites.

Snoopy was the first scientific aircraft to fly in the Kuwait smoke plume for extensive periods. Samples of the plume were taken and analysed and the British Met Office were the first organisation to produce a scientific paper on the results. The signs of smoke were still apparent on the aircraft despite many washes twelve months later. The crew of the aircraft were probably the only ones to fly in full NBC kit during the Operation.

Snoopy overflies the pollution in Kuwait

Another project was the Calibration and Evaluation of the European Met Satellite ERS1. To do this the aircraft spent two separate periods in Trondheim, Norway and two weeks in Ascension Island. Thus covering Temperate and Cold conditions (Norway) and Hot conditions (Ascension).

Such are the happenings of Snoopy and crew. A small unit remote from the mainstream of the Service, helping with experiments so that weather may be forecast more accurately, thus helping aircrew to fly more safely. (Oh, I forgot to tell you - we have our own specially built and fitted loos as well!).

CHAPTER 5

The Operational Record

Since the arrival of the first RAF Hercules at Thorney Island on 3rd May 1967, the aircraft has been involved in many operational and humanitarian tasks throughout the world.

The operational highlights of the past 26 years listed below reflect the inherent flexibility of the Hercules and the diversity of the air transport task:

1967
Withdrawal from Aden: 52 evacuation sorties to Bahrain, all but one achieving less than 30 minute turn-round times at Aden. Recovery of the RAF El Aden Desert Rescue Team from Kufra Oasis.

1968
Resupply of British TransArctic Expedition.

Recovery of Hawker Hind from Kabul, Afghanistan.

Unloading the Afghan Hind

1969
Deployment of Marines and police to quell Anguillan rebellion.

1970
Airlift of Red Cross relief support in Jordan, airlift of relief supplies to Turkey and Peru following earthquakes, and to East Pakistan following a cyclone disaster.

1971
Airlift of medical supplies to Calcutta to help stem cholera epidemic.

Indo-Pakistani War; extraction of British nationals from Karachi and Chakala to the safety of Masirah.

1972
Initial withdrawal of British troops from Malta.

Rapid deployment of troops to Belize to counter threat of invasion by neighbouring Guatemala.

Assistance with typhoon relief in the Phillipines.

Emergency airlift of relief supplies to Nicaragua (on Christmas Day) following earthquake.

Resupply of the International Scientific base at McMurdo Sound, Antarctica by RAF Hercules operating out of Christchurch, NZ.

1973
Mercy missions to famine areas in Southern Sudan, Mali, Senegal and other areas of West Africa.

Operation Khana Cascade: a four-aircraft detachment to Nepal to airdrop food to the starving people of remote, mountainous and relatively inaccessible West Nepal. 1,964 tons of food were airdropped in 29 days.

Airlift of 900 non-British troops into Cairo to establish the UN peace keeping force in the wake of the Yom Kippur War.

1974

Relief supplies airdropped to St Helena. Assistance given in the Darwin area following its devastation by Cyclone Tracy, and further famine relief in North Africa.

Coup in Cyprus and Turkish Invasion: intensive airlift to extract Service families and international tourists from Kingsfield Airstrip, Dhekalia, to the safety of RAF Akrotiri and thence to the UK. A total of 5,148 people of 46 nationalities were evacuated to the UK.

1975

Evacuation (under mortar fire on one occassion) of the British Embassy Staff from Saigon immediately prior to the fall of the city.

A further reinforcement to Belize following a heightening of tension in the area.

1976

Relief supplies flown to the Van area of Turkey following an earthquake.

1977

Rapid, and very effective airlift of Harriers, Rapier and troops to Belize to counter the seemingly imminent invasion by Guatemala.

1979

Evacuation of British and other Western nationals from Teheran and a minor airfield in the south of Iran following the overthrow of the Shah.

Relief supplies airlifted into civil war-torn Nicaragua.

Disaster relief flights to Yugoslavia following an earthquake.

Support of the Red Cross in Mapuchea, ferrying food and medical supplies to refugees in Phnom Penh from Bangkok.

Advance elements of the Commonwealth Ceasefire Monitoring Force airlifted to Rhodesia.

1980

Operation Agila: In-theatre as well as external support for the Commonwealth forces in Rhodesia.

Operation Khana Cascade '80: a re-run of the '73 Operation to bring famine relief to the inhabitants of Western Nepal.

Eight Hercules deployed to Vanuatu, New Hebrides, following a coup attempt by minority factions. Known as the "bring-a-bottle-war".

1982

Support British Forces during Operation Corporate - the return of the Falklands to British sovereignty. This has resulted in a Hercules detachment based on the Falklands ever since.

1983

Deployment and subsequent withdrawal of British elements of UN Peace Keeping Force in the Lebanon.

1984

Famine relief sorties flown to Upper Volta, transporting lorries as well as relief supplies.

Operation Bushel: RAF Hercules detachment established at Addis Ababa to conduct airland relief operations to remote strips in the drought stricken areas of Ethiopia.

1985

Operation Bushel continued to the end of November, developing into airdrop operations as well as airland. Some 32,000 tonnes of relief supplies were delivered by the RAF during Operation Bushel, of which 14,000 tonnes were airdropped.

1986

Disaster relief missions to Mexico City and Columbia.

Operation Balzac in support of the rescue of refugees from Aden.

1990

Support for the Electricity Board following the January gales.

Relief supplies flown to the Island of Montserrat following Hurricane Hugo.

Assistance to Western Samoa following a typhoon.

Operation Granby. The support of Allied forces following Iraq's invasion of Kuwait.

1991

Operation Granby - Provide Comfort. Air dropping relief supplies to the Kurdish refugees in Northern Iraq.

Operation Haven. Support of Royal Marines operations to provide safe areas for the Kurdish Refugees in Northern Iraq.

1992

Operation Warden. Extension of Operation Haven.

Operation Cheshire. Humanitarian & food aid flights in the former Yugoslavia.

Operation Jural. Deployment and resupply of Tornados for Southern Iraq Deny Flight.

Operation Hanwood. Delpoyment of Army Medical Corps to Bosnia.

Operation Grapple. Deployment and re-supply of Army in Bosnia

Operation Vigour. Famine relief sorties in Somalia.

1993

Operation Deny Flight. Deployment and re-supply Tornados for Bosnian Deny-Flight.

Routine Air Transport Operations. The preceeding list does not reflect the more routine Air Transport operations in support of all British Forces around the world. In addition there were the exchange programmes with foreign squadrons and international airlift competitions together with the support for British Diplomatic Staff world-wide plus the impromptu search and rescue operations and, of course, our own requirements for training and categorisation.

Aden - 1967 - Operation Jacobin

The Gulf of Aden stretches about 550 miles long and about 300 miles wide and lies to the western side of the Arabian sea. The shipping lane runs through this stretch from the Mediterranean to the Indian Ocean. Its chief ports are Berbera and Djibouti on the southern coast and Mukalla and Aden on the northern coast. Aden had a predominantly Moslem population of a quarter of a million people in 1967. Great Britain annexed it in 1839. It then became a colony and later a British protected state and was one of the members of the former Federation of South Arabia. It was a main port which had a large commercial sector and also had facilities for the refining and storing of oil. It became the capital of the People's Democratic Republic of Yemen in 1967. However, the transfer of power during independence, was not a smooth one due to skirmishes by the tribes along the coast and inland area. Many of these were targeted against the British.

In November 1967 a big shuttle was planned between the staging post at Muharraq in Bahrain and the forward airfield at Khormaksar, Aden. Tension had been building in the Aden area for some time and the idea was to airlift all British civilian and service personnel safely. The distance between Khormaksar and Muharraq is 1,000 miles, so it was planned to use the RAFs long range VC10 and the Britannia as the strategic transport airlift from Muharraq to the UK. The airlift operation was known as Operation Jacobin. The MOD had notified the requirements to the then HQ Air Support Command. Meetings were held at very high level which included HQ Middle East and RAF Khormaksar.

Four phases were set out with the Hercules Fleet being used extensively in the last one - the tactical phase - which was to last for the final 36 hours of the withdrawal of Army and Air Force personnel. This operation was a major test for the Hercules Fleet as the first Hercules had arrived only three months earlier. Fifteen Hercules were positioned at Muharraq of which No 36 Squadron, based at RAF Colerne and in the process of converting from Hastings, provided four crews and six aircraft. Two further aircraft were supplied with crews from No 48 Squadron, Changi, Singapore. The balance aircraft and crews were from No 242 OCU, Thorney Island. The entire assembled fleet of Hercules aircraft was commanded by Wing Commander J D Payling, OC No 36 Squadron. At this stage Nos 24, 30, 47 and 70 Squadrons were not equipped with the Hercules aircraft. The experienced crews were obviously those from No 36 Squadron with approximately 200 hours each followed by No 48 Squadron with 100 hours each. The technical groundcrew were limited to doing only the first line servicing.

The order to move came sooner than expected on 18th November 1967. The flight to Muharraq was about 12 hours non-stop and the first aircraft took off only 10 hours after the order was issued. At one hour intervals the 12 aircraft arrived safely by the morning of the 20th November. The unlucky 13th had to wait for diplomatic clearance from Akrotiri, Cyprus. There was nearly a "punch up" at Cyprus between the Cypriot Greeks and Cypriot Turks and the two nations of Greece and Turkey nearly went to war over this incident. On the 25th the last two aircraft arrived from Changi. During the early phase of 20th to 26th November, when other plans were put in full force to reduce the Garrison to a minimum, only a few flights were authorised for the Hercules fleet to fly to Khormaksar and return.

This was to familiarise the operating crew with certain procedures to enable them to get out of Khormaksar safely should the "natives" decide to harass the withdrawal during the final hours. Also the tactical loading and taxying procedures were learnt. The tactical loading involved loading with the two port engines running at low speed and shutting down the two starboard engines. This enabled speedy and safe loading from the starboard para door and the ramp with a safety man on the port side to prevent anyone walking towards the live propellers. The taxying involved manoeuvring the aircraft between two rows of stacked 45 gallon oil drums filled with water. These rows of water-filled drums were supposed to give some protection to the aircraft and passengers.

The fleet mounted 37 sorties to bring back passengers from the 26th to 29th November. This was nothing compared to the last 12 sorties on 30th which involved one sortie every 30 minutes. Only one flight was delayed due to a technical unserviceability but its place was taken by another one in less than five minutes. Some aircraft operated on a pure freight role whilst most of them took 75 passengers with their kit weighing about 5,000lbs. The turnaround for each aircraft was 30 minutes initially but as the ATLO and the Air Movement teams became experienced in these conditions they had trimmed it down to a fine art taking 10 minutes on the last two aircraft. The crews were also trained to land and take-off on only three serviceable engines but none were given the opportunity to try the method out. The mighty Hercules would not allow this and the crews encountered very few unserviceabilities. When the exercise was over all the aircraft returned to their home bases in the UK and Singapore.

Thirteen Britannias of Nos 99 and 511 Squadrons (which have since disbanded) from Lyneham, three VC10's of No 10 Squadron and two Belfasts of No 53 Squadron (now also disbanded), all from Brize Norton, were utilised for this operation. The VC10s and part of the Britannia fleet were utilised on the Muharraq to UK sector. In addition, the Argosy transport aircraft from No 70 Squadron were utilised between Muharraq, Khormaksar and other stations in the Gulf. For aerial protection and reconnaissance an umbrella of RAF and RN armed Wessex helicopters patrolled the perimeter of the airfield day and night. The RN had also positioned the Assault Ship HMS Intrepid for close support work and should they be required they would be assisted by RAF Hunter ground attack fighters.

Exercise Jacobin was successful because the liaison between aircrew and groundcrew was second to none. An important and vital contribution to the operation was made by the In-Flight Catering Section at Muharraq as well as the UKMAMS teams from Abingdon, Air Movements, ATLO, not forgetting the signals unit, No 2 Field Squadron (a Para unit) and No 37 Field Squadron (RAF Regiment).

East Pakistan - 1970
By mid-December the airlift of relief supplies and equipment by the RAF's Far East Air Force to cyclone-striken East Pakistan had already topped 1,400,000lbs, and Hercules aircraft had flown some 160,000 miles on the mercy missions.

Since the massive airlift was launched on 19th November, the RAF FEAF and Air Support Command Hercules had made 55 flights from Singapore to Dacca and Chittagong to air-drop fuel supplies, rice, milk, medical stores, clothing and blankets which had comprised the bulk of the relief supplies flown from Changi. The Hercules fleet had already delivered 1,400,000lbs of supplies, stores, equipment and passengers comprising British and Singapore Services aid teams to East Pakistan. The Hercules carried helicopters, boats, vehicles and trailers, motor-cycles, bicycles, fuel, radio and other

Some survivors near Dacca occupy a small island as refuge from the the floods

equipment and tents in addition to the huge loads of relief supplies. No 48 Squadron also air-dropped mail to Royal Navy ships taking part in the relief operations and also dropped fuel loads by parachute to the Navy's forward helicopter bases which were established near the cyclone disaster area, at the mouth of the River Ganges.

Stocks of vaccine against cholera and typhoid were flown in to the RAF airhead at Chittagong where a FEAF team ensured a smooth flow and turn-round of the Hercules flying in Red Cross and other stores and supplies from Singapore.

The author at Dacca Airport, East Pakistan

ANZUK - 1971

HMAS "Vendetta" a Royal Australian Navy Daring Class destroyer of 3,400 tons on deployment to ANZUK had completed visits to Subik Bay, and Cebu in the Philippines and was anchored in the Turtle Island group about three hours sailing from East Malaysia. The upper deck was being prepared for an all ranks "beer and barbecue" when the Captain, Commander Alan Ferris, called his second-in-command Lieutenant Commander Max Sulman and told him he was going to his cabin as he felt unwell.

An hour later the commander called for Lieutenant Bill Gason, Vendetta's doctor and said that he was feeling worse. Lt Gason, anxious about his captain's condition, advised Lt Cdr Sulman to make for the nearest shore hospital where a fuller examination could be made. The ship sailed at maximum speed to Sandakan in the north east of Sabah, East Malaysia where the commander was taken by ship's boat and ambulance to the local hospital. Commander Ferris became worse and the local medical staff decided that a transfer to the nearest military hospital was essential. The RAF Operations Room at the Singapore Armed Forces base, Tengah, was contacted and a request for a "casevac" (casualty evacuation) flight was made.

A Royal Air Force Hercules of No 24 Squadron based at Lyneham was staging through Singapore on a routine freighting mission and it was decided to use this aircraft. The crew of the Hercules was briefed to fly to Sandakan airstrip and return with the sick commander. The crew, Flight Lieutenant Dick Gould (Captain), Flight Lieutenant Dennis Cumming (Co-pilot), Flight Lieutenant Tom Norcross, (Navigator), Flight Sergeant Derek Lindegaard-Stewart, (Air Loadmaster), and Sergeant Pete Young (Flight Engineer), supervised the off-loading of freight and calculated the minimum amount of fuel required for the flight to Sandakan and to allow them to land on the short (4,500ft) runway there. The Hercules took off at 9 am with the casevac team of Lieutenant Colonel Ian Crawford, RAMC (Physician), Squadron Leader Jos Mitchell (Casevac Supervisor), the Senior RAF Medical Officer at Tengah, Flight Officer Pauline Gwythers (aeromedical sister), Staff Sergeant John Flynn, REME (medical technician) and Corporal Graham Elderfield, RAF, (ambulance attendant).

At 12.15pm the Hercules approached Sandakan airfield, which is normally used only for light commercial aircraft, and overflew the potholed runway. Considering the urgency of the situation and the amount of fuel on board Dick Gould decided to land off the second approach.

The aircraft touched down at 12.30pm, becoming the first RAF Hercules to land at Sandakan. The medical team examined the patient in consultation with the hospital staff and then took him to the aircraft. The Hercules took off again at 2.35pm for

Tengah. The waiting RAF Wessex helicopter of No 103 Squadron, crewed by Flight Lieutenant Martin Kaye and Sergeant Mike Maddison took Commander Ferris to the ANZUK Military Hospital at Changi.

Recovering, Commander Alan Ferris commented the following weekend that he was very grateful indeed for the first class co-operation and efficiency by the aircrews, medical teams and operations staff and gave his thanks.

Belize - 1972 todate

The Defence of Belize is conducted under the Defence Treaty between the Governments of Belize and Great Britain since 21st September 1981 - Belize's Independence. But over the years Guatemala has laid a claim to this, the only English speaking former British Colony. Mexico gained Independence in 1821 under Iturbide who gained temporary control of the Kingdom of Guatemala. Iturbide's sudden demise prompted the Provinces that made up the Kingdom of Guatemala to declare Independence in 1823 as the United Provinces of Central America. British woodcutters, former buccaneers, had been cutting mahogany from the river Hondo (now Belize's Northern border with Mexico) and as south as the river Sarstoon (Belize Southern border with Guatemala). The Western border was, and still is, from north to south from Garbutt Falls on the Belize river (an imaginary line). However, the border could have been defined much earlier with Spain if an orderly transfer of power had been given to her former colonies. The collapse of the Spanish Empire had a profound effect on the boundary settlement. The results of the Anglo-Mexican Treaty of 1826 resulted in Guatemala with her counter claims. This went on for many years, but in September 1864 the Imperial Commissioner for Yucaton (SE Mexico) published a decree that claimed Belize and parts of the Peten Province of Guatemala. The long-standing dispute came to an end after the Anglo-Mexico Treaty was signed in 1897, but the Guatemalan claim went on with the Treaty of 1859.

So who are the Guatemalans? More than half of the population are the original natives - the Maya Indians but they have no say in the running of the Government. The others are Mestizors (the Union of Spanish and Maya Indians) and a small minority of pure Spaniards.

The first Premier of Belize sums it all up in a speech made in August 1962................"Whenever there is internal strife in Guatemala, especially during election times or in times of economic collapse, this subject gives fuel for agitation".

So in early 1972 the Military Junta staged a military threat of an imminent invasion. All the five Squadrons operated the Hercules on a slip pattern via the Volcanic Islands of Santa Maria in the Azores in the Atlantic and Nassau in the sunny Caribbean. Large amounts of freight - armoured vehicles, helicopters and huge numbers of soldiers were airlifted to land at the short runway at Belize.

In 1975 there was a similar threat in which the squadrons were involved in taking supplies (stores) and troops by Hercules. But in 1977 the deployment by Hercules was a rapid one. It was very effective as Harrier strike aircraft were partly dismantled and each of them fitted neatly in the cargo compartment with space for the troops. Rapier anti-aircraft air defence batteries were airlifted with their ancillary service vehicles.

A Mayan temple in the jungle of Belize

What has not been mentioned is the large British Garrison known to the locals as APC (Airport Camp). It is a large camp with resident army regiments rotating every 6 months. Other army units are stationed there as is the small Royal Air Force unit. The Harriers and Puma helicopter operate from sites close-by while the Rapier sites operate from a camouflaged area. A further resident British or Gurkha Regiment, which is also rotated, is based at various other camps in Belize from where they patrol the Guatemalan border, most of which is jungle. At week-ends, or on the days off, the British soldiers would be at the pool or lying beside their "basker" to get a sun tan. However, the Gurkha soldiers would pool in some money to buy the odd pig and a handful of chickens to cook a "baht curry" in their recreational area.

Unloading a Hercules at **Belize City Airport**

Every six months the change-over of the resident army regiment takes place. They and other army units and RAF personnel are airlifted by the VC10 aircraft operated out of Brize Norton. However, the rotation of the Harrier fighters and Puma helicopters is conducted by Hercules and so are the "general" stores requested by the APC and courier mail service to the British Embassy at Belmopan, the Capital. There are weekly schedules, specials and 9 times out of 10 a Caribbean trainer is always routed through Belize to airlift the off-volume of freight. On exercises paratroopers and stores are despatched by airdrop to the designated drop zones. During Royal Visits the Hercules acts as a baggage truck and a Search and Rescue (SAR) aircraft.

Due to the current improved relations betreen Belize and Guatemala the size of the British Forces are progressively being reduced.

Antarctica - 1972 - Operation Deep Freeze

In 1972 the United States Navy had lost two of their C-130 Hercules which it used for operations in Antarctica supporting stations on the ice cap. The RAF agreed to send two aircraft and four crews from Lyneham to ferry cargo and passengers between the base at McMurdo Sound (Williams Field) and Christchurch in South Island New Zealand. A crew from each Lyneham squadron (then Nos 24, 30 36 and 47 Sqns) were deployed to the Operation Deepfreeze mounting base at Christchurch in mid November.

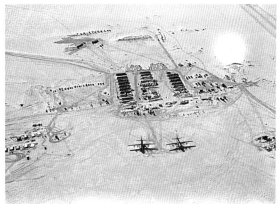

The two RAF Hercules at McMurdo Sound

The RAF crews carried large quantities of timber to Williams Field where it was transferred to a ski equipped C-130 which took the timber on to the South Pole Station. The timber was needed to build new accommodation at the South Pole as the existing buildings were being crushed by the weight of snow. The RAF Hercules could land on the smooth sea-ice runway of Williams Field but the other runways on Antarctica can only be used by aircraft equipped with skis or special tyres. However, on 8th December 1972 an RAF Hercules flown by the No 36 Squadron crew did fly over the true South Pole. The whole detachment returned to Lyneham on 19th December just in time for Christmas. It was not a white one!

Greenland - 1977

In 1977 a Hercules from Lyneham had been tasked to drop vital supplies of food and equipment to the Joint Services Greenland Expedition. It was also to drop supplies at four different sites for a Cambridge University Expedition which was due to begin in July. An additional task was to photograph the locations in order to assist the Cambridge Team to find the DZs (Dropping zones).

Despite bad weather conditions, the Hercules, captained by Flt Lt Ken MacLennan, and operating from Thule, attempted to drop its eight tons of supplies to the Joint Services Team at Carlsburg Fjord. Making an approach from the sea they managed to get into the Fjord entrance but the Drop Zone party with whom the aircraft was in contact confirmed that a drop would not be possible owing to complete cloud cover.

The Hercules then went on the Nordost Bugt, a Cambridge DZ, and successful drops were made on two different sites 25 miles apart at the base of the Roslin Glacier. Both of the remaining Cambridge DZs were unapproachable, one at 4,000ft at the top of the Glacier being in cloud, and the other's difficult terrain making approach impossible in the prevailing conditions.

The weather conditions did not improve that day and, after further radio contact with Flt Lt Tom Norcross of the Joint Services Team, the Hercules crew made tracks for Keflavik in Iceland. After an overnight stop in Keflavik the weather was even worse and it was not until two days later that the crew set out to make contact with the expedition at Carlsburg Fjord.

The conditions were still poor with snow and a 25 knot wind. Because of a delayed arrival at the Fjord, the Expedition took the precaution of going on to half rations in case the drop was further delayed. After four hours the weather showed no improvement, and having considered the possibility of a high "blind" drop through cloud, the aircrew resolved to carry it out the next day if there was no improvement.

The weather forecast was bad but there was a possibility of a slight improvement and the optimistic crew, through local knowledge gained on earlier flights, were hopeful of a visual drop.

A "blind" drop was planned but take-off delayed in order to take advantage of the latest Met forecast. With this forecast slightly more hopeful the Hercules departed from Iceland. About 10 miles from Greenland the dropping zone area was visible through broken cloud. Much to the relief of the Expedition and the crew, a direct approach was made and the drop was accomplished. Once complete the Hercules went on to the remaining Cambridge University DZs to survey the area.
The Roslin Glacier was still unapproachable due to cloud and the necessary stores were dropped at the base of the glacier DZ. The final drop was completed without incident.

Nicaragua - 1979

Flight Lieutenant Christopher Kemp, a Hercules Captain of No 30 Squadron was detached, in July 1979, to Panama as commander of an aircraft tasked

to assist with Red Cross famine relief operations in Nicaragua following an outbreak of civil war.

On 18th July, Flt Lt Kemp and his crew arrived at Managua airport on Task Red Cross 88 for what should have been a routine resupply mission. However, shortly after landing, a number of vehicles occupied an adjacent dispersal and armed troops boarded two C-46 and one DC-6 aircraft; in the turmoil which followed, the Hercules crew heard shots being fired. The C-46's and the DC-6 aircraft quickly started engines and took off. Simultaneously, sporadic shooting was heard from around the airfield. At this time the off-loading of Flt Lt Kemp's aircraft was nearing completion. The crew noticed signs of mounting tension at the congested airport Terminal building as combat troops joined the large numbers of troops and civilians already congregated outside the terminal building.

The Detachment crew stand by their aircraft. Note the markings by the crew door plus the AK47 and grenade symbolising this mission described here

When the unloading of Red Cross 88 was completed, the aircraft's auxiliary power unit was started prior to departure. Unfortunately, the noise attracted the attention of the onlookers and a number of troops and civilians ran to the aircraft and attempted to force their way on board. At the rear of the aircraft the Loadmaster managed to frustrate this attempt by closing the ramp and door. The Ground Engineer was instructed to board the aircraft immediately, but he was followed onto the aircraft by seven soldiers and civilians who attempted to force their way onto the flight deck. They were prevented from doing so by the Flight Engineer and

Navigator. Although a machine-gun carrier supported by armed troops was deployed to cover the front of the aircraft, Flt Lt Kemp started Numbers 3 and 4 engines, the remaining two could not be started because of the presence of people under the propellers. Meanwhile, the armed intruders were threatening to destroy the aircraft if the crew members refused to take them out of the country. The tension was further increased when a pin was removed from a hand grenade to emphasise the hijackers' intentions. Orders were given by the

Numbers 1 and 2 engines whilst his crew ejected the remaining intruders from the aircraft. The troops and gun carrier were still near the Hercules, but Flt Lt Kemp was able to jump the chocks by using a combination of forward and reverse power and taxy at speed to the end of the runway, pursued by two gun carriers. He made an emergency take-off to facilitate his escape. Meanwhile, to illustrate the determination of the troops and civilians, it is worth noting that the Red Cross DC-8 on the adjacent dispersal was successfully hijacked.

Flt Lt Kemp receives the trophy from the then CinC RAF Strike Command, Air Chief Marshal Sir David Evans, in the presence of the President of the RAF Escaping Society, Air Chief Marshal Sir Lewis Hodges together with the rest of the aircrew for this eventful flight

soldiers to open the ramp and door of the aircraft, but the crew refused to comply. Simultaneously, people outside the aircraft attempted to force open the rear para doors, but the crew had already foreseen this possibility and had secured the doors from the inside. At this stage a Red Cross DC-8 on an adjacent bay started an engine and the crowd rushed the dispersal in an attempt to climb on board. Flt Lt Kemp took advantage of this temporary respite and, with the propellers now clear, he started

The Citation

Flt Lt Kemp's cool and efficient management of his crew in tense and potentially dangerous circumstances was exemplary; by his authority and decisiveness in command he successfully averted an attempt to hijack an RAF aircraft. Furthermore Flt Lt Kemp and his crew displayed both courage and devotion to duty by continuing with the resupply operation into Managua even after this hijacking attempt. The actions of Flt Lt Kemp and his crew throughout this incident were in keeping with the best traditions of the service and amount to an outstanding feat of leadership and survival which emulates the spirit that inspired the great wartime escapes.

The RAF Escaping Society

The Royal Air Forces Escaping Society was formed in 1946, after the end of the Second World War. Its aim is to maintain contact with those, throughout the World, who helped members of the Royal Air Forces and Allied Air Forces to evade capture and so return to their units. Help was given at a staggering cost; penalties were severe; execution by firing squad, torture and imprisonment in a concentration camp was the lot of those caught. The number of helpers was vast and nobody knows exactly how many died, but they achieved wonderful results; In Europe alone 2,803 aircrew were brought to safety. The society is a registered charity which, whenever it is found that a helper is in need, responds at once with practical or financial assistance, as appropriate. Only successful evaders or escapers can become members of the Society and the crew of Red Cross 88 are now numbers among those whose courage and cool-headedness have earned for themselves life, freedom and this singular accolade.

Cambodia - April 1975

A hard won souvenir earned by No 48 Squadron was a piece of shrapnel collected by the crew of Hercules XV181 "hot from the barrel" of one of the weapons which were lobbing rebel bomb salvoes on to Phnom Penh airfield as the Lyneham fliers made an emergency dash to airlift refugees from the beleaguered Cambodian airport, and rush them to safety in Singapore.

An approach to Phnom Penh on a peaceful day

When the Hercules crew, headed by their Captain Flt Lt Len Marshall, arrived back at the Wiltshire base from their Far East adventure which had, incidentally, started out as a routine flight to Tengah, they were met by a crowd of pressmen and TV cameramen, mingling with their waiting wives and children. Also there to congratulate the No 48 Squadron crew on their performance were the AOC No 46 Group, Air Vice Marshal Norman Hoad, and the Assistant Chief of Air staff (Ops), Air Vice Marshal D B Craig, who were visiting Lyneham at the time, Station Commander Gp Capt Dennis Slade and the Squadron CO, Wg Cdr Ken Baynes.

An RAF Hercules at Phang Rang, S Vietnam enroute to Phnom Penh. A Mohawk and Caribou of the US Forces together with Providers in the distance are also visible

Flt Lt Marshall said two engines of the Hercules were kept running while the aircraft was on the ground for 40 minutes at Phnom Penh, and rocket and mortar bombs were hitting various parts of the airfield at that time.

Sharing the excitement were the Co-pilot Flt Lt Peter Stacey, who was on his his first overseas flight with No 48 Squadron, together with Navigator Flt Lt David Brown, Engineer Sgt Michael Higgins and Air Loadmaster Sgt Andrew Hegarty.

Rhodesia - 1979/80 - Operation Agila

"The Labours of Hercules" - was a headline in mid January in The Herald - Salisbury's sole daily newspaper. This preceded an article on the tasks of the Lyneham Hercules Detachment based at RAF New Sarum, the military side of Salisbury International Airport.

The Lancaster House Agreement set midnight on the 28th December 1979 as the start of the ceasefire to

XV213 lands at one of the many Rhodesian strips

Air-dropping supplies to one of the 16 Assembly Points during Operation Agila in Rhodesia

be followed by a seven day period in which the forces of the Patriotic Front were to come, without hindrance, into sixteen Assembly Points. At these Assembly Points would be elements of the Commonwealth Monitoring Force drawn from the Armed Forces of the United Kingdom, New Zealand, Australia, Fiji and Kenya.

The Assembly Points were spaced throughout Rhodesia and consequently some are a considerable distance from Salisbury. Rhodesia covers an area roughly the same as that covered by England, Wales, Scotland, Northern Ireland and Eire including the Irish Sea.

What then were these "Labours of Hercules"? The initial task was to help in the deployment of the Monitoring Force Teams throughout the country, between the signing of the Lancaster House Agreement just before Christmas and Ceasefire on the 28th December. During this period the Detachment of five Hercules flew forty-one sorties and carried over half a million pounds of freight.

It became evident during this phase that regular access to the Assembly Points by road was going to be more difficult than anticipated and that contractors were unlikely to wish to commit their vehicles and drivers to roads, which hitherto had been mined and subject to ambush, until they were more confident of the Ceasefire.

In consequence on the 29th December the Detachment was increased to seven aircraft and the second phase of the operation began to supply tentage and camp stores to each of the Assembly Points. By the deadline of the 4th January some 20,000 armed patriotic Front members had arrived at the Assembly Points and the Hercules Detachment had airdropped tentage, cooking equipment, and

blankets into each of the sixteen Points. In this period further 44 sorties were flown and over 400,000lbs of supplies had been delivered by parachute or free-drop.

The soldiers of the patriotic Front may be male or female under the terms of the Lancaster House Agreement. Only those showing evidence of regular service and formal military training were to be counted. Broadly this meant those armed with, and skilled in the handling of modern weapons, usually the AK47. Women soldiers with rifles slung over their shoulders and babies on their backs were not an uncommon sight. The forces of the Patriotic Front normally travel light, merely carrying weapons and ammunition, depending on villages in their area for food and shelter. Consequently, on their arrival at the Assembly Points, which are two-kilometre squares surrounded by a 500 metre cordon sanitaire, they needed to be provided with food as well as shelter if they were to remain at the Assembly Point. Furthermore the Commonwealth Monitoring Teams in the Assembly Points who had been living on compo rations for the preceding week, required fresh food and there was still no sign yet that until the contractors had sufficient faith in the Ceasefire to put their vehicles onto the road.

For the next 17 days the Hercules Detachment was to be fully employed in the airdrop or airland (where a suitable airstrip existed) of supplies, principally food. Feeding 20,000 plus people is quite a task and by the 21st of January the detachment had flown a further 78 sorties and carried 830,000lbs of freight of which some 250,000lbs were air-dropped.

This intensive airdrop phase was not without its lighter moments. The stores dropped included some unusual items, 50,000 pairs of underwear, all the same size but a choice of three different colours. To their surprise the Australians at one Assembly Point received by airdrop a consignment of 2,000 coat-hangars, very useful items in the Bush! They never discovered who was responsible for that particular supply error. At another Assembly Point a cow, which wandered onto the Dropping Zone, was killed by a fast moving 2,000lbs free drop load of tentage - providing a boost to the Monitoring Team's diet that day. On another flight a load of blankets broke free from their harness in mid air and were spread all over the Dropping Zone draped on bushes and trees as if hung out to dry.

On the 21st January the Hercules Detachment carried out the last routine air-drop sortie of rations. The contractors had now assumed the task by road, therefore, the detachment was reduced to three aircraft.

What had been achieved? In all, 163 sorties had been flown with just one significantly delayed by unserviceability, 1,700 passengers had been carried and 2,000,000lb of freight uplifted of which 700,000lbs had been airdropped. This record was achieved by the joint efforts of the ground crews with the air despatch crews, UKMAMS, TCW flight watch and the aircrews, all of whom worked together magnificently as a team. At 0815 on the 16th January it was possible to get them all together for 10 minutes for a photograph outside XV176 (Flak Alice), the aircraft that was hit by a bullet in the early days of Operation Agila. The efforts of the Hercules Detachment in the first month helped to ensure that men, equipment and supplies were in the right place at the right time.

One of the Detachment crews in Rhodesia. For Operation Agila a white cross was applied to the Hercules

Nepal - 8th May/27th June 1980 - Khana Cascade

Interspersed amongst the daily dropping sorties were the more unusual tasks, including VIP flights for the Governor and Lady Soames. In addition there were the return of 60 detainees from Beira who sought the crew's permission for a singsong which turned into a celebratory dance when they were told that they had crossed the border from Mozambique into Rhodesia - and meat runs from South Africa. This last task was to uplift 90 tons of frozen meat from Johannesburg to supplement the rations being provided to the Assembly Areas. The task was completed in six lifts, the last one managing to pack 37,000lbs of beef carcasses into the freight bay.

Perched between India and China, Nepal is one of the poorest countries in the world. It is land-locked, has few natural resources and suffers from an extremely formidable terrain. The depletion of forest resources and the associated problem of soil erosion greatly aggravate Nepal's difficulties. Most of the country's 13 million people derive their living from subsistence agriculture. Apart from the relatively wealthy agricultural lands along the thin belt of the Terai plains, the land is poor and extremely difficult to farm. Many farmers endeavour to scrape their living from a few square yards of hill terracing.

Hercules operating from a base at Bhairawa

Nepal's greatest potential lies in harnessing its water resources, but the construction of hydro-electric dams and large scale irrigation projects require a level of funds which the Nepalese Government and foreign aid donors can only accumulate gradually. Once the waters are harnessed they could generate power which could be sold to India, but meanwhile Nepal's chief source of foreign earnings are tourism and the provision of Gurkha soldiers for the Indian and British Armies.

Air Despatchers preparing pallets for loading

Although, in 1980, the Nepalese Government and a number of aid donors, including the UK, were running projects to improve agricultural production and food storage in the long term, in the short term Nepal's food problems were getting worse. At one time, Nepal produced enough food to feed itself and also to export rice to India, but a general decline in agricultural productivity caused mainly by soil erosion and a series of very poor monsoons made the country less and less self-sufficient. Even in the best years the people in the Western and Far Western Hills of Nepal did not produce enough food to feed themselves. They relied on the earnings of the young men of the area who seasonally moved to the Terai and India to earn money in casual agricultural and industrial employment.

The old and new means of transport meet to help distribute food to the starving on Khana Cascade

In 1979, the monsoon failed disastrously. No comparable records exist for Nepal, but in India the drought caused by the failure of the monsoon was the most severe since about 1896. Throughout Nepal, agricultural production was about 760,000 tonnes below that of a normal year. This represented a fall of 25%. The diaster was most marked in the Hills of the West and Far West of Nepal, where the shortfall was at least 40%. In the highest areas, where it is possible to grow only one crop, many farmers lost their complete harvest. The luckier ones in the lower hills were able to save their subsequent wheat crop but those further north had to wait another two months before their crop was ready. In April 1980 it was reported that deaths from starvation were already beginning in places like Dolpa and Simikot. It was certain that many other areas would have been similarly affected, without the advent of Operation Khana Cascade 80, and the number of deaths could have been extremely high. However, the efforts of the Royal Air Force, the Royal Nepal Army and Royal Nepal Airlines did much to prevent further deaths. Large numbers of people who would otherwise have died of starvation lived. The Operation was as crucial as that.

The Nepalese Government had produced a Special Action Plan to cope with the food deficit problem. This plan required large quantities of grain to be moved into the Hills by porter, lorry and other surface means. But somewhere between 3,000 and 4,000 tonnes had to be moved by air. The cost of such a form of transport was high but for many areas there was no alternative. Jumla is about 10 days walk from the nearest road head, Simikot another 10 days beyond that. A porter would not be able to carry more than 50 kilos and, in order to subsist, he would have to eat 2.5 kilos of his load each day.

Thus, by the time he arrived in Simikot he would have just finished the grain he had carried for the last 20 days. This was a telling demonstration of the absolute necessity of Khana Cascade 80.

Hungry villagers at Surkhet carry away the sacks of food from the Hercules during Khana Cascade

Britain had mounted a successful famine relief operation in 1973, air dropping 1,964 tons of rice and wheat grain, using Hercules aircraft from Lyneham, so it was no surprise when the Government of Nepal asked for similar help in 1980. Mainly because of strong financial restraints placed on the British Aid Programme, the operation mounted in 1980 was not as large as the 1973 effort which, over the period of 29 days, had involved four Hercules aircraft, a Puma helicopter and a total of 144 RAF and Army personnel. It did, however, bear the same name as its predecessor - Khana Cascade. A most appropriate title, because "khana" is Nepali for food.

Khana Cascade '80 consisted of one in-theatre aircraft, flown by two crews from No 70 Sqn, a seven man engineering support team, thirteen air despatchers of No 47 AD Sqn, RCT, a Mobile Supply Flight corporal and a medical officer, all under the command of a Squadron Leader, also from No 70 Sqn. The detachment was based in the capital, Kathmandu.

The agency responsible for coordinating the efforts of the RAF Detachment and for selecting the dropping zones was the Nepal Food Corporation. Dolpa, Jumla, Safi Bagar and Doti were the dropping zones selected. While each DZ was unique they nonetheless shared common features - all were remote, all were well above sea level and all

were surrounded by some of the most daunting mountains in the world.

The approach to the Dolpa DZ, for example, was particularly awe-inspiring because it involved flying along a valley, at an altitude of 8,000 ft, with peaks, towering up to 18,000 ft, on either side. At the end of the valley, a 90° turn to the right was necessary before the crew could catch its first sight of the DZ. Drops were carried out at Dolpa only in the early morning, because the sun's heat later in the day created unacceptably dangerous turbulence. Consequently, at 7 o'clock in the morning, the initial flight along the valley was carried out in a disconcerting gloom.

During the free drop the pallet splits and spreads over the DZ. This method saves time during the loading and preparing of pallets enabling a greater number of loads to be dropped

In common with the 1973 Khana Cascade Operation, initial supply drops of grain were carried out using parachutes but when supplies of these were exhausted the crews resorted to delivering the grain by a modification of a technique known as "free drop". Sacks of grain were piled on to and lashed to baseboards which were pushed, in pairs, from the ramp of the aircraft during a low pass (in the region of 50ft) over the DZ. This technique was not made any easier by the high true airspeeds of the aircraft, a direct result of the DZs being very high above sea level. Early problems, associated with sacks splitting on impact, were solved by modifying both the preparation of the sacks and the drop technique. It was most reassuring to be told that even the grain that was spilled on the DZs from the burst sacks was recovered by the starving villagers. Although the entire operation was carried out against the background threat of the onset of the monsoon season, only three sorties had to be cancelled because of weather. On a number of occasions, however, drops were possible thanks only to fortuitous breaks in cloud cover which permitted the crews to effect a safe descent into the DZ area.

During the first few days of the operation, the sortie rate was dictated by the load preparation time and was limited to just one sortie a day. However, once skilled help was received from the Nepal Army Parachute School and the drops became exclusively free drop, the load preparation time was reduced sufficiently to permit a rate of three sorties a day. For the majority of the detachment flights were carried out seven days a week.

XV182 overflies one of the collection points

The original concept of operations called for 200 tons of grain to be dropped in 60 flying hours. In 42 days, Operation Khana Cascade '80, realised a total of 77 sorties flown, each of between 2 and 3 hours duration. For a grand total of 185 in-theatre hours, 1,005 tons of grain were dropped onto four separate DZs. Full credit for instigating and securing Overseas Development Authority agreement to finance Khana Cascade '80 must go to Alex Sutherland, First Secretary (Development) at the British Embassy in Kathmandu. It was entirely due to Mr Sutherland that money for extra in-theatre flying hours was made available.

After the grain had been delivered by air to the various hill distribution centres it was received by the Nepalese Army and handed over to the Nepal Food Corporation. Distribution of the grain was supervised by the Chief District Officer, who worked with a District Food Management Committee. It was the responsibility of this Committee to ensure that grain was distributed speedily to those who needed it most. This was a carefully supervised programme.

The grain which was being distributed came from several sources. Most of the initial tonnage was from the Nepal Food Corporation's own stocks. The UN's World Food Programme provided at least 22,000 tonnes, the British Government 5,000 tonnes, Germany 2,000 tonnes and France and Switzerland 1,000 tonnes each. The total cost of Britain's contribution, including the Hercules aircraft, was about £650,000. This contribution was in addition to Britain's regular aid programme to Nepal which was running at about £10 million a year.

No other country has been associated with Nepal for as long as Britain. The ties between the two countries are lasting and strong and are illustrated by the large number of Gurkha soldiers who have fought for Britain since 1816. During the two World Wars and the Malayan Emergency, Gurkha soldiers have won thirteen VCs. Operation Khana Cascade was one of the many reflections of the continuing links between the two countries. In the early stages in the Operation, news came through about people dancing in the streets of Dolpa on the day of the first food drop. Such scenes were repeated at other places in Nepal as grain arrived in villages which had already given up hope.

Overall this was a successful operation which would not have been possible without the splendid cooperation of the Nepali agencies and others involved, together with the skill and dedication of the RAF and No 47 AD Sqn members of the detachment.

Vanuatu, New Hebridies - 1980 - Operation Titan
In June 1980, as a result of internal disturbances in the New Hebrides during the run up to

Independence, small peace keeping forces from the UK and France deployed to the Islands. The British force consisted of Royal Marine Commandos and two Hercules aircraft from Lyneham.

The arrival of the RM Commandos on the island of Vanuatu by Hercules attracts much interest from the local inhabitants

The New Hebrides had been an Anglo/French Condominium since 1906. During the '70s, the political direction in the Islands moved towards the nationalistic aspirations of the Ni-Vanuatu (native New Hebrideans) and away from the Colonial powers. The impetus towards independence increased throughout the '70s and, with the drawing up of the constitution in 1979, was finally set for 1980.

Progress had not been without its problems - caused in part by the diverse nature of the islands' peoples and the consequent differences between the political parties. As independence for a united nation dawned, one particular party - the Na-Griamel Movement, led by a self-styled chief named Jimmy Stevens, and prompted to some extent by doubtful outside business interest from the USA, declared unilateral independence in the northern island of Espiritu Santo as the Ni-Griamel Federation. The separate, but co-ordinated forces from France and Britain were deployed in order to help re-establish the status quo in preparation for independence as a single nation. They remained in the Islands until July 1980, departing after joining in the memorable Independence celebrations.

The Falklands - 1982 - Operation Corporate

In all honesty, how many civilian and service people actually knew where the Falkland Islands were prior to 2nd April 1982? When the news broadcast mentioned the invasion, some service wives remarked, "what are the Argies doing in Scotland?"

The Falkland Islands lie in the South Atlantic about 650 km north-east of Cape Horn. They consist of two large islands, East Falkland with Stanley as its Capital, and West Falkland. Numerous small islands are dotted all round, some inhabited. There is an enormous wildlife population whose way of life has not been disturbed by the Falkland Islanders as they understand their right to co-exist.

A Hercules overflies a typical farm house at Saunders on West Falklands

The Falkland Islands are the gateway to Antarctica and are the only inhabited British Colony. The population at the time of the invasion was approximately 1,800 and consisted entirely of British, either truly born Falkland Islanders or having one of their parents or grandparents was born in the United Kingdom. Life is not an easy one as the bleak cold wind blows for most of the year allowing no natural trees. Most inhabitants are farmers, not growing wheat or barley, but rearing sheep whose wool is world famous. The export of wool accounts for most of their trade. However, they also produce meat, vegetables, and hides. An abundance of fish and king krill exists around the coast but the Islanders do not possess large commercial fishing trawlers. Lots of ideas were put into practice such as the Kelp Processing Plant, although in vain. The Islands' shores are covered with kelp - a kind of seaweed which contains minerals. Most of the farmers have small holdings rented from absent landlords, in this case the Falkland Island Company (FIC). It has its office in the United Kingdom and owns about 40% of the land, controlling all export and imports and also the shipping round the islands. There are also numerous non FIC farms owned by absentee landlords and therefore most of the profits are not ploughed back into the islands.

Stanley still has the frontier spirit that is rare in the 20th Century and you may be sure of a warm welcome whether you are a visitor or a member of HM Forces.

Obviously the situation looked as though the Islanders had been left to their own devices with no small or large industries to offer alternative employment for their children. In the span of 20 years prior to 1982 there was a national feeling in Argentina of liberating these poor Islanders but the claim of these Islands goes back over 150 years.

Neither Conservative nor Labour Governments have ever said "Yes" or "No" towards these claims. The Islanders have been living under dispiriting conditions, with their future uncertain, whilst something was being conjured up on the mainland - Argentina. South of Mexico to Argentina the Spanish speaking colonies who did not receive their independence in an orderly manner have always found scapegoats for internal "problems". In this case the impatient Argentinians found themselves a new President - General Leopoldo Galtieri who thought the time was right to walk into Stanley and this he did. On 2nd April 1982 his troops hoisted the Argentinian Flags, thereby diverting their people's attention from their internal problems. This hasty action by the Junta was not taken about on the spur of the moment but was planned well in advance.

However, it was the incident at South Georgia on 19th March 1982 that sparked the invasion. A group of Argentine scrap metal workers sailed to South Georgia and raised their National flag when their initial intention was to collect scrap metal from the dilapitated whale factory. The UK foreign office protested after they had heard from a British Scientific party stationed there. This gave an excuse for the Argentine President to hasten the invasion. By 20th March 1982 a large fleet of Argentine war ships set sail in the South Atlantic with stores and Marines on board. On 1st April HMS Exeter, a Type 42 destroyer plus a frigate which was at Belize, Central America, headed towards the South Atlantic. In the early hours on the 2nd April after a fierce battle, the 67th Royal Marines and over a hundred Falkland Island civilian volunteers surrendered to the large number of Argentine Marines. On the 3rd the twenty two Royal Marines surrendered to the Argentine Marines following yet another fierce battle at Grytviken, South Georgia.

In the United Kingdom the British Government decided to send Naval Task Force 317 and this plan was named Operation Corporate. The unprovoked occupation by the Argentine Junta and the repatriation of the Governor Rex Hunt (now Sir Rex Hunt CMG) on 4th April 1982 came as a shock to the British people. It brought the nightmare of the fall of Singapore when the Japanese troops overwhelmed the British troops in 1941 (the author was born during the Japanese occupation in Ipoh, Malaysia).

Damage sustained by the Police Station in Stanley during the battle to free the town

The cost to restore British rule in the Falklands was going to take human lives as well as millions of pounds. However, there was very little opposition in the United Kingdon. The Argentinians thought that after the invasion their rule should be accepted as shown by the take-over of the former Dutch Colony, West New Guinea, by the Indonesians.

The view of the British Government changed overnight as honour and credibility was at stake. Spain never ruled the Falkland Islands nor did Argentina so this gave the impetus to the then Prime Minister, The Right Honourable Margaret Thatcher, that force would have to be used to retake the Islands if peaceful negotiations failed at the United Nations. On 5th April the Task Force set sail from Southampton and a massive airlift commenced to Ascension Island with the first Hercules leaving Lyneham on the 6th April. Lord Carrington, head of the Foreign Office resigned as the press revealed that the British Intelligence Service knew about the large Argentine naval build-up prior to the invasion. On the 8th the Labour Minister of Parliament Mr Anthony Wedgewood Benn refused to support the Task Force but the European Community (EEC) did. Diplomatic talks took place at the United Nations and the American mediator Alexander Haig commuted between the UK, USA, and Argentina to try to get a diplomatic solution. On 12th April the UK declared a Total Exclusion Zone of 200 nm around the Falkland Islands. The Task Force, already at sea, was only a week away from the rendezvous point at Ascension Island by this time.

Ascension is a solitary volcanic island which lies in the South Atlantic approximately 900 miles west of the coast of Africa. It is basically a 17,800ft volcano stood in 15,000ft of water. This island is the result of Volcanic activity over a period of thousands of years. It has numerous craters of which half a dozen of them had extensive lava flows. Juan da Nova discovered Ascension in 1501 and named it 'Conception' but his discovery was never published. Because of this the island was re-discovered in 1503 by Alphonse D'Albuguerque and named Ascension.

An aerial view of Ascension with the runway visible straight ahead

The British Garrison in the name of King George III claimed Ascension in 1815 and from then on it was continuously inhabited. Although the island is barren, the volcanic rocks do support a variety of plants especially around the base of Green Mountain. Here, the Royal Marines established a farm in 1815 and over the years it had been run efficiently and new crops and fruits were introduced. What Green Mountain is today is the result of the pioneers - "plant anything that will grow" was their motto.

The first aircraft landed on an airstrip built by the US Army Engineers in 1942 and about 4,000 servicemen mainly American, were stationed on the island in 1943. It was nearly 40 years later that more than 4,000 British servicemen were to participate in a different kind of conflict.

In 1956 the USA and the UK signed an agreement which permitted the former to use the airfield. Named Wideawake - the name of one of Ascension's native sea birds - the disused airfield was lengthened and improved to take the big jets. Its 10,000ft runway has been used by civilian charter jets, the USAF Lockheed C-141 Starlifter jet freighter and the Hercules. In the middle of November 1964 numerous USAF Hercules landed at Ascension to wait for orders before flying to the former colony of Belgian Congo, Africa. They carried the Belgian Red Berets who were going there to bring back European and American nationals, but mainly Belgians from the Capital Stanleyville. It was to be over seventeen years later that this airfield was to see a greater number of aircraft, especially Hercules.

The first Hercules left Lyneham for Ascension less than 24 hours after the decision was made to send a Task Force to the Falkland Islands. It carried six Mobile Air Movement Squadron members - the first of the hundreds that were to follow. This team had the difficult task of preparing for the loading and unloading of the many aircraft to follow.

The Hercules landed at Dakar, Senegal to refuel before taking off for Ascension. Dakar was a well known airfield as the Lyneham Hercules was used for relief work at Mali during the famine crisis a few years previously. Prior to 1982 a few training aircraft were often routed via Dakar for Ascension. Over 50 flights were made to Ascension during the first week, although some were routed through Gibraltar because they had bulky, heavy loads. The first crew had the frightening experience of a long run for the take-off from Gibraltar and they wondered whether the heavy aircraft would ever lift off. Such was the hair-raising flight out of Gibraltar, though further breathtaking flights were waiting for the crew out of Ascension towards the Falkland Islands a few weeks later. A slip pattern was set up such that some crews were positioned at Gibraltar and some at Ascension.

Only Ground Engineers and Mobile Servicing Squadron personnel were based at Dakar to refuel and fulfil a quick turn-around for the aircraft. The VC10 was the only other RAF aircraft that Hercules crew used to see at Dakar. At Ascension, the accommodation was at the Barracks of the United States Auxiliary Airfield. As the number of Hercules flights increased accommodation was improvised at the Georgetown hospital compound along with any empty bungalows owned by the Cable and Wireless Company. Other empty houses at Two Boats village sprang up. Mobile kitchens were found and the contract worker expatriates soon found that their peaceful life had been intruded on by the British forces - mainly Royal Air Force personnel, and the noise from the aircraft.

The Royal Navy Wessex were busy shuttling freight between ship and shore

A VC10 C.1 joins a pair of Hercules on the pan at Ascension

As the number of flights increased so did the members of UKMAMS to off-load the Hercules in the shortest possible time. By the time the Task Force 317 left for the Falklands the supplies/stores were building up at the perimeter of the airfield. Soon the Victor tankers and Phantoms arrived, followed by Wessex helicopters, at Ascension. Accommodation was a problem but this was alleviated by the quick construction of "Concertina City". The Americans had some portable accommodation packs stored in the desert which were utilised by their service personnel on exercises. The site chosen was beside the road directly opposite the USAF Base Headquarters about 50ft away on the other side of the road. The area of "Concertina City" was about 400ft x 200ft and each concertina pack was around 8ft x 12ft x 12ft. When it was pulled apart it stretched like the bellows of a piano accordion or concertina to around 8ft x 12ft x 24ft - instant accommodation for 20 plus people.

Soon the whole place was filled with "concertina" huts, "concertina" toilets and "concertina" bathrooms. The slip crew could not understand the layout of the toilets; there were six closets on each side in a portakabin but no doors or curtains. You either had a choice of a short or a long conversation with the other person(s) using the loo or you never went to the toilet until it was late at night or early morning. The showers were communal with 8 sprinklers in each cubicle. Initially everyone carried a camp bed and it was comfortable living inside the hut as it was air-conditioned. By using a plastic tube, normally made from dustbin liners the cold air was routed through a cardbox which became an instant refrigerator. The US Army provided some technicians to install electricity and 110v power points. It took a little longer for the water to boil in the English electric kettles. The dining hall was a few yards away where the civilian employees of USAF - those who worked at the airfield or for NASA - had their meals. It was a typically USAF in style, an all ranks dining hall - the American Colonel ate there along with the workers. It was a bit of a shock for some of the RAF officers who were not used to sharing the same table as enlisted airmen.

Slowly the population of the Forces increased on the island to an all time high so that accommodation and food, particularly in the Mess, began to dwindle. Corrective steps were taken before the Task Force arrived enabling them to pick their supplies up before proceeding to the Falklands. The local LUC shop was nearly empty before NAAFI set up their Expeditionary Forces Institute (EFI). This was controlled by NAAFI but the staff were in uniform.

As the number of Hercules flights increased, further aircrew were to slip at Dakar which alleviated the accommodation problem in a small way. By now the service flights were augmented by civilian charter flights to get maximum stores onto the island before the Task Force arrived. The Heavy Lift Belfast freighter were ex-RAF aircraft. They had been sold by the RAF after the defence cuts of 1975 prior to which they had been operated by No 53 Sqn. This aircraft brought standard and larger, bulky loads. The mountain of stores began to dwarf the airfield pan where numerous types were parked. All the Hercules were operated by Nos 24, 30, 47, 70 Sqns and 242 OCU. It was a nightmare for the Squadron that controlled the stock and its location for this vast amount of logistics. As the ships of the Task Force begin to trickle to the waters of Ascension the nightmare began.

Ascension does not possess a harbour that could provide docking facilities for large vessels, so most of the stores were loaded onto helicopters at Wideawake Airfield and were then flown to the ships to be man-handled. Various methods of loading were used but for speed most were piled on top of a net which was then lifted by its corners and dangled from a strop which hung from beneath the hovering helicopter.

A Royal Navy Sea King overflies a line of Victors on Ascension

What has not been mentioned is the high temperature on the island which is mostly above 90°F during the day and over 100°F on the pan. As the loaded ships proceeded south and south-east No 70 Sqn and the two Flights of No 47 Sqn were flying these sectors while Nos 24, 30 Sqns and 242 OCU were flying the UK to Ascension sectors. Initially the Hercules were air-dropping mail and very urgent

stores to the Fleet, but as they were getting further away the problem of fuel arose. The maximum fuel load is 62,900lbs and depending on the winds, it gave an endurance of approximately thirteen hours. By this time Lyneham Engineering Wing began to install two Andover ferry fuel tanks to the forward section in the floor of the cargo compartment which became known as the C.1LR2. Each of these tanks contained 7,000lbs of fuel.

A Hercules C.1P approaches the drogue trailed by the Victor K.2

The first refuelling probe was fitted to XV200 by Marshall of Cambridge on 29th April and A&AEE took it for trials. A successful wet coupling was made with a Victor tanker to enable the Hercules to receive fuel in flight on 2nd May. This Mark of Hercules which had the probe and forward fuselage tanks fitted was known as C.1PLR2. The OMEGA navigational aid equipment was added to the navigator's instrument panel and its aerial to the rear port side of the fuselage. XV200 arrived at Lyneham for the crew to do a few trial prods during which a new method was evolved called "Toboggan".The problem was that the Hercules, with a maximum speed of 230kts at 23,000ft due to its high load, was equivalent to the minimum speed of the Victor. The solution for air to air refuelling was that the Hercules would fly straight while the Victor approaches from astern and above. It would then overtake slowly and fly forward with its hose trailed. The Hercules would descend (toboggan) at 500fpm as soon as the Captain had visual contact and would be guided by use of a visual reference in the form of horizontal and vertical lines painted on the underside of the Victor's rear fuselage. The relative speed at this stage would be about 15 mph. The Co-pilot then guides the Hercules' probe to mate with the drogue by calling out left, right, up or down. As the

The Hercules approaches the drogue at the commencement of the toboggan. At this point the aircraft are just 85ft apart.

Hercules gets closer their relative speed now would be 3 mph and this is the critical moment as the probe must make contact within the circular basket whose spokes will guide it to be coupled for the fuel to pass from the tanker to the Hercules. Once the coupling has been made the Air Loadmaster operates the AAR panel monitored by the Flight Engineer who has to record the quantity of fuel received and balance it laterally in addition to watching the instrument panel and keeping an eye on the refuelling probe and the 80ft fuel hose connected to it. During the refuel this length of hose is at constant tension and the base is wound in or out by the Victor's Hose Drum Unit (HDU) whenever the Hercules' speed deviates from the Victor. Both then fly at the same speed of around 230-235kts for about 10 to 15 minutes. Fuel is transferred at the rate of 3,000lbs/min. To disconnect the probe from the Victor's drogue, the Hercules reduces its speed gently. This causes the hose to extend to its maximum, tension builds up and at the pre-determined level the hose disconnects. The pressure is less when the Hercules AAR probe nozzle engages the drogue and greater when it disengages. The Hercules then climbs back to its normal cruising level which is determined (in the Operating Data Manual) according to its All Up Weight (AUW).

The AAR course was held at Lyneham and training was given by personnel of Tanker Training Flight (TTF). Meanwhile, the C.1LR2 conversion, which had extended the range of the Hercules by approximately three hours duration was going to require an even further extension due to the position of the Task Force which was moving steadily south. This was achieved by fitting an additional two

7,000lb tanks aft of the two already fitted and this became the C.1LR4 and was then flown to Ascension. As the Task Force was now in the middle of the armed conflict with the Argentine Forces the first of these Hercules, which was additionally fitted with a refuelling probe making it a C.1PLR4, was about to make history (for the story, see "The First Operational Air-to-air Refuelling in the South Atlantic" on Page 69)

Ascension re-supply missions from the UK continued to be flown mainly by Hercules by Nos 24, 30 Sqns and 242 OCU augmented by Nos 47 and 70 Sqns whilst Nos 47 and 70 Sqns did the long non-stop flights to the Falkland Islands. By 3rd June the Hercules had logged 10,000 hours during Operation Corporate. UKMAMS had by then handled over 42,000 passengers and 18,000 tons of freight without any accidents.

By this time the first Hercules tanker was being fitted with a Mk.17 Hose Drum Unit (HDU) (similar to that fitted inside the Victor) by Marshalls of Cambridge (see page 39 for conversion details) The HDU was fitted to the Hercules C.1PLR4 and became known as C.1K. The long flights continued even after the surrender on 14th June and all airbridge Hercules remained airborne for around 26 hours. This was because the runway at Stanley was partly damaged and repairs were being done. Flt Lt Jim Norfolk was the first pilot to land at Stanley in XV291 on 24th June 1992 and took the first UKMAMS team to handle the freight that was to be air landed in the future. The next day, Governor Rex Hunt arrived in another Hercules piloted by Flt Lt Harry Burgoyne. After that the short, single runway was used by Hercules C.1PLR2 to ferry in men and materials.

From the 26th these airbridges were flown by members of Nos 24, 30, 47, 70 Sqns and 242 OCU members. Aircraft would leave Ascension with 62,900lbs fuel in the wings and the external tanks and 14,000lbs in the fuselage tanks. Seats were fitted in the narrow space beside the tanks and in the complete free space behind these two tanks. The fitting of these para seats is dependent upon the amount of freight carried.

The first AAR took place 3 hours after leaving Ascension and the Hercules took on about 20,000lbs of fuel, hopefully in good sunny weather. At the first rendezvous (RV) the second AAR took place about 9 hours later. The total fuel of 77,000lbs would be enough to reach Stanley and if the weather there was unsuitable (which it was at times) the aircraft had enough fuel to return to Ascension. If a landing is assured the Captain briefs the time the crew will dump the surplus fuel to reduce weight to enable them to land on the short runway. The Flight Engineer by this time had calculated the landing weight of 135,000lbs and the amount of fuel available for dumping from each tank except the fuselage tanks. When the Captain initiates the order to dump, the Flight Engineer lifts the guards to the dump valve switches. This enables the port and starboard dump valves to the fuel dump manifold in the wing section. The selected fuel tanks dump pump's switches are set to the "On" position. Fuel is dumped at 400lbs per minute through each pump. The ALM monitors the wings during this operation. When the landing weight is achieved the dump pumps are switched off and the dump valves are closed. The ALM informs that there is no more fuel coming out of the fuel dump manifold. During the landing phase in still air or low wind conditions the Captain will use his skill to make a smooth landing in the narrow short runway of 4,100ft length. Most of the time the weather was always bad - cloudy, fog, rain or snow. Landing with high side winds was a problem as although the wind drift is adjusted by heading towards the wind the last few feet of the touchdown required great skill and judgement. The navigator would continue to pass the wind speed - sometimes the aircraft would be offset from the runway by anything up to about 45°! In this case the Captain's two feet, two hands and his eyes are in constant movement to correct the heading and angle of the aircraft. When the wheels are a few feet above the ground the Captain gives a bootful of rudder direction and as the aircraft nose moves parallel with the runway the wheels make contact with the concrete below. Aileron control is assisted by the Co-pilot and full reverse is selected on the throttles with the Flight Engineer monitoring the torque gauges for any abnormalities in the engines. These flights would last between 13 to 14 hours depending on the wind conditions and the crew would stay for the night at Stanley. The aircraft would be refuelled and a fresh crew would take off late that evening and fly overnight without any AAR and land in the early morning at Ascension.

Sometimes there were two airbridges to Stanley each day. On one of these long flights the crew encountered head winds en route to Stanley and due to the severe adverse weather they had to turn back. Normally on the return flight, it is mostly tail winds that are encountered but on this occasion the headwind made the flight longer. By the time the crew touched down at Wideawake airfield the next morning they had made history with the longest flight ever recorded (with AAR) of 28 hours 4 minutes. The Captain was Flt Lt Terry Locke of No 70 Sqn.

Overshoot at Stanley airfield with abandoned Argentinian Pucaras and bomb damage visible

There was a period when the runway at Stanley was closed for the purpose of further repairs and runway extension from 15th - 28th August. Nos 47 and 70 crews reverted to the middle of June style flights of flying to Stanley to drop supplies and mail. They would then pick up the mail using the "grappling hook snatch" method technique developed by the Joint Air Transport Establishment (JATE) at RAF Brize Norton, and return to Ascension (see page 98). The round trip lasted 24-26 hours. These long flights were always augmented by an additional pilot and a navigator. Those who did these flights suffered from the "extra noise" of the aircraft. By now Hercules C.1K tankers began to augment the Victor tankers, and the tanker crew stayed at Ascension's "Concertina City". Their training was carried out at Marham, Brize Norton and Lyneham. The arrival of the Hercules tankers on Ascension provided relief for the strain on the Victor tankers and their crews. On the 29th August the Hercules freighters started to operate C.1Ps as it was now possible to land on a South American airfield in case of emergency. The new runway was "laid on" the existing runway which was lengthened to 6,100ft. The material used was known as AM-2 matting and consisted of sections of aluminium panels clipped together. This longer runway could now be used by the Phantom interceptors to augment the Harriers already based at Stanley.

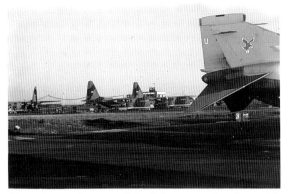

Hercules tankers and freighters at Stanley with the tail of a Phantom in the foreground

Hercules Tanker Operation

A typical Ascension to Stanley flight would be for the Hercules tanker to take off in the early morning. It would then circle Wideawake airfield to trail its hose for trailing checks and when all was satisfactory the Hercules freighter would then take off. They would then fly together as a formation and about four hours later the tanker would receive its fuel from a Victor. This would result in the freighter staying at its cruise height while the tankers had gone on a "Toboggan". The Victor would return to Ascension while the Hercules tanker would climb to its cruising altitude which would now, because of its weight, be lower than the freighter. After six hours the Hercules tanker would pull up to the left and above the freighter which would slow down. This allows the tanker and freighter to be in a good position. The crew would now do the final trailing checks which involves fitting their oxygen mask and the engineer depressurising the aircraft. When the aircraft is fully depressurised the ALM would remove the hose door (fitted to the ramp) to reveal the large rectangular aperture. The door is a two piece item which goes round the fuel hose as the basket is outside the ramp. The Engineer calculates the amount of fuel each of the eight tanks can give. By now fuel from the fuselage tanks would have been transferred to the wings in stages to keep the aircraft in trim. The Navigator operates the Hose Drum Unit (HDU) panel located at his station with the Flight Engineer monitoring for any abnormalities. This happens occasionally but the system is a proven one and most of the

unservicabilities are overcome by re-selection or operating the emergency circuit select switch. The hose is then trailed and the ALM keeps a close watch on its state through the aperture from his safe position. Before the tanker is ready the hose is primed to allow it to be filled with fuel for stability. The tanker's autopilot is now engaged, for "George" is always better and steadier than human hands and feet.

Hercules C.1P viewed from the hose aperture of the C.1K as it approaches the drogue

The freighter is now prepared to receive fuel but the Captain will maintain manual control. The clearance is given for the receiver to position for contact. The tanker's refuelling lights are switched to amber. Both aircraft fly at 230 knots around 20,000ft. Hercules to Hercules air-to-air refuelling is preferable to Victors because the Hercules refuelling basket (drogue) is also steadier at lower airspeeds. Some pilots have experienced a few misses during contact with Victors but most pilots have scored a "bulls eye" with Hercules tankers, that is the nozzle couples with the drogue without touching the outer rim or the spokes (this leads the nozzle to the drogue). When the nozzle is engaged and pushed the refuelling light changes to green. Transfer of fuel begins and when the correct amount is received by the freighter it informs the tanker, and reduces its speed slightly to break off. It then pulls back and moves to the starboard. The tanker Navigator will initiate the "hose wind" in from his HDU panel and complete his 'after tanking checks' along with the crew. The ALM fits the hose doors and the Flight Engineer starts to pressurise. The tanker now turns and heads for Ascension. When the cabin altitude reaches 8,000ft the crew remove their oxygen masks. "Anyone for coffee or tea?" asks the ALM. "Yes please!" answer the crew.

With the probe engaged fuel can flow to the C.1P

"Bumper" Rowley the Co-pilot of Hercules XV200 as it slowly taxied past the two QRA Phantom fighters parked just off the edge of Runway 14 of Wideawake Airfield on Ascension Island early on the morning of 17th May 1982. Across the cockpit, in the Captain's seat, Flt Lt Harry Burgoyne smiled wryly and reflected inwardly on what he and his crew had just been through in the course of an epoch making flight of 24 hours and 5 minutes from Ascension to the Falkland Islands and return. Between them the Flight Engineer, Flt Sgt Steve "Slug" Sloane wiped the grit from his eyes and passed the final fuel reading to Navigator Flt Lt Jim Cunningham who duly completed his navigation log and placed it in his bag. As the aircraft came to a halt Master Air Loadmaster Mick Sephton opened the door, stepped down onto the tarmac and gratefully filled his lungs with the fresh salt-laden Island air.

In the receiver aircraft the "after refuelling" checks would have been completed. With the autopilot now engaged, the Captain is offered a cold drink by the ALM without any request because the 15 minutes from start to end of refuel puts a lot of strain on him due mainly to the great concentration required, eased only by the Co-pilot's remarks - "Ease your fingers and wiggle your toes!". The freighter then proceeds to Stanley and about 3 hours away, reaches the critical point. If the weather is good at Stanley he will elect to proceed but if the weather is bad he can decide to return to Ascension as the fuel on board is sufficient. About twelve hours later the tanker lands at Ascension in the evening. Several minutes later the freighter lands at Stanley.

Those not mentioned are the Ground Engineers and the Servicing crews positioned at Ascension and Stanley who did a tremendous job. The personnel at Stanley suffered a lot due to the appalling living conditions in tents, portakabins and the adverse weather conditions where the rectifications had to be done in the open. The accommodation problem was alleviated when the floating hotels "coastels" arrived and these were moored in calm waters very close to the airport.

The First Operational Air-to-Air Refuel in the South Atlantic
"Oh for a nice safe job like being on a front-line fighter station". The line was delivered by Flt Lt Bob

As the props of the Hercules slowly wound to a halt and the all-pervading noise faded, Burgoyne extracted his aching body from his seat and stretched stiffly. It seemed a long time ago, yet it was barely 46 days, since that fateful day, 2nd April 1982, when it had all begun ....

Everybody on No 47 Squadron had been eagerly looking forward to the Easter weekend and a well earned break. Even the news of the Argentinian invasion had not made much of an impact, after all the Islands were over 4,000 miles from any usable airfield and unlikely have any impact on the Squadron. However, others had different ideas. The Boss, Sqn Ldr Max "Arthur" Roberts, had summoned everyone to work on the Saturday morning and it had been virtually non-stop from there as plans were made, changed, re-made, new techniques developed and rehearsals conducted at locations throughout the UK. Simultaneously two crews had been hastily detached to Ascension Island to commence a steady programme of parachute re-supply of the Royal Naval Task Force as it steamed Southward.

New equipment such as INS and NVG arrived daily and had been fitted and trialled in record time by the hard pressed Lyneham engineering staff. Ex-Andover ferry tanks had been mounted in the freight bay of several aircraft and experimental flights of over 12 hours had become commonplace. Burgoyne remembered vividly the effect of the SELCAL lights illuminating during one trial when the aircraft was IMC at 50ft over the sea at night! It has been demanding, arduous flying but it had never been boring!

By the end of April it had become apparent that the main task was going to be the re-supply of the Task Force which at that time was at the extreme range of the Ascension based Hercules fitted with the Andover fuel tanks. A means of further extending the range of the aircraft had to be quickly evolved and the answer was Air to Air Refuelling (AAR).

Although used by the USAF, AAR had not been seen as a requirement for the RAF Hercules and was therefore not so fitted. The decision to proceed was made on 1st May and Marshall of Cambridge Engineering, the designated Lockheed engineering authority, had set to with a will. Plans, drawings and modifications were made in record time and on the morning of 6th May Sqn Ldr Roberts, Flt Lt Burgoyne plus a composite crew and the Aircraft and Armament Experimental Establishment (A&AEE) were assembled in a briefing room at Boscombe Down to trial and learn AAR under the tutorage of test pilot Sqn Ldr John Brown.

Five days later all was complete! In that time the Hercules had been cleared to refuel from a Victor at weights above 155,000lbs and on four and three engines (two engine AAR had been attempted but had proved impossible at the high all-up weights involved). As a QFI and with four trips and five hours experience Sqn Ldr Roberts had been selected as the first Hercules AAR Instructor and had set about forming what would become the Tanker Training Flight whilst Flt Lt Burgoyne and his crew had hopped on a VC10 and detached to Ascension.

On their arrival on the morning of 14th May, Wideawake airfield had appeared initially to be a scene of total chaos. Apron space was at a premium with Nimrods, Victors, VC10s, and Hercules apparently shoe-horned into minute parking slots whilst overhead a never ending stream of buzzing helicopters went about their business. The predatory shape of a lone Vulcan bomber seemed to preside over this hive of activity and the Strike missiles slung menacingly under the wings only added to the sinister image. It was hot, dusty and the noise level was ear-shattering.

Hercules on Ascension disgorge their urgently required cargo

After an interminable wait for transport the crew had been driven the three miles over the stark volcanic plain and up the winding hill road to the relative calm and marginally cooler surrounds of the house in the Two Boats settlement which would be home for the next few months.

It was here that the new arrivals met up with the Captain and Navigator who were to augment them during the anticipated long flights South. Flight Lieutenants Jim "Grumps" Norfolk and Tom Rounds had been detached at the outset and consequently had flown several sorties to the Task Force. These two SF stalwarts provided a wealth of knowledge and experience regarding naval procedures, weather and operating the Hercules at weights well in excess of the manufacturers recommended maximum of 175,000lbs. They had also explained the rules of engagement (ROE) for the use of the bedrooms. Outbound crews had priority, returning crews were next and if neither of these were factors, the rule of first come, first served applied!

At this stage, aircrew fatigue had already become a major consideration which was causing some concern. Norfolk's crew were holding the record steady having flown almost 190 hours in an on-going 30 day period and most of the other crews were hovering around the 130-140 hour mark. (Normal peace time rules state that 120 hours should be the maximum). The RAF's Institute of Aviation Medicine had cleared temazipan sleeping pills for aircrew use and the "yellow perils", as they were affectionately known, had become a vital aid to sleep in the crowded, noisy, non-airconditioned environment. The doctors had forecast that these pills would work unaided but, being aircrew, most people had taken to speeding up the efficiency by washing them down with a can of Dr McEwans exported amber sleeping draught! This had actually created a memorable instance of levity in an otherwise serious situation when a rather tired navigator, Flt Lt "Paddy" Long, had actually fallen asleep while walking to his secluded sleep area in the garden and had an "utterly brilliant" pre-departure rest stretched out on the corridor floor! Unfortunately these lighter moments were the exception rather than the norm and while everyone put on a brave face it was obvious that as the Task Force entered the Total Exclusion Zone, the moment of truth for the crews of No 47 Sqn had arrived.

The morning of the 15th May had started normally as individuals awoke and joined the queue outside the bathroom in preparation for the ritual aircrew "three S's". Thereafter they had eaten a light breakfast, crowded round the small transistor radio for the 11 o'clock intelligence update courtesy of the world service of the BBC and had retired to the garden to read, sun-bathe or write a "bluey" home.

Around 1300 Flt Lt Burgoyne was asked to report, with his crew, to the AT Ops at the airhead. Following a lengthy transport delay they reported to the detachment commander, Sqn Ldr Nick Hudson, and were briefed on the next day's mission. This was to be an airdrop of eight parachutists and 1,000lbs of stores to the RFA Fort Austin at a position approximately 60 miles North of Port Stanley airfield. The drop was scheduled for mid-afternoon which, since transit time would be almost 13 hours, meant a take-off time of 0230, approximately 12 hours from now! Time had suddenly become very much of the essence.

Because of the acute shortage of manpower on the Island it was left to the aircrew to prepare the aircraft. Mick Sephton and "Sluggie" Sloane, aided by ALMs, Pete Scott and Roy Lewis, had departed quickly to commence the lengthy process. Fuel tanks had to be filled, equipment checked, survival suits and packs transferred from another Hercules and the 1,000lb load had to be prepared and carefully rigged for parachuting. At the same time the pilots and navigators had started flight planning.

Three hours later, as the sun sank behind Green Mountain, the highest hill on the Island, preparations were complete with the exception of the all important fuel and AAR plan. This had proved impractical to organise as the Victors, which would refuel the Hercules, were still airborne on another task. Navigator Jim Cunningham had volunteered to stay in the AAR cell and complete this task while the rest of the crew had returned to Two Boats to catch what sleep they could before the transport time of 2330.

Sleep had not been easy that night either due to aircraft noise, the 75° heat or more likely to sheer nervousness. However at the appointed hour the crew had assembled outside the block to await the transport which duly arrived 40 minutes late. Despite this inauspicious start, and having sacrificed breakfast, the crew rushed through an intelligence brief and eventually arrived at the flight planning tent. Here they had rejoined Flt Lt Cunningham who had worked throughout the evening and had finally completed his planning some 40 minutes earlier. Thanks to Flt Lt Norfolk's previous flights the pilot's performance planning was completed expeditiously - although most of the speeds had to be extrapolated from the graphs which did not cover the 175,000lb all-up weight of the aircraft. Flt Lt Burgoyne completed his brief and the crew had arrived at the aircraft with a few minutes to spare before start-up.

It had been a strangely quiet atmosphere as each man set about his individual pre-flight tasks. Parachutes were checked, survival suits unpacked and personal survival packs positioned ready for immediate use. There had been little of the usual friendly "banter", each was apparently engrossed in his own little world and as the last few minutes ticked away everyone seemed pre-occupied with their individual thoughts. However, at the appointed time, the familiar ritual of the pre-start checks had re-concentrated minds and the sleeping Hercules had been slowly nursed into life.

The take-off roll had been much longer than normal but in answer to the Captain's command XV200 had slowly risen into the soft night air. Following a long period of acceleration the aircraft was slowly eased into a gentle turning climb and as the aircraft settled on course, the Southern Cross appeared off the nose, clearly visible among the myriad of stars twinkling in the deep purple black of the night sky.

The next six hours had passed fairly routinely although all the crew had been kept busy with hourly fuel calculations and checks. ALM Mick Sephton had opened the galley and had produced egg and bacon sandwiches which, following the recent exertions, had been gratefully received and swiftly despatched. Dawn broke around 4 o'clock and this, combined with copious quantities of hot sweet coffee, had restored the energy levels in preparation for the airborne refuel.

Following the UK trials it had been established that the AAR would have to be conducted in a descent as the fully laden Hercules would be unable to keep up with the Victor in level flight. It was with some relief that Flt Lt Burgoyne noted the rendezvous area was clear apart from some small cumulo-nimbus clouds far below. As he adjusted his seat and restraining harness, the Captain mentally ran through the procedure which he was about to undertake for only the 5th time. His palms had glistened moistly as he slipped on his flying gloves and his mouth had felt distinctly dry.

He had been aroused from his reverie by the harsh intrusion of the radio call from the approaching Victor. Having taken off from Ascension some time after the Hercules the much faster tanker had gradually closed the gap and was now only 5 miles behind. Co-pilot, Flt Lt Rowley made a radio call in reply and after confirmation that all was ready the AAR commenced. The slim elegant shape of the Victor had overtaken the ungainly Hercules and on Rowley's command both had commenced the gradual descent. Juggling with the controls Burgoyne manoeuvred into a line astern position and

This sequence were actually taken during the first operational refuel. Here, the Hercules is moving into position behind the Victor

As the Hercules approaches the Victor the probe is aligned with the drogue as seen by the Co-pilot

commenced his hook up run. Under the Co-pilot's directions and with the engineer monitoring the engines the two giants had slowly closed until the probe on top of the Hercules and the Victor's dancing basket were only ten feet apart.

At last a successful contact was made and fuel could flow but this close formation had to be held for over 30 minutes for the 37,000lb transfer

AAR has been rudely described as "trying to take a flying something at a rolling doughnut" and this was no exception. Time and again Flt Lt Burgoyne had edged his aircraft forward but each time had failed to connect. Valuable fuel was being used up and the formation was getting lower and lower. Finally as they passed 17,000 feet and as the pressure became almost unbearable a successful contact was made and fuel began to flow. Over 30 minutes later, with 37,000lbs of fuel transferred, down to a height of just under 4,000ft and having navigated around several cu-nimbs refuelling was complete. Burgoyne eased back on the power and with a soft clunk and a slight spray of fuel a clean disconnect was achieved.

Having passed control to his Co-pilot, Flt Lt Burgoyne wiped the sweat from his eyes and drunk three cups of water. He then extricated himself from his sodden seat and retreated to the crew bunk. An air of euphoria pervaded the atmosphere and as the tanker completed an elegant sweeping turn and headed back North to Ascension, the compass needle of the Hercules had settled once more on South and towards the The Exclusion Zone (TEZ).

It had been over three hours before the Captain returned to his seat having spent two of those on the rest bunk in a futile attempt to sleep. In the meantime the rest of the crew had swapped around in an attempt to gain what rest they could. It was now only about one hour to the descent point and so, as each man returned to his station, he appeared dressed in a survival suit comprising a "mae-west" and parachute harness.

The descent to Stanley had been initiated about 250 miles north of the Falkland Islands. As the Hercules had levelled at 2,000ft the paratroop doors had been opened, observers from No 47 Air Despatch Regiment stood in them and a special series of checks were completed. As the aircraft entered the TEZ an air of tension and expectancy became apparent. Conversation was minimal and all eyes scoured the horizon for enemy fighters.

Conditions were not ideal. It was a grey foreboding day with a cloud-base of about 3,000ft, and a visibility of about 6km which decreased markedly in the widespread squally showers. It was bitterly cold and as Flt Lt Rowley established contact with the Royal Navy the sea temperature was reported as 2°. Luckily the wind was within limits and as the parachutists were wearing immersion suits it looked reasonable for the drop. As the crew homed on RFA Fort Austin, the hastily installed and primitive hand-held Radar Warning Receiver chirped and squeaked indicating that several radars were illuminating the aircraft although, thankfully, none of the fire-control radars had "lock-on".

The ship had been acquired visually about 2 miles out riding on a grey sea and with its recovery boat already in the water. The drop went exactly to plan, the parachutists being dispatched on the first run and the stores on the second. As the Hercules turned North into a gathering night time gloom a faint voice

The Hercules approaches RFA Fort Austin at the rendezvous point

had been heard over the radio thanking the crew for the small amount of mail that the ALMs had managed to include in the stores container. It had been a small thing for the aircrew but it had obviously meant a great deal to those so far away from their homes and loved ones.

By the top of climb darkness had once more descended and a new problem had arisen. Unforecast headwinds caused by a Jet Stream had developed and seemed likely to continue for some time. This had obvious fuel implications and a solution was required. In surmounting the problem the crew borrowed an idea, tacking, from the early sailing ships. The aircraft was allowed to drift east with the wind and was then turned hard into the wind until track was regained! Thereafter the procedure had been repeated until the wind abated. The most demanding and potentially hazardous portions of the flight had now passed and all that remained was the long eleven hour night flight back to Ascension. As the hours passed seats were swapped, meals were eaten (more to combat encroaching fatigue than from hunger), games were devised (anybody who was on the flight now hates "I Spy") and the BBC world service continued to provide hourly updates on the progress of the conflict.

Boredom had become a big factor. However this air of calm had been shattered about an hour out from Ascension when Jim Cunningham announced in a

With the parachutists dropped on the first run, the stores followed on the second

commanding voice that he had a contact on the radar at 10 o'clock five miles distance!

The pre-departure brief had mentioned the remote possibility of an Argentinian Boeing 707 being equipped with missiles and sent out on patrol. Indeed, prior to the outbreak of hostilities, the Boeing had formated on one of the RAF reconnaissance aircraft although on this occasion nothing further had developed.

Burgoyne had acquired a visual sighting almost immediately and confirmed it as a group of lights which appeared to be an aircraft in a left bank and turning towards the defenceless Hercules. Well versed in fighter evasion technique, the Captain had disengaged the autopilot, reduced the power and started an immediate turn towards the threat. Jim Norfolk had shot forward to the Captain's side and it was his timely intervention which avoided a possible catastrophe as he identified the lights as a string of refuelling Victors on climb out from Ascension. What had appeared to the exhausted Hercules crew was in fact a mass formation of tankers setting out on another Black Buck mission which had not been known about when the Hercules crew had briefed some 27 hours earlier! As a result of this incident separate arrival and departure routes were devised and used thereafter.

Following this hair-raising few minutes the approach and landing had appeared somewhat straightforward by comparison, although fatigue ensured that everyone monitored everyone else very closely as

XV200 finally touched down on Wideawake's Runway 14 some 24 hours and 5 minutes after take-off.

Flt Lt Burgoyne was brought back to the present as he was given the news that there was the usual welcome back. The bars were shut and transport was unavailable! At 0300, the only way to Two Boats was to hitch-hike.

Oh well, never mind, at least by the time they got to the block they would be regaled by Pete Scott, Roy Lewis and Andy Hegarty as they put the world to rights over another "Irish coffee". The most wide awake drunks in the South Atlantic would no doubt have ensured at least one beer was waiting in the fridge. Wouldn't they!!!!!

Hercules Detachment (HERCDET) at RAF Stanley, Falkland Is - 1982

A new chapter in the history of the Royal Air Force opened on 17th October 1982 with the arrival at Stanley of Hercules tanker aircraft XV192 and XV201, flown by Sqn Ldr David Farquhar OC Hercules Detachment (HERCDET) from No 24 Sqn and Flt Lt David Turner from No 30 Sqn. At the time, these aircraft were to become the workhorses of Lyneham's latest and most operational detachment, HERCDET at Stanley.

As the motto of the detachment "Support, Search, Save, Supply" indicates, the role of the Hercules Tanker, or C.1K, in the Falklands, is not only varied but also revolutionary. Never before had RAF Hercules been used to support Air Defence Operations. The primary role of C.1K was to give the Stanley based Phantom aircraft the capability, by air-to-air refuelling, to remain on Combat Air Patrol for extended periods. This capability greatly strengthened the Air Defence of the Falklands Islands Protection Zone (FIPZ). During 1972 the Phantoms were retired and replaced by the Tornado F.3.

The secondary roles of the C.1Ks are threefold; to provide Maritime Surveillance in and around the FIPZ, to provide Tactical Support through airdropping vital supplies and mail to the Garrison on South Georgia, and finally, to provide long range Search and Rescue cover for all military operations

A Phantom FGR.2 of No 1435 Flight during refuelling from a Hercules C.1K over the Falkland coast

The crew walk out to their aircraft for another sortie from Stanley. In the background is the old ATC tower while the Portakabin provides the Detachment with office space

in and around the FIPZ. In addition, and complimentary to the air-to-air refuelling role, a considerable amount of fighter affiliation was carried out with the Phantom. The affiliation provided attack training for the Phantom crews and vital attack evasion training for the C.1K crews.

Initial living conditions at Stanley were rudimentary. The detachment site was tented and, although reasonably comfortable, has been likened to a gypsy encampment on a rubbish tip, in the middle of a building site. The site subsequently had been the main holding area for Argentinian prisoners. Conditions improved when the detachment moved to a permanent Portakabin site. Because of readiness state, and Quick Reaction Alert (QRA) commitments, aircrew were spending two days and nights out of three at the airfield. The main accommodation was on board a ship anchored in Stanley Harbour. The ground crew fared slightly better, each man spending every third night at the airfield on QRA. By November 1982 personnel who were accommodated on board ship moved to the Coastell - a floating hotel with five persons to a room aboard a barge which was anchored half a mile from the airfield. Once both Coastell and Portakabins were available, a reasonable standard of both working and living accommodation was achieved.

Initial tour length for all HERCDET personnel was three months although this was later extended to four. In the early days few recreational facilities existed. The detachment built its own 3 hole golf course and det personnel often turned to bridge, Open University and Lingaphone courses to help pass the time.

Little publicity was initially given to the Hercules Tanker Force and its considerable operational achievement in the South Atlantic. Great credit was, and still is, reflected on Lyneham by the professionalism of the aircrew of Nos 24 and 30 Sqns and the groundcrew of Engineering Wing who have given a great deal to ensure the success of the new operation. From a military viewpoint, the close operational liaison which was achieved with the fast jet world brought to both Phantom and C.1K operators a new understanding of each other's

Radio 1 DJ - Ed Stewart visits the rudimentary detachment accomodation while collecting requests for his programme

problems, strength and weaknesses. Both found that in any future South Atlantic conflict their survival would be mutually dependent.

By early 1983 a standard Hercules C.1P had arrived to augment the two Hercules tankers. This aircraft was widely used on Maritime Radar Reconnaissance (MRR) and Search And Rescue (SAR) missions. At this stage the airbridge still continued to arrive on a daily basis. By the time the construction of Mount

Airbridge Hercules C.1P being unloaded at Stanley

Pleasant Airfield, about 35 miles away, took place plans had already started to increase the length of detachment to 4 months. Subsequently the number of airbridges were reduced. In that time the detachment at Ascension to fly the tankers in support of the airbridge still lasted three weeks and crews from No 24 and 30 Sqns alternated. The HERCDET crew at Stanley was also from No 24 and 30 Sqns. However, the airbridge was flown by No 24,20 47 and 70 Sqns. The HERCDET then became No 1312 Flight in November 1983 and it continued to maintain the high standard set by the initial crews. By now Stanley began to take shape as an RAF station and the airfield was cleared of most debris except the damaged Argentinian Pucaras and other aircraft which were laid at the roadside between the coastell and the ATC.

At Lyneham the aircraft is serviced by two separate lines, namely "A"Line (ALSS) and "B" Line

(BLSS) separately and the flying squadrons are allocated aircraft from both these lines for their daily tasks. At Stanley the detachment was like a family; aircrew and groundcrew together form part of the Squadron and as such there is no inter line or inter-squadron squabbles. They worked as a team successfully.

When Mount Pleasant Airfield (MPA) was opened in May '85 the Tristars of No 216 Sqn began to operate the schedules and the airbridge came to an end. No: 1312 Flight moved to MPA and was allocated their place of work on the north side of the airfield close to the Fire Section and the ATC. It had its own offices, accommodation for the QRA groundcrew and aircrew and a large storeroom in an area known as "Albert Square". The ISO containers outside provided a large storage room and portakabins provided a weekend recreational facility which was

XV213, a Hercules C.1K of No 1312 Flight at MPA is still awaiting a part in a certain TV soap!

known as Queen Vic! Here, there are two kitchens each forming part of the lounge/TV room/dining room. For some reason the aircrew prefer to do their own cooking rather than to eat in the aircrew feeder a few yards away. The duties are the same as they were before. Each crew does a QRA for 24 hours followed by a standby crew on 60 minutes call. The third day is free. During their four month detachment each crew gets a three day Rest and Recreation (R & R) which gives them an opportunity of a free flight and accommodation - good at any of the Islands' centres or to stay with a Falkland Island family.

Today RAF Mount Pleasant Airfield (MPA) is the home for Sea King HAR.3s and Chinook HC.1 of No 78 Squadron, Tornado F.3s of No 1435 Flight and two Hercules C.1Ks with No 1312 Flight.

The crew for Ascot 4165 from Lyneham which was the 650th and final Hercules Airbridge

Hercules C.1K overflies the new airfield at MPA

Hercules C.1K of No 1312 Flight currently provide tanker capacity for the Tornado F.3s of No 1435 Flight also located at MPA

Prepare to Ditch! - by Flying Officer Shields

These details were from a Report on Flight Ascot 8173 RAF Stanley to Wideawake airfield, Ascension Island on the 3rd/4th March 1984.

Crew:	Captain	Flt Lt Akister
	Co-Pilot	Fg Off Oborn
	Navigator	Fg Off Shields
	Eng	FS Dodd
	ALM	Sgt McDonagh

The crew of Ascot 8173 at Stanley.
LtoR: FS Dodd, Flt Lt Akister, Flt Lt Shields, (front) Fg Off Oborn, Sgt McDonagh

Ascot 8173 made her scheduled departure from Stanley to Ascension Island at 2210Z on 3rd March 1984. The Zero Fuel Weight (ZFW) was 98,000lbs and the Jetplan required 60,000lbs of fuel. The aircraft was fully serviceable apart from the No 4 Tank fuel gauge. On start up the estimated fuel load was 62,000lbs.

At Ascension the weather forecast was "FHAW 1212 13015 9999 3CYU 018 TEMPO 8000 80RASH 6CU012=". Interpreted, this advised the crew that the weather prediction requested was for the period 12.00 Zulu to 12.00 Zulu (Zulu being a military standard time throughout the world irrespective of the local time zone). The wind direction and speed would be 130° at 15kts and the visibility would be in excess of 10kms. The cloud would be three eighths cover at 1,800ft. Temporarily the visibility would be down to 8,000m in rain showers with six eighths cloud at 1,200ft. A fair weather forecast.

The Hercules load consisted of sixty passengers together with their baggage. These mainly comprised of returning Hercules and Phantom crews together with elements of No 16 Sqn, RAF Regiment who had been operating the Rapier missiles as part of the Falkland Islands Air Defence. The flight progressed as briefed - completely normal with just occasional clouds painting the Cloud Collision Warning Radar (CCWR) screen. At 0830Z, one and a half hours after sunrise and 200nm out, contact was made with Wideawake Tower on VHF radio and an updated weather report was received. The crew were happy as this was similar to the forecast received overnight from 81SU.

The radome removed exposing the CCWR

The final fuel estimate of 13,700lbs was made, giving the last approach fuel total of 10,500lbs to be available. Shortly afterwards a descent was initiated from FL230 which was calculated to position the Hercules 5nm out on finals for the TAC/VIZ approach to Runway 14. The TAC/VIZ is an approach procedure which uses TACAN to acquire the runway visually.

During the descent and at a range 75nm, Wideawake passed the latest weather as estimated by the controller, at this time there being no forecaster at the control tower. In common with most people at the time, he was stranded in the unexpected torrential rain at Travellers Hill. The weather was deteriorating rapidly with a 300ft cloud base with less than a mile visibility on the airfield due to the heavy rain. The wind was variable - over the next hour updates to the crew advised it as having been 6-10kts from almost every point of the compass.

The terrain at Ascension is inhospitable at the best of times never mind in bad weather

The Hercules was being flown along a tortuous route to avoid CB (Cumulo-Nimbus thunderstorms) which were building up to the South West of the Island. It was decided to follow the Tacan procedure from Colts which is the Final Approach Fix 10nm out from Runway 14.

At 1,000 feet on the Radar Altimeter the Hercules was in IMC (Instrument Meteorological Conditions) - in other words they were in cloud - so a let down to 800ft was commenced. The visibility from the tower was now down to half a mile due to the rain. The first approach was started at 0915Z with an estimated 10,200lbs fuel available. The ALM (Air Load Master) remained down the back of the aircraft with all passengers strapped in to the para seats, the two Phantom pilots being strapped in on the bunks for the remainder of the flight. By this time the CCWR was showing solid CB activity within a 30nm radius of Ascension indicating numerous thunderstorms around the island.

During the first approach the crew were forced to descend to 350ft QNH (height above mean sea level) to avoid extreme turbulence in the base of the storm clouds. The Radar Altimeter warning was set to 300ft. One and a half miles out and at 350ft a missed approach was initiated. At this point the crew were in visual contact with the sea but could not see the coast. They had just overflown the SS Uganda, which was later estimated to have been only a half a mile short of the runway threshold.

Just as the turn was started, the Engineer identified the approach lights in his 11 o'clock position. The aircraft was about 200 yards right of the centreline. The turn took the Hercules over the beach which the crew could just see through the Co-Pilot's windows. The controller in the tower glimpsed the vague outline of the aircraft during the missed approach.

The second approach was almost identical to the first, except the weather had deteriorated further and the lights were not seen. By now the Hercules was down to an estimated 8,000lbs of fuel, and with little hope of an improvement in the weather conditions the Captain suggested that Ascension try to launch a tanker so that they could hold off or divert to Dakar. In the event this may have proved impossible, as not only could the crews not get down from Travellers Hill, but a take-off may have been difficult due to flooding of the runway.

This shows the difficult terrain for landing in good weather at Ascension. In poor weather conditions this becomes potentially dangerous

After the second missed approach, the tower informed the crew that the Runway 32 threshold was in the clear and, with a wind of 330° and 6kts, suggested an approach to that runway. Using a combination of Tacan and Doppler the crew tried to set-up for an approach to 32. They found a large, clear gap 5nm SE of the Island, but between themselves and Ascension there was a solid sheet of water falling from the 300ft cloud base. They flew at 700ft QNH but could not start an approach to Runway 32 as the weather had closed and therefore returned to Colts.

The fuel state was now approaching 7,000lbs. The passengers were aware that all was not normal, but were reassured by the calmness of the ALM. Due to the extreme turbulence and humidity, many were being air-sick at this stage.

On the next approach to Runway 14 the Hercules came down to a mile and a half on the

Tacan/Doppler at 350ft QNH. By now the Island could not be distinguished from the cloud on the CCWR. The Tower gave an estimated visibility of 400 yards. The Hercules was in base of the clouds and continuous lightning was striking the sea around it. Again, on the missed approach the crew could just make out the land below them.

Co-pilots view of the threshold of Runway 14

At this stage the likelihood of a ditching was being considered since it was unlikely in the time remaining that a tanker would be able to launch or that a successful landing could be made due to the weather conditions. With the cloud stationary over the Island it was decided that it would be better using the fuel in continued approaches rather than holding. The severe turbulence and low heights that they were forced to fly to maintain positive control of the aircraft ruled out any possibility of shutting down an engine for fuel conservation. The fourth approach to Runway 14 was the worst from the point of view of turbulence, lightning and poor visibility. Again an initiated missed approach was commenced from one and a half miles, but the crew could not see the beach which was this time only 150ft below them.

Throughout the approaches the Controller in the Tower was passing the anxious crew his estimates of visibility and cloud ceiling which were of great assistance.

The sixth approach commenced at 1003Z with an estimated 5,900lbs of fuel remaining. The Captain informed the crew that he would transmit a Mayday call at 5,000lbs, order life jackets on at 4,000lbs and ditch at 2,000lbs. On this approach it was elected to overshoot at 1nm on the Distance Measuring Equipment (DME) and at 300 feet QNH. The approach was started at Colts, at 700ft and they had to drop to 300ft quite rapidly due to the cloud base. The Radio Altimeter warning was set to 200 feet. The crew did not see the Uganda on this approach. They later learnt that the Uganda had manned her lifeboats in order to offer assistance if they ditched. The Royal Navy helicopter crew was also trying to get down from Travellers Hill to assist, but were also stranded.

At just over 1 nm, with the Co-Pilot still at the controls, the Navigator called: "Prepare to overshoot". At this point the Engineer called, "Lights, 11 o'clock". The Captain then took control of the aircraft, turning left and descending slightly. As they broke through the rain they could just see the threshold. They landed at 1010Z on a flooded runway using propeller reversing to stop. The visibility, assessed from the flight-deck, was 100m in heavy rain. On shutdown the fuel-totaliser was indicating 3,000lbs, but with No 4 tank fuel gauge unservicable, the crew estimated the total fuel to be 5,000lbs. The tanks were later dipped and found to contain 4,700lbs. The total flight time comprised nine hours in night conditions and three hours daylight.

South Georgia and the South Sandwich Islands by MALM M.J. Clabby

During our four month tour of duty on the Falkland Islands, we were tasked to do three sorties to South Georgia. The last sortie included an airborne look at the South Sandwich Islands.

The runs to South Georgia fulfilled two roles. Firstly, the air-drop of urgent supplies and mail and secondly, to look at the old whaling stations for evidence of intruders.

As a bonus for the personnel at Stanley and other units on the Islands we used to take up to 26 passengers on the South Georgia trips. This was to get them off the islands for a day and to let them see how the Hercules helped in the defence of the Islands.

No 1312 Flight had a seat allocation to reward those people who had supported the flight in little ways like providing cement, timber, toilet fittings etc, for the non-stop building of "Albert's landing".

The day before the trip the men of No 47 AD, the despatchers, would build the airdrop packs and sort out the parachutes. Depending on the freight, every pack had to weigh about 100lbs but had also to float in the water long enough for the recovery boats to collect them. This usually meant that an old passenger life jacket was put on the pack.

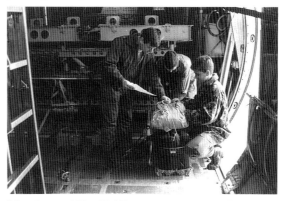

Members of No 47 AD prepare a load prior to the airdrop flight

Trip day meant an early start as take-off time was 0800. I had to check the aircraft, the load for dropping and the seats for the passengers. Then I collected the flight rations and on the way back I collected the assembled passengers. After briefing they were strapped in and given their ration packs.

Our first trip to South Georgia was as exciting for us as it was for one of the passengers. This passenger, a Mr Greg Brooker, was on board to see the mountain that his father had climbed first in 1950.

The drop was the primary task so we proceeded to Cumberland Bay. Our first run was at about 750 feet to check out our route, the wind sheer and to locate the recovery boats. We dropped one pack at a time from the port paratroop door and all our drops went without any problem.

After the last drop we climbed to 10,000ft and went to look for Mt Brooker. Due to the cloud that had appeared we went up higher to about 15,000ft and we turned back for the high ground. As if by magic the cloud cleared and Mt Brooker was standing in brilliant sunshine. The snow seemed to be in terraces, a bit like icing on a cake. All of the passengers were very impressed especially Greg, who was on the flight deck.

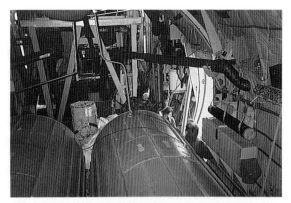

The Despatchers await instructions to make the airdrop from a C.1K. with most of the cargo compartment filled with the tanks and refuelling equipment leaving little space for freight

Due to the cloud at lower levels the harbour check was scrubbed so we headed back to Stanley. Once there, the crew presented Greg Brooker with a signed print of a No 1312 Flt aircraft.

Our final trip was to include a sweep around the South Sandwich Islands. It was decided to use a tanker to give us the extra fuel. This did however limit the number of passengers to two. I only had the one despatcher with me because of the same weight limits.

The Headquarters staff assigned the Officer IC the South Sandwich Islands to the flight which left us with only one seat. The crew decision was to take the hospital Matron. She declined and sent her deputy.

On the day of the flight we taxied out to the end of the runway. Once lined up, the Captain reversed under my advice to the very end of the runway. That gave us 6,000ft of AM2 matting together with Stanley harbour and the mountains in front of us.

Using the engines at full power, we lurched off down the runway getting airborne with sufficient runway left in the event of an abort. We passed over Moody Brook before we had enough height to turn right over Wireless Ridge. Once the hurdle was passed we headed South East for the South Sandwiches.

After four hours we arrived in the area of the Islands. A careful descent through the clouds brought us to a clear area near South Thule. We orbited the Island and took photographs of the old settlement still with it's Union flag flying high.

I was to take photographs of all the Islands where possible. It appears the Army Officer had the same brief as we fought for the best shots.

Then mother nature took over and sent in the low cloud. Up we went and the radar took over in the identifying of the Islands. The Officer IC the Islands was not happy with this, he was then informed of the results of hitting granite and the lack of rescue facilities in the area. Suitably subdued, he retired to the bunk.

Later on we entered clear air again and visually identified some more of the Islands. In all we saw Southern Thule and Bristol island with a quantity of large penguins on it. We flew round twice as we didn't believe it the first time. We also saw Visokoi and Zavodoski islands and took plenty of photographs. The Army was now happier!

Having found all of our "passengers" charges we headed for South Georgia. This time we followed the coast from St Andrew's Bay going north west. The drops at Grytviken went without problems apart from me having to do manual labour and heave them out.

A volcano on one of the South Sandwich Islands gently simmers away

The sunken Argentinian Navy submarine - the Sânta Fé - off the coast of Grytviken

The Hercules of No 1312 Flight provide the only alternative means of re-supply to a lengthy sea voyage to Grytviken

That done we followed the coast and took a good number of photos of all the harbours, the British Antarctic Survey base on Bird Island and a sunset shot over the mountains.

We landed at Stanley 10 hours after take-off; it was dark and wet. We now had only 17 days to do - time to plan the "GOZOME" party.

Ethiopia - November/December 1984 - Operation Bushell

During October 1984 the world's media highlighted the plight of millions of starving people in northern Ethiopia. Their situation had become critical after drought and civil war had caused widespread malnutrition. The British Government was amongst the first to offer aid, and more importantly, a means of distributing the aid in the form of two RAF Hercules aircraft.

On 1st November 1984, two aircraft, together with four aircrews and support personnel, deployed to Ethiopia. The crews were at first drawn from Nos 47 and 70 Sqns, although after six months Nos 24 and 30 Sqns also sent crews to join the effort.

The detachment set up an operating base at Addis Ababa International Airport, which it shared with a squadron of twelve "Aeroflot" An.12 aircraft. Personnel spent between three and four weeks in theatre before rotation. Initially, aid in the form of blankets, tents, grain and other supplies were airlanded, as the airdrop of aid had not been politically approved. Subsequently, a typical load of 42,000lbs of grain would be prepared at Addis or Assab on the coast, and airlanded the aid at Axum,

The British Military Detachment at Addis Ababa

Gondar, Mekele, Asmara or Alimata. The inland landing strips were high altitude -3,500-7,500ft - and usually had a gravel or sand surface. Axum in particular, had a rough rocky surface which caused one aircraft, piloted by Flt Lt Paul Spears, to burst a tyre on landing. As no spare was available, the aircraft was flown safely back to Addis on three main wheels.

Undercarriage repairs with minimal support

Of the 2,500 tonnes of supplies moved by air in the first month, 1,700 tonnes were flown by the RAF. The squadron of "Aeroflot" An.12 - "Cubs" (see page 19), - concentrated their efforts on the "relocation" of refugees from the drought area to new settlements in the south of Ethiopia. During this time there was much rivalry, friendly and otherwise, between the RAF and Aeroflot crews. On all airland sorties each Hercules carried an Ethiopian secret service "minder", to ensure that the crews kept out of trouble and did not fly to unauthorised locations.

Towards the end of January 1985, it became clear that the best way of delivering aid to the more isolated areas was by airdrop. It was decided that the most efficient method of despatch was to free drop (no parachute) the grain from a height of 12ft. The first airdrop was flown by Flt Lt Jim Norfolk on the 26th January 1985. The drop zones were located adjacent to several remote villages approximately 100nms north of Addis, and at altitudes around 9,000ft. The loads were manually despatched by

Delivering load which usually consisted of grain, biscuits and cooking oil. The aircraft and crew were invariably mobbed by the locals wherever they landed

members of No 47 AD. Three drops were made per sortie, and crews flew up to six sorties per day. The drop zones were prepared and manned by No 47 AD personnel, who were flown in daily from Addis by two Polish Air Force Mil Mi-8 "Hip" helicopters. A typical contribution was that of Flt Lt Voute and crew from No 47 Sqn, who over a three week period flew 92 hours, airdropped 844,000lbs, and airlanded 504,000lbs of grain.

World attention was kept on Ethiopia and its starving, by the frequent visits of celebrities most of whom were flown in RAF Hercules aircraft. These

Initially the airdrops were made from 50ft but these were later reduced to 25ft

Experience in containing damage inflicted by the rough landing strips proved useful during the Gulf War

ranged from Germaine Greer and Neil Kinnock to Bob Geldoff and Mother Theresa.

For the bulk of the Operation, detachment personnel were accommodated on the campus of the International Livestock Centre of Africa (ILCA), a World Bank sponsored agricultural college in Addis. Operation Bushel took its full toll in terms of aircraft wear and tear, with most suffering serious stone damage from repeated landings on rough strips. However, all those crews who took part were grateful for the opportunity both to help the starving of Ethiopia, and to experience the challenge of airdrop and airland operations in the hot and high environment.

A birdstrike can result in substantial damage to the aircraft besides being fatal to the bird, some of which actually try to attack the aircraft!

One of the Detachment crews in Ethiopia for Operation Bushell

The Ethiopian Experience by Cpl Marsh of No 47 (AD), RLC

The world saw the plight of the Ethiopians by the media coverage in the last few months of 1984. The No 47(AD),RCT (later to become RLC (Royal Logistics Corps)), initially sent two crews out in January 1985.

I actually arrived in Addis Ababa in May 1985. By this time the operation had been going for nearly five months. Therefore things were getting into a routine. The first thing that hit you was the smell, then the heat. We landed at about 1400 hrs and we were greeted by a mass of smiling faces and a haze of white free-drop bags. We parked right beside the rigging area, where I saw the main local workforce.

The Air Despatch detachment of No 47(AD) consisted of one Officer, one SNCO and four-man AD crews. It worked out that a day would amount to one crew flying, two crews rigging, one crew on day off and two men would run the DZ courtesy of a lift by a Polish helicopter.

It took about four days to acclimatize. The flying, rather than the load rigging, was most tiring. We had to be at the aircraft at 0700 hours ready for a take off at about 0730. The aircraft would be loaded for the first sortie the night before. The Hercules C.1 took 16 one ton Nepal free drops. Each Nepal free-drop contained about 20 individual free drop sacks weighing about 140lbs each.

The drop zones were about an hour's flying time away. We flew at low level for speed. The fuselage was stripped of all unnecessary equipment, including seats, lifejackets, unused chains, couplings and floor points. On route to the DZ we sat on the Nepal free-drops. On the return trip however, we sat wherever we could through total exhaustion.

The DZs would be prepared and run by No 47AD

About 15 minutes out from the DZ we would get a call from the air load master. Once helmets and belts were checked we would position ourselves in despatch stations. As soon as possible the aircraft ramp and door would be opened in order to position the load and to get some cool air. The type of drop we were doing was called Block 4 Nepal free-drop. On the load master's signal we would move two Nepal free-drops down into despatch stations by using chocks and strength. Despatch stations were usually about tie down row 27 - the closer the load was to the edge, the more accurate the drop.

Once the first pair was in position and secured with chocks we would then move forward to bring down the next pair which would be positioned immediately behind the first pair. We would then join all four containers together using cord ties and end up with one final tie going to a floor point which, when cut, would release all four free- drops at once.

By this time we were then usually about 2 minutes out from the DZ. The next call would be 15 seconds, action stations. My No 2 and I would take out our aft most chocks so that the only thing restraining the four-free drops was that final tie going to the floor point. We all then positioned ourselves forward of the load and pushed on the Nepal free-drops to get tension on the final tie.

The pilot began a slight climb to assist us with this and at only 50 feet, I think I would want to climb. "RED ON", 5 seconds to go "GREEN ON", a signal to the No 4 by me followed immediately by a scream of "cut" and the No 4 despatcher would slice through the 7,000lbs cord holding the loads in.

The No 2, No 3 and I would push with all our might to get the stores out and onto the ground as soon as possible. We would stop pushing at about tie-down row 26, so by the time we had come to a halt we were at the ramp edge.

The four 1 tons were no sooner out of the back that they were hitting the DZ splintering into about 80 individual free drops, travelling at some 60 to 90 mph. A few seconds to observe the drop then back into action for the next four followed by the next four and finally the last four. Hence, as soon as the doors were closed we fell to the floor exhausted prior to landing back in Addis Ababa. Twenty to

thirty minutes to reload, then off again. We usually did about four sorties a day.

Gulf - 1990/91 - Operation Granby

The region around Iraq has seen conflicts both small and large scale long before the birth of Christ and in the case of the Moslems, long before the birth of Islam. History books are full of epics by great leaders and their men. Conquerors came from the east of Iraq, from Europe, the Mongolians from the north, the Persians from the east and a host of other nations subsequently.

The last major power to subdue this region, in actual fact most of the Arabian Peninsula, were the Turks who in 1288 founded a Moslem state by Othman I. Their expansion took them to Asia Minor, parts of Europe, the Balkans and South Russia. Their region also extended to the areas of the Tigris and Euphrates right up to the Persian Gulf. The Great Chinese Philosopher once said, "Everything that goes up must come down". No power lasts forever and the decline of the Ottoman Empire came because of greed, negligence, tyranny and corruption which in turn led to a weaker position. They lost their Empire after the First World War. Although under the Treaty of Lausanne Turkey lost all the Arab parts of the Ottoman Empire, it resented having lost the Mosul Villayet where the Turkish forces were not defeated - they withdrew because their discredited Sultan had signed the armistice and honour was at stake. The population there was partly made up of Assyrians and Persians, but mainly Kurds. There was speculation that oil was in the region. In 1926 the Anglo/Iraq/Turkish Treaty was signed which settled the Mosul Villayet along the Brussels line. Having failed to dislodge Great Britain from Kurdistan they were offered 10% of the oil revenue and from 1930 royalties started to arrive.

A No 30 Sqn Hawker Hardy at Hinaidi, Iraq

The British position at the end of the First World War was that its Forces, supported by Faisal's Arab troops in Syria, had conquered and occupied Palestine, Jordan, Syria, Lebanon and Mesopotamia and the RAF's No 30 Sqn had bases in Mesopotamia, Northern Persia and the Persian Gulf. Air power here played a vital part. Britain had two interests in Iraq; oil and its strategic importance - a direct route from Egypt to the Far East. Where does Kuwait feature in all this? It was an autonomous region within the Ottoman Empire under the direct rule of the Al Sabahs.

The nation of Iraq was created in 1920, by the League of Nations created Iraq in 1920 and involved the three regions of Baghdad, Basra and Mosul. previously belonging to the Ottoman Empire and occupied by the British in 1918. In the Islamic society of the Arabian Peninsula the way of life is complex. The family unit is of paramount importance and they live in groups or communities as a tribe. The life style of the nomadic tribe is to wander from place to place, or in the case of the coastal tribe it would be to farming and fishing. Obviously commerce became a way of life for them. Every tribe had a leader, as organised raiding played a great part in their society; he became a man of power and the surrounding land belonged to his tribe. They would attack not only another tribe but also caravans that were in that area. As time went on, due to the discovery of oil, a leader became distinguished only through the income he got from oil. As long as some wealth was distributed the masses were happy. However, income from oil amounted to millions of pounds in the past and since 1970, billions. The income people received in these "tribal" areas was far higher than in other areas that had no oil. Prior to this, the coastal towns had flourished and commerce built up in a small way, but inland in the desert, there was not even this.

There has never been a place where wealth has been so unevenly distributed as it is in the Arabian Peninsula. Poverty exists particularly where the Palestinians are. If Mosul had not been included the Kurdish people would have a nation and the Gulf War would not have happened. In 1932 Iraq became independent with a much larger area than before.

With oil in the surrounding nation of Iraq, power and politics went hand in hand and arms were sold to whoever had the huge sums of money to pay for them. Iraq started producing oil from 1927 and Kuwait in 1946 and by 1948 it was producing twice as much as Iraq. The foreign oil companies were also profiting until some Arab countries like Iran started to nationalise and they lost their monopoly.

The Libyan leader's forceful approach and that of the Oil Producing Countries (OPEC) made sure that oil prices were increased to bring further wealth to that area. This ensured that the Third World countries became poorer still as they had to pay the same price as the affluent European and American nations. The founders of OPEC, Saudi Arabia, Iraq, Iran, Kuwait and Venezuela, had a virtual monopoly and their authority went beyond the control of oil prices. It was only after the Arab/Israeli "Yom Kippur War" that the process of nationalisation was speeded up.

Once OPEC started imposing restrictions it was not only non-members who increased their production, but also one or two of their own members. In the Gulf area the United Arab Emirates (UAE), consisting of the seven Sheikhdoms and Oman, were producing oil after the 1960's.

Until then their defence was undertaken by the British but due to the change of Government in the United Kingdom this altered. The then Labour Government decided that huge savings could be made by abandoning that region's defence and in 1967 the cuts were implemented. In 1971 the Sheikhdoms became independent and transformed these countries from nothing to a modern society with free education, health, employment and distribution of some of the oil income. This created problems such as how to fill jobs that the Arabs were not prepared to do, which in turn created an influx of workers from the Asian countries with the technical and managerial jobs going to the Western countries. All of the affluent nations in the Arabian Peninsula have reached the 20th Century in terms of wealth, advancement of their society, industry, and defence in less than 20 years.

Where do Kuwait, the USA, the West, the former USSR and Iran feature in the Gulf conflict? The West sold arms and this income helped their balance of payments and employment. The USA promised help to any country in that area to keep out communism. The USSR armed the nations who were sympathetic or supported communism. Iran moved into the 20th Century in 1960 at which time the late Shah and his family were loved by their people. The USA sold arms and equipped the Iranian armed forces, but greed and corruption caused the Iranian people to overthrow the Government, the Shah and his family. At this time the West, including the USA sold and equipped arms to Saudi Arabia. After the Iranian Revolution the Iranians became anti-American and this shifted sympathetic feelings to Iraq; arms to Iraq flowed in from the West, the USSR and China. The Iraqi Government had an agreement with the Shah for the use of the facilities at the confluence of the rivers Tigris and Euphrates - the Shatt-al-Arab Waterway. All this changed with the arrival in Iran of their spiritual leader the late Ayatollah Khomeni in 1979. From 1980 the long and futile war between the two Moslem countries of Iran and Iraq took place. It lasted for eight years and nothing was gained but death and bloodshed to innocent civilians.

This was watched by the Arabs living around Iraq and although the United Nations (UN) and the West tried for a peaceful solution, nothing happened. How could the Islamic Republic of Iran take heed of any mediation from the UN and the West when they consider non Moslems as infidels? Both countries, Iran and Iraq, possessed an arsenal of 20th Century weapons but only a fraction of them were used, as conventional weapons were used heavily and so it became a trench war - reminiscent of the First World War. When surface-to-surface missiles were used they fell out of range and landed in mainly populated areas on both sides. It was only after oil was affected in The Gulf of Homuz that the course of the war changed. Iranian missile batteries and mine-laying brought a sympathetic view of Iraq which now had many friends in the West. The war between them ended on 20th August 1988.

Everyone talks about the poor Palestinians. The unequal distribution from the profits of oil export from the Arabian Peninsula along with the entire cost of this eight year war could have made each Palestine family a millionaire!

Why did President Saddam Hussein invade Kuwait? The answer once again is power and money. Iraq was rich and had a surplus of balance of payment but after the war the Iraqi Nation had a deficit of over £70 billion. Kuwait lent the most money and as oil prices started to fall there was no way Iraq could repay anyone. So, a scapegoat had to be found. Firstly Saddam Hussein accused the Arabs of plotting to sell oil at low prices in order to make Iraq poor and at the same time he accused the Kuwaitis of pumping oil from the Neutral Zone. No amount of "Arab" diplomatic shuttles and conferences would appease Saddam. So on his own initiative, about 30,000 Iraqi troops were sent to the border with Kuwait. When Iraq was about to attack, Kuwait agreed to write off her loan to Iraq and provide compensation on 27th July 1990.

The inevitable happened on 1st August 1990 when Iraq walked into Kuwait with about 100,000 troops and tanks. The Iraqi forces encountered a small opposition which was crushed and in a few hours they were in Kuwait City. By this time the ruler of Kuwait, members of the Royal Family and those who had the means, travelled south to escape to Saudi Arabia. The Iraqi troops never having seen such affluent amenities as the Kuwaitis had been enjoying all those years, practically stripped everything in the department stores/shops of luxury goods. The Bullion market was stripped of all the gold and a host of atrocities were committed. The Asian and Egyptian foreign workers were forced out of Kuwait and Iraq, followed by a systematic rounding up of the Westerners, these people becoming "hostages". They were used as pawns to enable the Iraqi armed forces to build a defensive "wall" in Kuwait and to install these civilians around key installations in Iraq and Kuwait. All this was going on during the period of many meetings in the UN. The UN made a few resolutions against Iraq, namely sanctions and the nullification of the annexation of Kuwait by the end of the first week. Why Iraq did not enter Saudi Arabia and walk into the rich countries of Bahrain, Qatar, the UAE and Oman is anybody's guess. The Government of Saudi Arabia decided after a number of meetings to invite the American Forces and Western Allies for a variety of reasons.

RAF Hercules flew from Lyneham as well as other stations in the UK and Germany, picking up freight and personnel from squadrons that operated Jaguars and Tornados, taking them, via Cyprus, to Riyadh. After unloading they would return to Lyneham. In Saudi Arabia Hercules of the Riyadh detachment

One of the numerous Hercules missions into Riyadh. Along with most of the RAF attack aircraft some of the Hercules were given nose art

were utilised to transfer these stores to various locations in The Gulf. Only two Hercules at Riyadh were used to do the round trip within The Gulf. By this time freight was also brought in by VC10s and Tristars from Brize Norton. The detachment personnel were accommodated at the city's hotel and "compound" - comprising of three blocks of flats in the city's suburb near Sulaimaniya/Dalla Olaya. Transit aircrew also stayed in hotel. The WRAF aircrew had to wear the Abaya - the women's compulsory long black overdress which covered the whole body exposing the face and hands only. This was a concession as the native Saudi Ladies had to wear a further layer which covered their entire body with a semi-transparent piece designed to cover their eyes.

The British Government decided to send troops to the Gulf and so began Operation Granby. Within 48 hours the first three crews departed on a VC10 from

Despite the hot conditions the WRAF aircrew had to wear the Abaya to observe Saudi customs

Hercules aircrew at Brize Norton armed with side arms await the flight to Akrotiri

Brize Norton to Cyprus on 8th August and a slip pattern was set up at Akrotiri. Within three days, crews were operating between Lyneham and other parts of the UK and Germany to Akrotiri and to various locations in the Gulf. The number of slip crews varied at Akrotiri. The operating aircrew did a 5-10 days slip. The crew from Lyneham would fly the fully laden aircraft to Akrotiri where they would get off and one of the slip crews there would fly to any of the bases at the Arabian Peninsula and return. (The bases there were Riyadh, Dhahran, Jubail, Tabuk, Bahrain, Minhad, Seeb, Thumrait, Victor and Masirah, and later on to King Khalid Military City and Quasimah). They would then slip at Akrotiri, and 24 to 48 hours later they would fly once again to the Gulf before returning to Lyneham for 24 to 48 hours stand-down. The Engineering Wing ground-crew did a 28 day detachment to Akrotiri which was increased later and their numbers varied as the weeks went by. This also applied to UKMAMS. The aircrew sent to Akrotiri for Operations desk duties did a 28 day detachment. Accommodation at Akrotiri was doubled and sometimes tripled but the worst part was trying to sleep either during the day or at night. Crews were coming in and going out at all hours and some crews were noisy. Each crew member that left Lyneham had two green bags laden with all the necessary Nuclear, Biological and Chemical (NBC) Kit plus an air and ground respirator, as well as a protection helmet in addition to their normal flying and overnight kit. These had to be carted and manhandled to every destination at which they had to night stop.

The arrangement for the Hercules ground Engineers servicing crew and UKMAMS varied in each

Aircrew wearing the hot and heavy but potentially vital NBC kit as well as NVG

location. Some did a 28-day detachment and returned to the UK while others moved to another location within the Gulf area. Accommodation was either in tents, compounds or hotels.

As the pace increased the Hercules were required to carry a wide range of loads from troops to armoured vehicles

By the end of August some crews were flying from Akrotiri to the UK - normally to Coltishall and Marham in Norfolk - and returning on the same day. Their crew duty would be anything from 20 to 23 hours. By September the units deployed in The Gulf area had to be re-supplied with stores and rations. By now the Army units from the UK, but mainly from Germany, started to move in full force to the Gulf. The intensity of operations continued as the build-up of the Army developed and the first of the strange items of equipment, which eventually

became so familiar, began to appear. The area inside the outbound hangar at Lyneham became full and boxes for equipment were piled haphazardly in the open air awaiting their return.

A third of ALSS and BLSS were on detachment to Cyprus and to all the locations in the Arabian Gulf. The Ground Engineers also shared the detachments. During this period normal schedule flights went on unhindered. The aircrew did long flights in the slip pattern. During the first month they flew from Lyneham to Akrotiri and handed the aircraft to the next crew who took the freight to any of the locations in The Gulf and returned either empty or laden with unserviceable equipment. The aircraft was then flown to Lyneham by another crew. Sometimes the crew that left Lyneham did a long flight, after refuelling at Akrotiri, to the Gulf, particularly Minhad in Dubai, for a night stop.

By the end of August the Egyptian refugees had left by land to Jordan and went by ship to Egypt through the Gulf of Aquaba or by Hercules aircraft of the Egyptian Air Force. Asian refugees had been left stranded in desert camps in Jordan. Offers of help for them were slow in coming. By the time the Indian Government took steps by sending ships to bring back their nationals safely, there was no sign of a peace settlement and there still seemed no real sign of a let-up.

Instead, the first Hercules detachment in-theatre formed when three aircraft, six crews, twelve ground engineers and twelve movements personnel under a Detachment Commander established themselves at Riyadh International Airport. The aircrew did a three

Some of the Detachment ground engineers based at Riyadh keeping paperwork up todate

week detachment. The Tristars of No 216 Sqn moved personnel and freight to Riyadh where they were distributed by the Detachment Hercules to various airfields such as Tabuk, Dhahran and Jubail around the Gulf. The Lyneham to Riyadh Hercules flight took mainly freight but sometimes passengers.

November was a similar month but December ensured no return of the troops to the UK for Christmas.

Various resolutions were now passed by the UN, all of which were ignored by Iraq. As a result the USA prepared to enforce Resolution 678 which had been set on 29th November and gave the right to use force. The deadline for Iraq to withdraw was 15th January 1991.

On the 16th January the Air War started and no transport aircraft were allowed to fly on that day in the skies of Saudi Arabia. The crews were still on standby and most of them crowded round the TV sets to watch what was happening in The Gulf. This glorious relaxation did not last long and within 24 hours later crews were operating the slip pattern again.

The detachment in Riyadh had grown to seven aircraft and fourteen crews who worked round the clock flying to the major airfields and further north to support the Army directly.

Over 7,500 hours were flown in support of the Operation alone. The Air War was prolonged for a longer period than the Allies envisaged. Just like a bull fight in a Spanish Arena where the bull is weakened before the kill, this ensured the Iraqi ground troops were demoralised. It was thought, from the onset of the build up, the casualty rate would be high so preparations were made to fly them to the nearest hospitals which were being set up. When the ground war started on 24th February the Hercules fleet fortunately did not have the unenviable task of flying the injured back to the UK.

The flights into Jubail, Dhahran and Riyadh, Quasimah and in the strips, were now becoming dangerous due to enemy attack and also due to the anti-aircraft, notably the Patriot missile batteries. Some crews actually saw the spectacular "fireworks display" when the Patriot missile destroyed the unpredictable Iraqi Scud missiles.

While this was happening in the Gulf, Akrotiri had a relatively peaceful time, none of the personnel had to carry respirators or tin helmets. However, the three sections, TASF, Air Movements and Operations were extremely busy.

While Akrotiri was away from the threat of attack, its was kept very busy with movements

The Hercules that were operating from airfields such as Riyadh and Dhahran, which had concrete runways, had few problems apart from the hot weather from August through to September.

During the pre-conflict period most aircraft were put through their paces including fighter evasion

Fortunately, those aircraft that were required to fly into desert strips close to the border encountered minimal unserviceability as they were given the necessary protection. This was as a result of experience by some of the crews from the Ethiopian operations where they had previously been operating in similar conditions. One of the main problems was that of belly damage from debris thrown up during the landing and take-off runs from the desert strips. During the early planning briefs at Lyneham a programme was drawn up to help reduce the damage factor. To prevent the type of damage encountered in Ethiopia a material, which looked similar to car

While concrete surfaces had the minor problem of sand being blown onto the runway, this was nothing compared with that at the desert strips

The Hercules were required to operate from desert strips which usually became rutted and required attention by the Army engineers

Due to the nature of the runway surface, using the brakes to stop the aircraft ripped the tyres therefore reverse thrust was carefully applied to avoid excessive dust

underseal, was applied to the underside of the aircraft and the belly aerials and landing lights wrapped up. The additional problem of desert operation means that aircraft would be subjected to very hot, dry, windy and dusty conditions. The sand and dust has a habit of getting into virtually every position. It is highly abrasive and so special care has to be taken to reduce the problem. Vital areas such

as hinge points, bearings, landing gear oleos, engine cowling and intakes required special attention. Before departure from the UK as much of the surface dirt and greasy areas were cleaned especially around the wheel oleos to prevent sand sticking.

A partial solution was the application of an underseal like material to the underside of the aircraft which absorbed much of the damage

Once in the Gulf the normal internal checks included the removal of dust deposits on instrument panels, switches and on and around the flight and engine controls. During external checks the area around the control surfaces and flap areas were inspected for sand and dust. The seals around the oleos were cleaned of sand. Further precautions were taken by the aircrew during taxying and steering on the ground. Landings required special attention as the ground was often uneven and could be soft in places. Cautious reverse power was required as dust could easily be blown forward which would restrict the visibility as well as debris being sucked into the engine intakes.

The Air War continued for a longer period than expected and those detached to Dhahran, Riyadh, Jubail, Quasimah and other forward areas had many sleepless nights due to the air raids and having to don respirators in case one of the Scud missiles contained any Chemical weapons. By the time the land war started, flights to the forward bases and strips near the War Zone increased to replenish the supplies. Fortunately, although the Ground war started in the early morning of 24th February it had finished by the 28th.

The Hercules was the first fixed-wing aircraft to fly into Kuwait where it delivered the first men to secure the Embassy. Two days later the Ambassador returned to his rightful place. The fleet now went into full swing as the Saudi Government gave 30 days for all foreign forces to leave. Most of the equipment went by sea, but the pertinent ones were airlifted. Soon the materials that were piled outside the Lyneham Cargo hangar began to disappear. The detachment personnel went to operate from Bahrain before returning to Lyneham. The civil war in Iraq

An aerial view of the burnt out ATC tower at Kuwait City Airport with some US aircraft and helicopters in the foreground and the City of Kuwait at the rear

did not last long as some of Saddam Hussein's Elite Guards who were kept for a rainy day in a safe part of Iraq went into full swing. They were able to deal with this situation as they had the armour, machinery and men and were fully trained to deal with unarmed and armed civilians, in the North - the Kurds and in the South - the Shi'ites.

USAF A-10 escorts a Hercules during the airdrops of food and tents to the Kurds in Northern Iraq

By late March the Shi'ites were taking refuge in Iran but the plight of the large numbers of Kurds led to the requirement for assistance which was provided in the form of Operation Provide Comfort and Haven. The massing of the starving Kurds in the mountains along the Turkish/Iraqi border triggered

an aid programme in which food and tents were air-dropped by Hercules which in turn were escorted by USAF A-10 Thunderbolt aircraft for their own protection. Assisted by the 47 AD who were responsible for the loading and despatch, over 1 million pounds of supplies were air-dropped by the end of April.

By the middle of May Operation Haven was in full swing to provide safe camps within Iraq. The conditions in the mountains were appalling as well as difficult for the delivery of aid to the refugees and so an incentive to persuade the Kurds to return to their homelands was given by providing a ground force. These troops were to ensure that Saddams forces did not harass the returning Kurds.

All of these extra movements resulted in more technical tradesmen being attached to ALSS, BLSS and AES to undertake the necessary increase in servicing created by these additional flying hours.

The success of our Forces throughout Operation Granby was due, in no small measure, to the support provided by the Hercules. The adage "first in, last out" certainly applies to the Hercules and all her support personnel, of which Operation Granby and Operation Haven were prime examples.

It is unfair to single out any single squadron or one achievement throughout the campaign. Suffice to say that our success story, as a result of professionalism, loyalty and dedication of the aircrew and groundcrew alike, both in the Middle East and at Lyneham, as well as the motivation and determination of those attached to Lyneham throughout the campaign, speaks for itself and should represent an achievement to which we can all be proud.

Free Kuwait! by Flt Lt S T A Sharpe
Imagine the scene, it's 2am in the morning and an American with a blue enamel bath and an M16 has just pitched up at your door wondering if he can trade the bath for a 10 man compo rat pack. Well, that was just one of the scenes from Kuwait City just after Saddam's Army had left in a hurry.

In late February, I was happily spending the war at Riyadh, dodging Scuds, runaway forklifts and the most dangerous thing in the Gulf, - Saudi drivers.

The ground war was well advanced and most people were thinking that it would all be over soon, and we would all soon be back in England with a pint of beer. These happy thoughts were quickly dispelled on the 26th February when I was chosen along with a team of eight to go into Kuwait to open the RAF airhead. We spent the night preparing equipment and were ready to go the next morning. However, for various operational reasons, our departure was held up and we eventually flew into Kuwait International Airport on 28th February 1991.

A Hercules takes off from Kuwait while smoke billows up from the oil wells set alight by the Iraqi forces before they withdrew

The scene on the way in was like Dante's Inferno; oil well fires pouring flames and smoke, wrecked tanks and the lunar landscape created by B-52 saturation bombing. On landing, our Herc was met by an American riding a motocross bike who guided us to a safe taxiway. When the engines stopped we piled down the ramp to have a first look at the Airport. In front of us were the burnt out remains of a British Airways Boeing 747 and littered all around were items of broken aircraft handling equipment, shrapnel and burnt out vehicles. We offloaded Albert and set about finding a site to work out of. However, though it was only 1pm, it seemed to be getting awfully dark. By 2.30 it was pitch black. It was impossible to see the headlights of the Landrover at more than 20 metres. Shortly after that it started to rain. Have you ever been in a paint storm? The smoke from the oil well fires had turned the rain black and given it the consistency of watered down treacle.

We eventually pitched camp underneath a baggage hall in the main terminal, deciding to hit the maggot at approximately 1800, as it was dark and with no electricity there was not much else useful we could

do. We awoke the next morning to find a bright sky as the smoke had drifted north. Some army EOD types happened to pass by and ask if we were the RAF Det? On giving a positive reply we were advised that we had an immediate problem. A check of the area revealed we had spent the night sleeping beside a booby trapped vehicle. Two hours later and 2 large explosions, we returned to the tent with our enthusiasm somewhat dampened.

During the day we managed to take a look at the Airport in an attempt to find a suitable site to conduct operations. During our exploration the extent of the damage wrought by the Iraqi troops became clear. Everything of value had either been stolen, burnt or vandalised. The strangest thing was that every vehicle had its wheels removed, why not steal the car intact? However, that was the logical solution, and by the end of the day nothing seemed logical anymore. Our travels did reveal one definite find, a battery of four Anti-Aircraft guns, one of which is now on display outside UKMAMS HQ.

A Hercules crew pose for a photo in front of their aircraft and burnt out buildings at Kuwait City Airport

Life settled down for the next few days until 2nd March when the American air transport personnel started to arrive in force. In poured men and equipment and on the 4th March the first Lockheed C-5 Galaxy arrived. Judging by the crowd round it we all thought that something pretty important had arrived. Closer investigation revealed that the Americans had flown in a Wolfburger mobile hamburger bar, a sort of combat McDonalds. This amazed most of us, here was Kuwait, no water, electricity and a severe lack of food or supplies and the US were trying to corner the fast food market.

The arrival en-masse of our Colonial cousins brought a whole new meaning to the word barter. Their MRE or Meal Ready to Eat was a sort of baby food in a bag, some of which could be quite nice but in general I would rather go on hunger strike. It would appear that the Yanks felt the same, even to the extent that they would sell their Granny for a box of our Compo (hence the bath mentioned earlier). Over the next few days we acquired a shower block, a toilet block and a generator and lighting set (on loan for the duration), all for a few tins of compo, more to the point, we could now get clean and start to feel human again. At this stage we were unsure as to how long we would be in Kuwait so the team needed to find accommodation of a more substantial nature, explorations revealed that the Met Office was abandoned and with a bit of work could be made habitable. The Americans had cleared the place of IEDs (earlier experiences were still quite vivid) so the UKMAMS cleaning team sprang into action and by the end of the day we had some quite civilised living quarters.

The US Army had set up an Aeromed Huey Flight next to us, all the personnel being Reservists called up for Op Desert Storm and we quickly developed a friendship. Their Senior Pilot, Ron McCullough an Ex Vietnam Vet, now an under cover drugs cop with LA PD took a shine to the crazy Brits next door, offering to fly at least one of our team every day. These forays into the desert all at a height of about 30 feet revealed just how ill equipped the Iraqis

One of the Aeromed Flight Hueys at Kuwait City

were against a modern army. Tanks and equipment were strewn across the desert, some damaged where they had been hit by an unseen enemy. The rest just abandoned in panic. The Kuwait Air Base at Ali Al Saleem used by the Iraqi Air Force had been devastated. Every HAS had been blown apart most by a single hit from a smart weapon. The road at

Multa Ridge (The Basra Road) provided a gruesome and vivid demonstration of the full killing power of modern warfare.

Just one of the many Kuwaiti AF large Hardened Aircraft Shelters (HAS) which were destroyed by the Allies when they were occupied by the Iraqis

The spell at Kuwait helped us develop new skills; we became air traffic controllers. When the smoke reduced the visibility to less then 1 km the US Marine Corps would shut up shop and refuse to talk to inbound aircraft, turning off the runway lights to make sure the crew could not see the airfield - "sorry Sir, orders from the Colonel, we can't talk to any aircraft today". Off would go two UKMAMS with Landrovers, park on either side of the end of the runway, lights pointed towards the oncoming aircraft, a few words on the radio and in came Albert. Not to be outdone the Mobile Servicing Squadron (MSS) team from Brize would then head off to the other end of the runway in the Supercat (a sort of 6 wheeled dune buggy, acquired from the Army) with a cardboard follow me sign to collect the Herc which was now usually lost in the gloom.

We became chauffeurs, if an aircraft turned up that was not either British, French, Kuwaiti, or American, the "helpful" Marines would either deliver it to us - the standard excuse was "well it didn't belong to anybody else and you guys are good at handling foreigners". Inevitably it would turn out to be another ambassador returning to reopen an embassy, with nobody to meet him. Out would come the UKMAMS Landrover to act as VIP transport into Kuwait City. By the time we came to leave, the lads were quite familiar with the diplomatic sector of Kuwait City.

By week three the decision had been taken to airlift the remaining British Troops from a dozen new desert strips as the smoke clouds round the city were preventing flying two days out of three. The decision was made shortly after this to close down the Kuwait International Airport Det and after four weeks we closed up shop. The range of activities carried out by the team during our stay in Kuwait was vast, we off-loaded aircraft with generators to restore electricity to the city, Red Cross relief supplies and unfortunately had to send dead and wounded back home. We did much more than just handle aircraft. The feeling when we first arrived and saw the carnage was one of despair, by the time we left, positive steps to reverse the damage were being taken. A lot of effort was going into rebuilding a shattered country and its people after the ravages of war, and though we only played a small part in its reconstruction we all felt proud to have been there!

After the massive effort to deploy the Allied forces to the Gulf and free occupied Kuwait the transport fleet were tasked with withdrawing the troops back home

Turkey - 1991 - Operation Warden
This was an extension of Operation Haven. It involved the protection of Kurdish camps from the air and the policing of the No-fly zone in Northern Iraq, from Adana in Turkey. The Hercules re-supply was achieved by extending the normal Akrotiri tasks.

Yugoslavia - 1992 - Operation Cheshire
Commenced in July in support of the UNHCR in the former Yugoslavia. One Hercules aircraft was deployed to Zagreb on 25th July and commenced relief flights into Sarajevo on 3rd July. The deliveries totalling 78,000lbs of composite rations were made on the first day. Because of the increasing danger to the flight crews the RAF detachment was moved to Ancona in Italy in early February. During the first 13 months some 1,600 hours had been flown during 760 sorties at the rate

of up to 3 per day. In excess of 25,000,000lbs of food, medicines, clothing, fuel and general goods had been airlifted into the besieged city of Sarajevo on behalf of the United Nations.

Hercules at Zagreb loading UNHCR aid to be airlifted into Sarajevo

Saudi Arabia - 1992 - Operation Jural
This operation commenced in August and involved the deployment of six Tornado F.3s to Dharhan to police the Southern No-Fly Zone in Iraq. The Hercules was initially required to fly out the Tornado support and spares kits during which some 1,550 hours were flown in addition to the months scheduled tasking of 2,177 hours. These operations continue for the Hercules with a twice weekly re-supply schedule linked with that of Operation Warden.

Bosnia - 1992 - Operation Hanwood
This involved the move of medical personnel and supplies of the Army Medical Services to Bosnia

Yugoslavia - 1992 - Operation Grapple
This was the deployment and continued re-supply of the army initially in Zagreb and later Split. The Army units in the former Yugoslavia are working with the UN Protection Force (UNPROFOR).

Somalia - 1992 - Operation Vigour
Hercules were deployed on 10th December 1992 to airlift relief supplies into Mogadishu and the hinterland of Somalia as well as support of the US

Marine Corps. The first relief flight took place on the 12th December from Mombassa and 6,619,600lbs of aid were delivered in flying 1,458 hours before the 90 strong detachment arrived home on the 10th of March.

Italy - 1993 - Operation Deny Flight

This deployment of six Tornado F.3s and two VC.10 tankers to Italy in support of the Bosnian No-Fly Zone involved Lyneham flying 37 tasks totalling 370 hours flying time in two and a half days. It also has generated another re-supply flight each week.

Lyneham is also currently involved with the Conventional Forces in Europe (CFE) inspections which are the result of the Vienna Treaty, CSBM and INF Treaties. Lyneham is a point of entry for incoming inspections. There are also three to four outgoing inspections per month. These have included flights from Lyneham to Moscow, Kiev, Minsk, Bucharest, Warsaw, Budapest, Prague, Moldovia, Sofia, Yerevan, Baku, Tbilisi and Tirana.

Loading sacks of humanitarian food onto a Somalian lorry for distribution during Operation Vigour

The snatch method of recovering mail from the ground was developed by JATE. It was used extensively from August to October 1982 when the runway at Stanley was closed. The round trips Ascension - Falkland Islands - Ascension, lasted anything from twenty-four to twenty-eight hours non-stop.

After dropping the mail at Stanley, the arduous and dangerous job of snatching the mailbag is as follows:-

1. The grappling hook dangles at about 25ft. (AGL)
3. As the aircraft flies over the marker panels, it descends lower and the hook makes contact with the rope.
4. Once the hook has grabbed the rope, it is wound in by an electric motor by the ALM., and a member of the army 47 AD Sqn. grabs the mailbag.

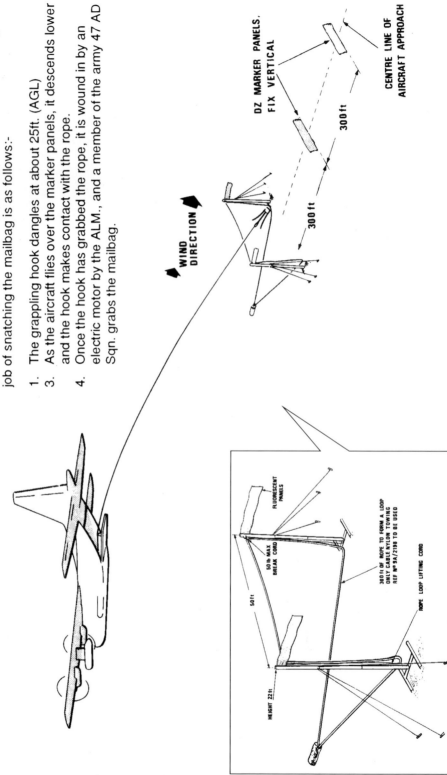

WIND DIRECTION

DZ MARKER PANELS. FIX VERTICAL

300 ft

300 ft

CENTRE LINE OF AIRCRAFT APPROACH

FLUORESCENT PANELS

50 lb MAX BREAK CORD

50 ft

300 ft OF ROPE TO FORM A LOOP ONLY CABLE NYLON TOWING REF Nº 9A/2198 TO BE USED

ROPE LOOP LIFTING CORD

HEIGHT 22 ft

CHAPTER 6

Crew Duties

The Captain/Co-Pilot/Navigator - TS TASKS

Transport Support (TS) tasks can be a singleton or multi-ship usually in multiples of three Hercules. Unless they are the lead crew of a formation the Captain, Co-pilot and Navigator will meet about 2-3 hours before take-off to plan the route. If they are the lead crew they will generally come in an hour before the other crews and have the planning ready for the other crews to copy. The planning for a TS task, particularly for the lead crew, can be quite hectic. Firstly the crew will decide on a route, with particular regard to weather, avoidance areas and length of time allowed for the task. Once the route is decided the Co-pilot and Navigator will spend the time planning the specifics such as tracks, distances, safety attitudes while the Captain supervises the general planning, such as type of load to be dropped, weights and speeds.

The Captain, Co-pilot and Navigator in Flight Planning to preparing for their task

About two hours before take-off the Captain will carry out a crew/formation brief covering all aspects of the task. The crew will generally arrive at the aircraft about 45 minutes before take-off where the Captain will carry out a further brief with the flight Engineer, Loadmaster and the Despatcher - if stores are to be dropped this will be a member of 47 Air

Despatch Squadron or a Parachute Jump Instructor (PJI) if paratroopers are to be dropped. Take-off time is worked out by the Navigator to the minute to achieve the desired time over the Drop Zone.

Aircraft in a formation will take-off at 15 second intervals and once airborne will take up their formation position as soon as possible. There are two types of formation flown on the Hercules - usual or SKE (Station Keeping Equipment). SKE is an American system which allows up to 36 aircraft to fly in formation safely in cloud at medium level. It takes a great deal of concentration by the crews, monitoring a special radar screen and other indicators, to maintain position. The lead aircraft can send commands, such as turns, climbs or descents using the SKE equipment. Visual flying is by far the easier formation to fly.

The Captain's position. The box at the top of the instrument panel is the UHF HOMER. Nose wheel steering is via the small wheel to the left. The four sets of instruments are for the engines

The lead crew have the hardest job navigating and carrying out communications for the formation while the other aircraft follow, although they are required to monitor the lead crew and be prepared to take over should the lead have a problem and need to abort.

The Co-pilot checks his oxygen supply

Navigating the Hercules at low level is achieved by close co-operation between the Navigator and Co-pilot. The Co-pilot map reads and gives position updates for the Navigator to feed into his equipment. Over featureless terrain the Navigator will keep the Co-pilot updated on distance to go and position left or right of track until such time as the Co-pilot can get a good fix. The Captain flying the aircraft makes sure he and his formation keep clear of towns and other sensitive areas while keeping a close eye on the weather ahead.

The Navigator at his desk continually monitors the aircraft position

Approaching the Drop Zone (DZ) the aircraft or formation has to be slowed from its cruise speed to a speed at which it can open the doors and then eventually down to the speed for dropping the stores/troops. Slow down is achieved at a specific time or way point and the checklists called. Utmost care and monitoring by the crew is required to ensure that the correct heights, flap settings and speeds are flown. On the run-in to the DZ the Captain will be concentrating on hard flying, while the Co-pilot will be calling the DZ for clearance to

drop, navigating and looking ahead for the DZ markings. The Navigator will be assisting the Co-pilot as well as positioning himself behind the Captain or Co-pilot (depending on drift) to operate the drop lights at the correct point. The RED-ON light is operated 5 seconds to go and the GREEN-ON light is at the correct point. This is the executive command for the stores to be released or the troops to start jumping. Once all troops or stores have been dropped further checklists are called to close up the doors, bring flaps in and the aircraft brought back to cruise speed.

Recovery back to Lyneham in a formation is normally for an overhead break to land.

The Route Flight Engineer

Having decided on the forthcoming month's tasking, Strike Command supplies the necessary details to RAF Lyneham. The amount of flying is proportionately divided amongst the four Squadrons. The task is allocated a four figure callsign and supplied to the squadrons, usually, by the middle of the current month. A monthly "seats conference" is held among section leaders to decide on additional seat requirements for training purposes depending on task itinerary. Signals are received by each squadron giving a breakdown of load and passenger details and any special requirements needed.

The Engineer Leader, or his deputy then allocates the tasks to section engineers depending on a pecking order for routes going outside the normal European Theatre, such as trips to the USA, Canada, Africa, Far East, Caribbean, and occasional Specials. The engineer who is top of the respective ladder would then be allocated the route provided he was not already tasked, on leave, on detachment, or course.

A folder containing all the flight details including updates and itinerary changes, is held in squadron operations and is consulted by all crew members for that task. Where there are special considerations for a task the Captain of the proposed flight will usually hold a crew brief within the previous 48 hours of departure time.

On the day of the flight the crew meets at the entrance to the passenger terminal, familiarly referred to as the "CO's End", some two hours

Two Loadmasters visiting Station Operations to collect aircraft and load details

before the planned departure time. The Engineer together with the Loadmaster then goes to Station Operations where the aircraft details and load breakdown are obtained. A short visit is made to flight planning by the Engineer to check on NOTice of Air Movements (NOTAMs) which might affect the flight. The Engineer and Loadmaster get transport to the line servicing squadron which maintains the mandatory servicing of their aircraft. Here, the Engineer looks through the aircraft servicing documents referred to as the Form 700 paying particular attention to aircraft role limitations, acceptable deferred defects, servicing validity and recurring problems. The aircraft key is signed out and a starter crew is booked for 30 mins before proposed departure time.

A trainee engineer and checker read the Form 700 to confirm that the aircraft is fully servicable for the task and that previous problems have been rectified before booking out the key

The Engineer and Loadmaster are then driven out to the aircraft to perform their remaining pre-flight duties. Baggage and individuals' kit is off loaded at the aircraft and the Engineer unlocks the aircraft and does a quick walk-round looking for obvious

abnormalities and checking that the aircraft is correctly chocked, earthed and a fire extinguisher is in place. The ground power set is started, the Engineer climbs on board and a few safety checks are carried out in conjunction with the Loadmaster prior to external power being connected.

The Flight Engineer plugs in the ground power while the Loadmaster boards the aircraft

The Engineer methodically checks various systems including fire detection, fuel, de-icing, flight control, compass and navigational systems. External and internal checks looking for loose panels, screws, fasteners, leaks etc. are carried out before he completes his engineer's log. This initially shows the Zero Fuel Weight (ZFW) plus fuel load and distribution giving the All Up Weight (AUW) of the aircraft. Using his Flight Reference Cards (FRC) the Engineer obtains the corresponding decision speeds for rotate, one engine inoperative, flaps up safely, and immediate landing. In the event of the weight of the aircraft being above that for normal maximum landing then a fuel jettison plan is written down on the back of the log together with any speed limitations governed by the varying aircraft weight.

Once the remainder of the crew arrives the Engineer advises the Captain of the current aircraft status and presents the servicing certificate for signature. To complete the engineer's pre-flight log the Navigator informs the Engineer of flight plan time and required fuel together with cruising flight level and International Standard Atmosphere (ISA) deviation. The Engineer can then calculate the target speed, fuel flow and engine torque for the proposed flight level. The Gas Turbine Compressor (GTC) is started and a bleed air leak check carried out to ensure the integrity of this system prior to engine start. An inverter is switched on providing electrical power to various engine instruments. As each engine is started

The Flight Engineer carrying out his fuel checks

in turn the Engineer monitors engine RPM, fuel flow, ignition, oil pressures, hydraulic pressure and peak Turbine Inlet Temperature (TIT). Once stable at Low Speed Ground Idle (LSGI) the Engineer calls the peak TIT and then brings the engine to Normal Ground Idle (NGI) again monitoring for excessive TIT. The engine driven generator is checked for correct voltage and frequency and brought on-line. A second inverter is switched on powering the Captain's and Co-pilot's Altitude Direction Indicators (ADIs). Once all engines are running normally, the GTC is shut down, air conditioning switched on, the Engineer checks out the electrical, engine and propeller anti-icing and fuel systems as required.

With taxying checks complete the Engineer is ready to begin the take-off checks; this involves the re-positioning of switches affecting electrical, anti-icing, fuel and pressurisation systems. Once safely airborne the Engineer synchronises and syn-chrophases the propellers, sets the pressurisation for the desired flight level, monitors all aircraft systems throughout the climb. This also includes a check of

the leading edge de-icing for the wings and empennage. At the top of the climb the first full column of the engineer's log is completed. This covers writing down instantaneous values of various engine parameters, fuel left and electrical output. Having obtained the ISA deviation the target speed, fuel flow, engine torque, 3 engine stabilising height and endurance are calculated. A partial log entry is completed every hour and a full log every 2 hours.

The Form 700 contains flight time, average cruise height and speed, number of pressurisations and landings, servicing required and this is completed for each sector flown. The Diary contains actual itinerary and flight times, type of let-down and amount of instrument flying while the Squadron History Form, which duplicates the Diary, contains additional information on type of load and passenger carried, is completed by the Engineer.

Throughout the flight all systems are monitored by the Engineer and, when problems arise, he will advise the Captain on remedial action where appropriate. An important part of the Engineer's role is the careful monitoring and use of fuel as there can be up to 8 tanks, any one being able to supply fuel to any engine. It is necessary, therefore, to maintain a symmetrical balance of fuel within the wing. At the top of descent a landing fuel figure is calculated and landing weight with corresponding landing speeds for 50% and 100% flap obtained from the FRCs and agreed with the pilots. During the descent pressurisation is set such that upon landing the aircraft will be depressurised. Engine torque is closely monitored in order to maintain positive output from each engine. Snags for malfunctions of various systems are written up in the Form 700 and a Techwarn message is passed by the Engineer to Station Operations.

After the landing run is complete, anti-icing, pressurisation, electrical and fuel systems are set for taxying to the parking bay. After engine shut down all outstanding paperwork is completed by the Engineer, the flight deck checked for tidiness and the personal kit offloaded on to the crew bus. If the aircraft has been overseas the crew visit HM Customs and, when cleared, proceed to the line servicing squadron to assist in the technical debrief of snags that have arisen during the flight. Once complete the Form 700 is handed back to the line chief and the crew returns to the "CO's End" where details of individual's stand-down are obtained before the crew members disperse and go their separate ways.

The Flight Engineer on the TS Role

In addition to his normal responsibilities, the Flight Engineer during the Transport Support role carries out extra duties in order to assist the crew to complete the mission.

Above the ADI is the SKE box

During his pre-flight checks he would carry out additional functional checks of aircraft equipment or systems which are required during the task. Prior to start-up he attends the final crew brief in order to confirm timings, drop altitudes and any other relevant information.

In flight, the Engineer reads all support role checks, as challenge and response, at the appropriate times. He keeps a good visual scan outside the aircraft for hazards such as other aircraft, birds, pylons, masts etc as well as his usual instrument scan during which he pays particular attention to ADIs, altimeters, ASIs and pressure settings. If possible, he updates pressure settings on HF on the hour as well as monitoring HF for airfield cloud states and en route

diversion weather. During the run in to the drop he will revise and update drop weight and minimum drop speed and advise the Captain. He monitors speed and flap settings at all times but particularly at the slow down point.

If Station Keeping Equipment (SKE) is used during the mission, it is the Engineer's responsibility to carry out a thorough pre-flight check of the SKE installation checking all range markers, proximity warning alarms and track while scanning indications for various along and across track parameters. In flight it is his responsibility to call all Flight Command Indicator (FCI) indications and to operate SKE controls as directed by the operating pilot. He will inform the Captain of any SKE malfunctions and advise on appropriate remedial action.

At the end of the mission he will attend the post flight debriefing.

The Air Loadmaster on Route

It all begins when the Loadmaster's office allocates a "route" trip to a particular Loadmaster. On the last working day before the route trip's departure, the Loadmaster involved is required to make preparations by finding out what load will be carried, its weight, (important for the pilots and navigators) where it will be going and last, but by no means least, finding out what each member of the crew wants to eat. (Some trips may last as long as sixteen hours although during Operation Granby some crews were flying for as long as twenty three hours, a long time to be without food).

First stop on the Loadmaster's journey to prepare the trip is a visit to the Squadron Operations where the names of the rest of the crew members can be found from the Route board. Also shown is the trip callsign which will give the Loadmaster a clue as to the mark of Hercules - CMk.3 aircraft begin with a five. From the "Transop" - a signal showing the route details - the Loadmaster can see the destinations and times of arrival and departure, the planned load details and any special instructions such as a visa which may be required for certain countries. Once the Loadmaster has found as much information about the trip as possible at this point, a visit to Load Control is called for.

At Load Control, the Loadmaster is required to check any last minute changes to the trip and to fill out a form requesting any additional role equipment required. This depends on the loads to be carried. An extra 10,000 lbs net or extra restraint chains may be needed or if the destination is Norway, during winter, then Arctic Survival Packs need to be ordered

Once this has been done the next step is In-Flight Catering where food for the flight is ordered. On most of the squadrons, the crew members' meal requirements are listed on a board. This information is transferred onto the Catering sheets. If the length of the trip means that the crew is entitled to take three meals each but only two will actually be eaten then a cash allowance is given with which to buy coffee, tea bags, milk and so on. These Catering Forms are then handed to the Catering Office where they are checked and also any passenger numbers are notified.

Two hours before the start of the trip the Loadmaster reports to Load Control where he inspects the cargo manifests to see that all is correct. A check is made on the the aircraft trim sheet - a list of where items have been loaded on the aircraft, therefore determining the balance of the Hercules. When this is done, it's off to the aircraft for the flight. With one hour to go to the departure time, the food should arrive and when it is all checked, it is stored away until it is required.

The two In-Flight catering staff are delivering meal boxes

When the rest of the crew arrives, the Loadmaster tells the Captain the aircraft weight and runs through the load telling him if anything dangerous is on board. With this done, it is time to go.

The Loadmaster positions himself outside the aircraft to supervise the start. When the engines have

started he climbs aboard and has a last look around at the load and the aircraft before take off. When airborne, the look-around is then repeated and after this is done the Loadmaster can settle down to preparing all of his paperwork for the next destination.

The Loadmaster positions himself where he can see all around the aircraft during the engine start. Here he is indicating to the rest of the ground crew that Number 2 engine is about to start

Air Loadmaster on a Parachute Sortie

Prior to reporting to the aircraft two hours before departure the Air Loadmaster (ALM) collects the Hung Up Parachute Release Assembly (HUPRA) from the Safety Equipment Section. This is a device for releasing parachutists accidentally suspended outside the aircraft. The aircraft engineering document (F700) is checked for correct Parachute Role Fit for the task.

On arrival at the aircraft the ALM commences his parachute preflight and aircraft check lists which include important items such as strops (the parachutist's life-line between aircraft and parachute), anchor cables and exit doorways. An aircraft trim sheet is prepared which gives weight and balance clearance for the flight. During the flight to the Dropping Zone (DZ) the ALM is responsible, together with the Parachute Jump Instructors (PJIs) for the welfare of all troops and that all Standing Operating Procedures (SOPs) covering both routine despatch of the paratroops and any emergency procedures that may occur, are carried out expediently and correctly.

Thirty minutes before the drop, final preparations commence which includes folding seats and loose equipment strapped down. Parachute Static Lines are connected to the cable and require checking while the parachutists make buddy-buddy checks on each other. Movement to the open exit doors require careful control and is completed at P hour minus two minutes. Any stores or the wedge will be dropped immediately before the troops.

When all of the troops have left the aircraft the empty parachute bags, which remain attached to the anchor cable by the Static Lines, are recovered from outside the aircraft.

If the Wedge Airdrop System (WAS) is to be used, the ALM will be required to report to the aircraft four hours before departure to supervise the loading. If the sortie is to include the dropping of large platform loads the ALM will be require to report to the aircraft up to six hours in advance of departure.

Tea For Who? - a Loadmaster's tale by M ALM Birkin-Hewitt

It was half past five on a cold, dark, wet and windy February morning and Sergeant Jimmy McCabe was just starting his day. As he turned the key in the padlock on the door of Hercules XV219 he pondered upon the day ahead - if all went well, if the load arrived on time, if the aircraft would stay serviceable, if the weather stayed good for the duration of the flight and the drop, and if the loading vehicles - Condecs - stayed serviceable he just might be finished by three in the afternoon. Then a quick call into the Loadmaster section on the Squadron to check his mail slot and the next day's programme - an hour in the gym and then home for a break before meeting the new girlfriend at the local. But all of that was some way off and right now he needed to turn his concentration to the next seven hours.

With his flight bags on board he started the ground power set, turned on the aircraft's electrics and opened up the radios with Station Operations using the tactical callsign for the day - 2MO 14J.

His airdrop load today was a double, Medium Stressed Platform (MSP), the largest, heaviest and arguably the most spectacular airdropped load regularly exercised by Lyneham's TS (Transport Support) squadrons. Each rigid based platform is a large, open sided, metal-skeleton box which can carry loads in excess of eight tonnes and, when fully rigged can be over 20ft long, 7ft wide and over 8ft high. A typical load secured into an MSP is a landrover and a trailer, with related stores and equipment lashed against the metal framework sides of the platform. This type of load would be dropped as essential stores for previously dropped paratroops - MSPs cannot be dropped from the same aircraft as troops. With two platforms loaded into one aircraft the Hercules is at its maximum capacity both in bulk and in volume. Each type of airdrop requires a totally different role fitting.

Loading a completed MSP onto a Condec by members of No 47 AD

A quick fix of hot black coffee from his flask (it was some six hours before the in-Flight Caterers were due at the aircraft) and Jim was ready for action! Armed with several check lists he now had less than two hours to complete the pre-flight and pre-loading checks, two hours which usually seemed like thirty minutes, especially if during the checks he found any faults, which was not uncommon. Today was good, he needed the Role Equipment fitters to attend the aircraft for just a couple of minor faults. Satisfied that his checks were complete Jim then started the paperwork: an Airdrop Check List Certificate with his signature to confirm the completion of all the required checks so far and an aircraft Trim Sheet, an essential before-flight document which, when completed by the Loadmaster, computes the aircraft's weight and balance, and trim condition throughout the flight - important information for the flight deck crew especially on airdrop work.

The army installation team together with the MSPs loaded onto two condecs arrived on time at 0730 - things were obviously going well. A quick check of the load manifests, a short briefing with the Army Installation Commander (AIC), Corporal Davey Cone, spiced with a lot of early morning ribald banter between "Crabs" and "Brown Jobs", and the task of emplaning the loaded platforms began in earnest. The AD boys were glad for the activity to help ward off the early morning chill. Davey and

Jim had previously worked together and each recognised each others responsibilities for the onload, so experience and familiarity replaced the need for rank which allowed each to get on with his own part of the ensuing team effort.

Onloading the two platforms took almost four hours.

The Condec loaded with an MSP is driven up to the Hercules ramp

The time normally allowed, with everything running smoothly, is three and a half hours, but a number of faults had been found and had to be rectified, each

The deck of the Condec and Hercules are rigged with rollers enabling the load to be pushed easily into the hold once they are accurately lined up

taking its toll against the tightly run time schedule. For Jim and the army team it had been a busy morning. Sometime during the last four hours the dawn had broken, but Jim didn't recall noticing the sunrise. It was still cold but not so wet and the wind had dropped. Perhaps the Met Man was telling the truth after all! Jim had received the weather check over the radio hours ago. The Met Man report stated that the weather should be OK for the whole area for the two hours of low level flying and for the drop at 1400 onto the DZ at Keevil. At the time of the report it was blowing a fair gale and he had heard these

optimistic reports many times before. Disbelievingly he shrugged his shoulders, sucked his teeth and told the army team to continue with the onload. Once loaded, if the task was then cancelled, it would take another hour to offload but this time it would have been with a very disgruntled team of "Brown Job Squaddies"!

In between the endless checks on the platforms, on the loads, the aircraft functional systems, the rigging and the parachutes, Jim had also dealt with the Role Equipment Fitters (more signatures!) groundcrew "lineys" who'd been sent to do a fuel uplift - this meant stopping the loading while the ramp was raised, and then the Flight Caterers said they couldn't find the aircraft because they had been give the wrong bay number! Nevertheless the arrival of the hot water flasks was a welcome event. Jim's coffee flask was long since empty and a fresh brew was definitely a must.

Amazingly the Flight Engineer appeared at the aircraft steps just as Jim was stirring sugar into the steaming brown liquid. "Orr Jim!.. just what I need, two sugars in mine mate" Jim's predictable but good natured Scottish lilt was lost in the wake of another Herc taxying past "F......! Ahm bezzy.." was all the Engineer heard!

The thirty minutes of flex which Jim had built into his load planning had been soaked up by the faults found on the load, so with just 35 minutes to go before scheduled chocks time of 1205, there was still plenty to do and he knew full well that the flight deck crew would be on the aircraft early. They would have been into the Flight Planning Cell at a gentlemanly time of ten o'clock and spent a while clearing the low level route around the Cornwall and Devon areas. Jim often wondered just what the three of them actually did. Two hours of fine professional mapping and planning and yet within twenty minutes of being airborne he could almost guarantee they'd be lost at some stage! Then, hungry and bored and eager to get airborne "a few minutes early in case we lose some time on the route!" they'd arrive at the aircraft hunting for their lunch boxes, wanting drinks and looking for some sport, generally known as baiting-the-loadie.

Jim had finished the trim sheet apart from the "Finals" signatures, one from himself and one from Davey, so the two of them worked together, Davey reading off the check list guide while Jim physically checked each item in turn. This was the final check, a last look at the entire installation rigged inside the aircraft and, when completely satisfied that the two MSP's were loaded correctly and "in accordance with the book" the two of them signed the relevant certificates on the trim sheets - any faults after that would be Jim's responsibility. Jim had some difficulty signing the certificate - his fingers were crossed!

The pilots and the Navigator appeared just as the army team were leaving, for now their job was finished. However once back in the hangar there would be many more loads to prepare for the next day, from ammunition-box sized Harness Packs to more MSPs. The boys of 47 Squadron (AD) RLC were never idle for very long.

With just fifteen minutes to go to the chocks time the Captain, Flight Lieutenant John Williams, called the crew together for a briefing. Firstly he called a time check to ensure everyone had synchronised watches, and then announced the details of the task, "..a timed take off at 1214 and 30 seconds, a South Westerly route for one hour and forty-five minutes of low level ending up at Keevil at 1400 for a double MSP. For the drop we'll be at 600 ft AGL, 125 knots, with 75% flap for our drop weight, you to monitor please, Eng, and after the drop we'll come straight home, on the ground at about 1420 or thereabouts... your brief please Jim...". Although he'd already given a briefing sheet to the Captain and the Navigator so that they had the load weights and parachute information necessary to calculate the aircraft's dropping parameters, Jim went through a quick resume of the drop sequence, confirmed once again the heights and weights as advertised and requested the Navigator to advise him of the pre-drop timings; a 20 minutes call, "Prepare for Action", 10 minutes and 5 minutes for "Pre-drop Checks" and "Final drop Checks" at which time the cargo door is opened, and 2 minutes "Action Stations". He also reminded the crew that after the two minute call the Safety Line would be removed, (this is a cord attached to the extractor parachute and is designed to prevent an accidental release of the extractor drudge) the load would then be "Live" and any faults thereafter would have to be treated as an emergency condition. This requires the operation of a manual override system, by the Loadmaster,

making the extractor parachute inoperative, and thereby making the load "Safe" ... Six tonnes of assorted metalwork landing in someone's back garden would mean an awful lot of writing for the whole crew!

Jim finished his briefing with a run through of the various load emergencies and finally the Navigator gave his lights-brief, "..the sequence will be RED-ON followed by GREEN-ON at which point the drop is to commence. Any subsequent RED-ON, stop dropping. In the event of a lights failure we will drop on my verbal commands, if the intercom fails there will be no drop ....". Jim couldn't help smirking at the brief, once the MSP drop system had commenced it would take no more than eleven seconds for the two platforms to be divorced from the aircraft and become airborne, and a six ton mass travelling at a separation speed of approximately 150 miles per hour will not be stopped, especially not by "... any subsequent RED-ON.."! However, that was no reflection on the Nav; his briefing was a regulation standard procedure which had to be complied with whether the drop was for MSPs or paratroops.

At last, all pre-flight preparations were complete, all paperwork was signed and completed, all the checks were done and all the required briefings were out of the way. Headsets On!

Apart from the Co-pilot missing the weather broadcast, he was more interested in the new WRAF controller's voice in Air Traffic Control, and the Engineer spilling his tea in the Captain's nav bag, which caused a lot of swearing and a flurry of paper towels. The aircraft start up and the taxying out to the runway was routine and uneventful.

Take-off, though, was almost late. The pilots anxiously counting down the minutes to their "timed take off" were frustrated by the honey voiced controller who denied them access to the runway line-up point to allow a Route Inbound to land first - they do have priority! After landing the Routie then continued all the way to the furthest end of the runway, eating away even more precious seconds. Only when the aircraft was completely clear were they permitted to "Enter and line-up". By now the honey voice had a mocking tone - so the Co-pilot's earlier wisecracks had been heard! With the time

The Captain taxis the aircraft out of the parking space

ticking away the Captain steered the aircraft into the middle of the runway - the sound of the Navs voice in his ears "...ten seconds, five, four, three, two, one, brakes off.." and with the Engineer monitoring his every move, applied the power. At 110 knots the Herc strained into the air and, with the gear and flaps retracted, changed from a lumbering truck to an almost elegant machine in its favourite element - a Herc at low level has no equal.

Low level flying is confined to low populated areas and is required to provide realistic training to enable the aircraft to be flown below radar and avoid detection by the enemy

Being a singleton meant the aircraft was on a "free-play" mission, following a promulgated and cleared route, but without the constraints of an aircraft formation nor any exercise injects from AWACS or controlling ground agencies. Having completed his paperwork and without much to do until the 20 minute call Jim knelt by the windows to the left of the Captain where he adopted the role of an observer - an extra pair of eyes to scan the horizon for any possible threat to the aircraft. This quiet position was only occasionally broken with subtle quips from the rest of the crew such as "..dry ol' trip this

inn'it.." and he would have to break from his sight-seeing tour to produce a cup of coffee to regain the peace.

As the time approached 1340 Jim glanced at the Nav, pointed to his watch and gave a questioning thumb-up; the Nav nodded and thumbed agreement, "20 minutes, Captain...". "Roger, 20 minutes Jim .. prepare the load .." Jim unplugged his headset from the intercom and left the flight deck -they'd use the public address system if they needed him urgently. The aircraft was still see-sawing its way along the meandering low level route so once he was in the freight bay, Jim picked his way carefully, stopping to hang on to overhead anchor cables whenever sharp turns or changes in "G" threatened to bowl him over. His pre-drop preparations involved removing two in-flight restraint chains from each of the MSPs, a thorough inspection of the platforms and the area in the freight bay aft of them, ensuring that nothing had come adrift during the flight, and finally a quick check of the aircraft systems. This was the last real chance he'd have to inspect the working parts of the aircraft before the drop sequence commenced. Satisfied, Jim made his way back to his despatch position at the forward end of the bay. Cursing at the weaving manoeuvres and the ankle-trapping roller conveyor he secured his harness to the anchor cable and called in on the intercom; "Loadie on, ... the load is ready..".

As the Captain turned the aircraft onto its final leg the crew's workload increased and the Nav's ten minute call was almost lost amongst the chatter. With six minutes to run to the drop the Captain asked for the "Pre Dropping Checks" and as soon as they were completed the Nav called for the slow down, a reduction from the average low level speed of around 210 knots to the drop speed of 125 knots. Once at the correct speed and with the flaps set accordingly "Final Dropping Checks..." were called for by the Captain. As the Engineer reached "Cargo Ramp and Door" on the check list, Jim watched the ramp area and confirmed "You're clear to open". Daylight flooded into the freight bay as the ramp and door separated, forcing Jim to shield his eyes. At the same time the Co-pilot called "I have the DZ!" The ramp, held by two fixed arms, stopped in its horizontal position but the upward opening door strained towards its uplock, nudged it, and then hovered provokingly just beneath it! Jim swore under his breath. This often happened, the single hydraulic jack fixed near the doors hinged end couldn't always cope with the inflight demands and until the door was safely up-locked the drop could not go ahead! There were still checks to do and the Engineer was getting concerned that he still had the Ramp and Door button depressed but without the comforting illuminated "OPEN" indicator and the DZ was getting closer by the second.

Jim was about to call for a "bunt", (the pilot applies negative "G") which sometimes works on a reluctant door, when the aircraft hit a patch of turbulence. Almost by magic the uplock engaged and the Engineers call was heard "Open light ..ON!".

The remaining checks were quickly completed. " Two minutes... Action Stations!" Jim acknowledged the warning command and began removing the safety line, at first carefully and slowly, pulling the 120 ft of cord hand over hand and rolling it into a neat loop, and then it snagged, on something not seen, a couple of tugs and it came loose but time was now dribbling away so he pulled faster, two yards of cord at a time. The cord seemed endless and then one loop caught on his wrist, then one on his boot, then a piece caught on a seat clip and another round the knife on his leg..! Cursing as he fought to rid himself of two handfuls of living spaghetti he called "Safety line removed .. Live Load!" threw the defeated cord behind the seats and stood by the Emergency Handles.

The Nav moved to the Captain's left elbow so that they could both see the Impact Point on the DZ, from that position he also had access to the drop-light controls and after assessing the aircraft path to be slightly off the ideal for the CARP (Calculated Air Release Point) he gave fine course corrections. The previously noisy flight deck was now totally silent, everyone concentrating on the job in hand, all waiting for the Nav's next two calls. The stop watch showed 1400 and 30 seconds as the Nav called "RED-ON!", the Co-pilot's left hand, positioned by the extractor parachute release control panel, twitched in readiness, the Captain prepared to maintain firm control on the yoke and ride the trims as the platforms were expelled from the aircraft, and Jim, his gaze firmly fixed on the Extractor, braced his hands on the Parachute Release Emergency Handle. "GREEN-ON!" the Co-pilot fired the

Extractor button. Jim, seeing that it was a good release, followed with a running commentary, his words punctuated by the tumultuous racket of the two escaping platforms, like two trains being sucked out of a tunnel by some immense but unseen vacuum. " Extractor released! .. extractor deployed! Main chutes released.. aft load moving .. aft load gone! Main chutes deployed ... forward load moving .. load gone! Loadie going aft to observe the drop!" As he hurried towards the back his intercom long lead fouled on a floor beam tugging his head and hindering him he yanked it free and rushed onto the ramp to watch the vertical flight of the MSPs, all the while something else pulling at his right leg! He chose to ignore it.

The noise from each of the MSPs departing was like a train being sucked out of a tunnel

Whilst watching the two platforms drift gently to earth Jim reported their descent to the flight deck and reflected upon his day so far. He'd been at work almost nine hours, and had flown for two. It had taken four hours to emplane the platforms and about ten seconds to offload them! All that was left to do now was to close-up the aircraft and return to Lyneham, on the ground in about twenty minutes and then away to the gym. He turned away from the panorama to close the ramp and door but found that his right leg wanted to go the other way! He quickly investigated the restriction, "What the ...?" two loops of the living spaghetti had tightly coiled around his leg knife and had refused to let go .. the remaining 110 ft of cord had followed him down the length of the freight bay and was tangled on every possible catch and hook. "Oh B.....!"

"Any chance of a cup a'tea Loadie?"

The Aircraft Ground Engineer

Hercules aircraft departing RAF Lyneham on most route taskings have an Aircraft Ground Engineer (AGE) allocated to them. The AGE is an aircraft technician who has undergone specialist training encompassing all the aircraft trades. This training enables him to work completely independently on all systems whenever the aircraft is away from base. The allocation of AGEs to route tasking is basically on a "who is available" basis and this results in an extremely varied and interesting life-style. Currently there are forty two AGEs to cover all the tasks which results in AGEs spending, on average, 200 days a year enclosed in a metal tube - the freight bay of a Hercules on route.

An AGE checks a snag on the ADF box

An AGE becomes part of the crew for the particular task for which he is nominated. His role in flight is that of a passenger; consequently AGEs become very adept at sleeping in the most obscure places within the freight bay of the aircraft, and they have the annoying habit of asking for food and drink at the most inappropriate times. When the aircraft reaches its destination the AGE, after a pleasant flight being waited on hand and foot, commences work.

The amount of time being spent on the ground depends on the work that has to be undertaken. Sometimes the aircraft lands mainly to pick up fuel or freight in which case the depth of servicing undertaken is minimal, frequently only a refuel and a cursory look around the aircraft. Usually, however, a night stop is involved in which case more in-depth servicing is required.

When the aircraft is stopping overnight somewhere in the world, the amount of time the AGE spends at the aircraft can vary tremendously. On the odd occasion, when the aircraft has landed in a serviceable condition, the AGE will carry out an after-flight servicing, any out of phase servicings and all replenishments necessary before joining the rest of the crew at the hotel or on-base accommodation. Invariably though, various problems have developed throughout the flight and after being debriefed, usually by the Flight Engineer, the AGE will carry out any rectification necessary. This is not always that simple; the amount of spares carried can vary from next to nothing to at best a limited amount. Resourcefulness, ingenuity, the infamous yellow tool box and whatever is hidden in the bottom of the bag are called upon in many situations. In most cases a "fix" of some form can be effected that will enable the aircraft to continue safely on task the next day. The time spent reaching this point depends on the amount of work to be done, if it takes all night so be it, but usually a few hours will see the aircraft fully serviceable and ready to go again.

Should a fault with the Hercules prove to be beyond the capabilities of the AGE then spares have to be requested from base. The AGE is responsible for liasing with the local handling agents (who may not speak English and not many AGEs can converse in many other languages) and for requesting the correct spares. Once the spares are received, after successfully negotiating the Customs bureaucracy, the AGE will, hopefully, be able to make the aircraft serviceable so that it can continue on its way. As soon as the aircraft is airborne the AGE assumes his usual position, curled up somewhere fast asleep after begging for more food and drink from the Loadmaster. Normally he dreams of an even bigger wallet and far away places with strange sounding names with the prospect of another night spent on an airfield trying to fix some obscure fault.

The 47 Air Despatchers routine

The Air Despatchers assemble ready for the day's work to be allocated. Today it is 16 x 1 ton air drop containers and this commences at the home of No 47 (Air Despatch) Sqn RLC, at B Site at Lyneham. There are two Air Despatch troops located in B2 hangar which is commonly known by Air Despatchers as the pleasure dome though no one knows why.

A view inside the pleasure dome on B Site showing a quantity of loads ready for an exercise

The task starts with the preparation of 1 ton Air Drop container kits. Bridport nets are used to give the container a flexible height up to 60 inches. Wooden baseboards 52 x 43 ins provide a sturdy base to construct on and give a smooth surface ideal for the ease and flow as the containers roll out of the aircraft on a roller conveyer Baseboards once found unserviceable have numerous other uses as part of rabbit hutches and could make excellent flooring in lofts. Dufalite (honeycomb paper) provides the load with a cushion for impact, this arrives as logs and the air despatcher spends many hours pulling and gluing sheets in the jig and for this he earns the pleasure of blisters on thumb and forefinger. (there is nothing like the technical approach). To keep our load restrained within the net freight straps shrink wrap is used to great effect. Once prepared we now await for the stores to arrive. Training loads are constructed with old ammunition boxes full of stones, the container weight being a maximum of 2,500 lbs. The enjoyment comes with the dropping of live stores tested more recently on Op Haven which provided a great deal of variety and a great challenge, everything from sleeping bags to medical supplies and numerous amounts of plastic shelters were dropped. Our stores are moulded to within the size of the container much like a jigsaw puzzle but applying packing principles. Each item of equipment is weighed and accounted for; there's no chance of getting away from the paperwork, even at this early stage. The containers once constructed are checked by the Despatch Crew Commander who assembles them in stick order on roller conveyor. The despatch crew will then work on the connection and preparation of parachutes including disconnects which automatically release the parachute on landing to prevent it from being dragged around the Drop Zone.

Our 16 containers will be despatched in blocks of 4 in four runs across the DZ. The load is despatched manually - pushed by the crew members. To achieve this final restraint cord, 7,000 NBC is prepared prior to loading.

The containers now prepared are given a thorough check by the Crew Commander, load details including weights, para serial numbers are recorded for insertion on the load manifest and detailed packing reports are completed to account for supply drop equipment and the stores themselves. Once satisfied our despatch crew will transfer the containers on to 5-ton mexi trailers, restrained and sheeted against inclement weather prior to movement to the airfield. The Despatch crew commander will complete a floor loading plan and co-ordinate via load control, the movement of the load to the aircraft. The final stage sees a crew brief prior to the convoy departing for the aircraft. On arrival the first two trailers are parked near the aircraft with the vehicle returning to collect the remainder of the load. Following a brief from the ALM the crew now loads with well rehearsed drills and procedures under the control and guidance of the Crew Commander. The load is restrained in its appropriate load station, parachute static lines are connected to overhead cables and The DCC and ALM complete the final checks before departure.

For the next few hours the Despatch crew deal with low level tactical flying by a tried and trusted method from old - everyone sleeps. Not easy with a full compliment of air drop loads.

Loading a 1 ton airdrop container onto the ramp of the Hercules

At P minus 20 (P is the precise time that the load will be dropped) the crew prepares for action, connects the harnesses up and prepare the load.

The crew attach the restraining chains to the load to ensure that is secure

Chocks are placed forward and aft of the load prior to removal of the restraints. The containers are then moved into despatch stations, an extremely difficult task when the aircraft is continuing to manoeuvre with unpredictable turns. The despatch crew remain in control with well practised drills. At 2,500 lbs a runaway container can make a disastrous mess of the crew and aircraft alike. The final restraint is tied off and the crew await further commands from the DCC. The cargo doors are now open and the breath of fresh air is very welcome. At 15 seconds its action stations; the chocks are removed and the crew start to push. The Number Four of the crew will prepare to cut at "RED-ON" and cut the final restraint tie at "GREEN-ON". The remainder of the crew will continue to push until the load falls away over the ramp. The parachutes deploy (it can be very disappointing if they don't) and the despatchers see the fruits of their labour arrive safely on the DZ. They continue to despatch the remaining loads before the aircraft returns home where the Despatch team checks in at the Pleasure Dome for the next batch of containers requiring preparation.

With harnesses around their waists the Air Despatchers push the 1 ton pallets out the back of the Hercules on the instruction from the ALM

29 Regiment, RLC

South Cerney, the home of No 29 Regiment, RLC, has had a long and rewarding association with the Hercules. The Air Mounting Centre (AMC), operated by No 55 (MC) Squadron and the two away squadrons, Nos 50 and 59 (MC) Squadrons, all deal extensively with the Hercules fleet at nearby Lyneham. No 47 (AD) Squadron and No 80 (PC) Squadron also form part of the Regiment.

The AMC's principal role is to receive, process and despatch passengers, vehicles and freight on operations and exercises for flights from nearby Brize Norton and Lyneham. Freight arrives at the AMC where it is weighed and checked against the manifest. The check involves 10% of normal freight and 100% of Dangerous Air Cargo (DAC). The freight is then reloaded on the Unit's vehicles and despatched to the waiting Hercules at Lyneham. The Unit's vehicles and trailers are weighed on the AMC weighbridge and vehicles and contents are checked for proper storage and prepared for air shipment. Once prepared the vehicles are shipped by Chalks Lyneham where they are again checked by the Air Transport Liaison Officer (ATLO), who is a member of No 29 Regiment and then turned over to the RAF for a final check and loading into the Hercules.

Concurrently, passengers and/or parachutists are also processed. A manifest is produced, baggage checked for DAC, weighed and Next of Kin details compiled. Once check-in has been completed, passengers are either despatched directly to the waiting Hercules at Lyneham in chalk loads or are fed and quartered. Up to 1,600 passengers can be processed at any one time and are despatched, as required, to meet the flow of the Hercules. Personnel of No 55 (MC) Squadron are also directly involved with the Hercules away from South Cerney when squadron personnel are required to supplement the normal away squadrons in such exotic places as Bosnia, Canada, the USA and Kenya to mention just a few.

The other two Movement Control Squadrons, Nos 50 and 59, primarily work with the Hercules at airfields in foreign countries. The Squadrons provide the movement control expertise to receive UK based units which are proceeding on operations or exercises to countries where there is no resident British support. The Squadrons deal mainly with deployments and/or recoveries of AMF(L), No 1

(UK) Armoured Division, No 3 (UK) Division, No 5 Airborne Brigade and No 3 Commando Brigade. The Squadron personnel must be full conversant with airfield operations and the capabilities of the Hercules to make the maximum use of the limited airlift which is assigned to any operation/exercise.

No 29 Regiment, RLC, through its many changes over the years has had a long and rewarding association with the Hercules both throughout the myriad of exercises worldwide and the operations in which the UK has found itself over the years.

The "Albert" and the "Movers" have been and will continue to be inseparable.

No 80 (PC) Squadron, Postal and Courier Service

The Postal and Courier Service (PCS) is responsible for postal and courier support to the Royal Navy, Royal Air Force as well as the Army. RAF flights have always been important to supplement the civil air mail service. Indeed the Service has a close liaison with the RAF and in the 1950s recognised the possibility of improving air-drop facilities to ships at sea. A special Lindholm container was developed for this task and the Hercules was the despatching aircraft.

During the Falklands War a Lindholm container was dropped to a submarine which failed to pick it up. The container was eventually washed ashore on the coast of Brazil and handed over to the authorities

Loading Forces mail onto a Hercules by No 80 PC personnel

who returned it to the UK. The mail was completely dry and ultimately delivered to the addressees only six weeks late!

In August 1982, while repairs were being made to the runway at Stanley on the Falkland Islands, the mail was dropped by Hercules. Collection was by a "mail snatch" method involving dangling a hook at the end of a rope. Surprisingly no mail was lost in the process.

The Hercules has always been a tremendous aid to the Services and has helped the mail get through. Wherever there are servicemen receiving mail the Hercules is never far away. Commitments during the Gulf War, Northern Iraq and Bosnia have all been supported by the PCS with the invaluable help of "Fat Albert".

CHAPTER 7

History of the Squadrons

No 24 Squadron

No 24 Squadron is the senior Squadron at RAF Lyneham. It was formed at Hounslow on 1st September 1915. Initially it was equipped with the Bleriot, BE.2C and Vickers Gunbus aircraft. It moved to France in February 1916 to become the first squadron to operate single seater fighters (DH2 Scouts) in combat. The Squadron's first permanent CO was Major L J Hawker VC, DSO who won great distinction for himself and the Squadron, but was later shot down and killed by Baron Von Richthofen. However, the Squadron extracted ample revenge during the rest of the war by destroying no less than 297 enemy aircraft.

A replica of a No 24 Sqn DH2 Scout

During the inter-war years, No 24 Sqn was engaged in communications duties, a role which it continued and developed during the Second World War. As one of the premier Squadrons of the newly formed Transport Command, it was privileged not only to carry His Majesty King George VI, but also to operate Winston Churchill's personal Avro York. Moreover, in recognition of its 323 flights in unarmed Lockheed Hudson aircraft into a besieged Malta, No 24 Sqn was accorded the great honour of delivering the Island's George Cross Medal.

In 1947, the Squadron reorganised on a Commonwealth basis, and, until 1962, many of its Commanding Officers and members were drawn from the Air Forces of Australia, Canada, New Zealand, and South Africa. During 1948-49 the Dakotas of No 24 Sqn played a prominent role in the Berlin Airlift.

Throughout the post war years the Squadron transported many VIP's including Field Marshal Viscount Montgomery, Marshal of the RAF Lord Tedder, and many foreign dignitaries. A change of role gradually took place after 1950 with the acquisition of the Handley Page Hastings. More special and scheduled flights were flown whilst the number of VIP flights decreased.

A No 24 Sqn photograph with the Hastings

In March 1954, No 24 Sqn was awarded its Standard, the first transport squadron to receive such an honour.

No 24 Sqn moved to RAF Lyneham from Colerne in January 1968 when it re-equipped with the Hercules CMk1. Operations using this versatile aircraft have included famine relief in Nepal in 1973 the evacuation of refugees from Cyprus in 1974; the airlift of medical supplies to the earthquake victims of Turkey in 1976; the transport of Red Cross supplies into Phnom Pehn in 1979; the evacuation of refugees from Iran when the Shah fell also in 1979, and the airlift of the peace keeping force into Rhodesia, now Zimbabwe, in 1980. The massive airlift of support equipment for the South Atlantic Task Force in 1982 and the distribution of famine relief supplies in Ethiopia in 1984/1985 have all featured amongst the Squadron's recent exploits.

In the aftermath of the Falklands campaign some Hercules were converted for Air-to-Air refuelling duties as tanker aircraft. No 24 Sqn crews were in the forefront of this developing role and were actively engaged in operating tanker and airbridge aircraft from Ascension Island and the Falklands...culminating in participating in Operation Granby, Operation Provide Comfort and Operation Haven, Operation Vigour, Operation Grapple, and Operation Jural.

The Squadron's ability to undertake tasks such as these, in addition to its everyday world-wide, troop and cargo-carrying roles, owes as much to the versatility of both the Hercules and its crews. Today, as always, No 24 Sqn stands ready to live up to its motto "In Omnia Parati" translated as "In All Things Prepared", or more colloquially "Ready for Anything".

No 30 Squadron

No 30 Squadron, Royal Flying Corps, was formed at Ishmalia on 24th March 1915 with five Farmans engaged in reconnaissance, bombing, fighter and Army co-operation duties vital to our successful defence of the Suez Canal. It carried out its first bombing mission just three days later. A second flight formed at Basra in April 1915 and supported the British advance up the river Tigris and was joined by the first flight in October. No 30 Squadron was the only RFC unit in Mesopotamia and fought continuously and intensively throughout the war.

The following year, in appalling heat, No 30 Sqn was tasked to supply the Garrison at Kut-el-Amara where 13,850 troops and 3,700 town Arabs were besieged by the Turks. 5,000 lbs of food a day was needed. A desperate maximum effort was mounted, starting with four BE2Cs, one Henri Farman, one Voisin and three Short Seaplanes dropping loads of 150 lbs, in the first ever air-supply operation. The seaplanes proved of limited use, but despite unserviceability, losses due to enemy action, and crashes with overladen aeroplanes, 140 sorties were flown in two frantic weeks, dropping 19,000 lbs in all. But it was not enough, and sadly the Garrison had to surrender on 29th April. 5 Officers and over 30 NCOs and Airmen of No 30 Sqn were captured but few survived. The effort utterly exhausted the Squadron but, strengthened by some new personnel, they bounced back in July and by the end of August had regained their air superiority which the Germans had seized after Kut, and the Squadron gave essential support to the Army who drove the Turks northwards.

In the Official History "The War in the Air", H A Jones records: "The Squadron inflicted damage (by) bombing enemy troops and lines of communication, but the outstanding feature of its work was reconnaissance the pilots had quickly asserted their superiority. The British troops went forward with the knowledge that the Turkish dispositions and movements could not be concealed from the British aeroplanes. The pilots and Observers did all that was asked of them, but their work would not have been possible without the untiring spirit and skill displayed by the Air Mechanics...the aeroplanes were kept serviceable under the most primitive conditions in the face of extreme climatic and physical difficulties".

No 30 Sqn was joined at the front by No 63 Sqn in November 1917 and in March 1918 by No 72 Sqn. The campaign against the Turks ended on 31st October 1918, but No 30 Sqn was engaged in active operations in Persia until May 1919.

From 9th April 1919, No 30 Sqn was again the only squadron in Iraq. Unrest was endemic and when No 6 Sqn arrived in July, No 30 Sqn detachments were already on operations at Kasvin (in Persia) and Mosul. From June to December 1920, No 30 and 6 Sqns were fully stretched fighting the Iraqi uprising.

In 1921, flying DH9As from Mosul, they were engaged against Kurdish rebels, and from Hinaidi against tribesmen in the south. They also played a major part in the arduous pioneering of the important Cairo to Baghdad air route; indeed a No 30 Squadron DH9A was the first aircraft to fly from Baghdad to Cairo in one day. No 30 Sqn was heavily involved in the campaigns against the redoubtable Sheikh Mahmoud and against Saudi tribesmen intruding into southern Iraq.

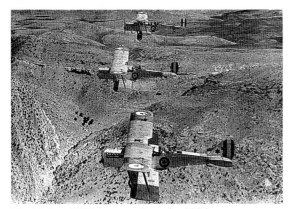

No 30 Sqn DH9As over Iraq in 1924

Re-equipped with Wapitis, No 30 Sqn was based at Mosul from October 1929 for the next seven years where they were still heavily engaged in the final campaign against Sheikh Mahmoud and against Skeikh Ahmed - indeed No 30 Sqn saw active operations in each of its first 17 years. In 1935 they re-equipped with Hardys and in October 1936 it was the first Squadron to move to Habbaniya. In January 1938 they re-equipped with Blenheims. At the end of August 1939, after 24 years in Iraq, the Squadron moved to Ismailia, its original war station.

A Hawker Hardy of No 30 Sqn over Iraq in 1936

No 30 Sqn was used in the Western Desert, mainly in the fighter role, with a pack of 4 Browning guns fitted in the bomb bay. When the Italians invaded

Greece on 28th October 1940, No 30 Sqn was ordered to move to Eleusis near Athens. They flew in on 3rd November - the first British fighting unit to arrive in Greece - and flew their first operation the next day. During their five and a half months in Greece No 30 Sqn flew over 400 operational sorties, dropped some 80,000 lbs of bombs, sunk an Italian Destroyer, destroyed or probably destroyed 10 Italian and 5 German aircraft, and damaged at the very least 30 more, for the loss of 12 aircrew.

Hitler declared war on Greece on 6th April 1941. In good spring weather they swept all before them. Most of the RAF's 80 combat aircraft were quickly overwhelmed and destroyed by 900 Luftwaffe aircraft. Within two weeks the British faced a second Dunkirk-like evacuation. On 17th April No 30 Sqn was ordered to Maleme in Crete - with them were also No 33 Sqn with a few Hurricanes. With their longer range and endurance, the Blenheim's task was the air defence of convoys moving between Greece, Crete and Egypt.

In 4 weeks the Squadron worked stoically under increasingly difficult conditions, with a dwindling number of Blenheims and few spares. They still flew some 100 sorties during which they destroyed 4 enemy aircraft and damaging at least another 33 for no loss of aircrew or ships. Churchill declared that Crete must be held at all costs and Hitler too considered it essential to deny us Crete as an air base. The only way the Germans could invade Crete was by Airborne Forces. Britain and the Commonwealth were then fighting Hitler alone and so soon after the Battle of Britain, and with a menacing threat to Egypt and the Canal, no more fighters could be spared to reinforce Crete.

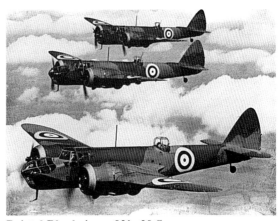

Bristol Blenheims of No 30 Sqn

Maleme the nearest airfield and was defended by the 22nd Battalion of the New Zealand Regiment and by those remaining from No 30 Sqn (some 4 Officers and 114 men) plus No 33 Sqn. Many RAF men did not even have a rifle, and those who did were woefully short of ammunition. The end was sudden and violent, during bitter fighting, sometimes hand-to-hand, against superior numbers and weapons, 29 men from No 30 Sqn were killed - many acts of great bravery are told. In the ensuing chaos Pilot Officer Crowther led some men to Sphakia on the south coast, whence they were evacuated by the Navy, who did heroic work at heavy cost, with exhausted crews in damaged ships, able to operate off Crete only in darkness. Some 60 of No 30 Sqn's men were taken prisoner.

After Crete the Squadron was re-equipped with Hurricanes and fought again in the Desert. In March 1942 it embarked on HMS Indomitable, for Ceylon, arriving at Ratmalana, Approximately five miles south of Colombo, on 23rd March. Admiral Nagumo, with his Air Striking Force which had attacked Pearl Harbour so successfully, approached Ceylon, aiming to destroy British sea power in the Indian Ocean. This threatened India itself, and our vital supply line round the Cape. Churchill once called this "The Most Dangerous Moment in the war".

The attack came on 5th April. 22 out of 23 Hurricanes available to No 30 Sqn were on readiness from 0400. No radar warning was provided, and at 0740 a force of some 125 bombers appeared over Ratmalana, with escorting Mitsubishi Zero fighters. No 30 Sqn was caught on the ground, and many of their 21 pilots who managed to take off did so as bombs were falling, some were bounced by Zeros as they got airborne, 8 out of 30 Sqn's Hurricanes were shot down, five pilots being killed and two seriously injured. A further eight aircraft were damaged and that evening, despite prodigious efforts, the Squadron could only muster 7 Hurricanes. No 30 Sqn pilots had destroyed fourteen Japanese aircraft, probably six more, and damaged another five.

No 30 Sqn remained at Ceylon on air defence duties until in February 1944, it took its Hurricane IICs to the Arakan front in Burma, flying close support operations and was withdrawn to Yellahanka in India in June 1944. It re-equipped with Thunder-

bolts, returning to the Arakan in October to fly long range bomber escorts, fighter sweeps and interdictions as well as close support tasks. In April 1945, from Akyab, it supported the invasion of Rangoon, and after the Japanese had been driven out of Burma, was withdrawn to India to prepare for the invasion of Malaya planned for that autumn. Fortunately the Japanese surrendered in August.

No 30 Sqn re-equipped briefly with Tempest IIs in the summer of 1946, but was disbanded for the first time ever in December 1946, ending then the longest period of overseas service of any RAF Squadron. Eleven months later it was reformed at Oakington with Dakotas. Completion of their work-up was timely, for in June 1948 Stalin tried to force the Allies out of West Berlin by cutting all surface routes. But he misjudged the British and American resolve and their resources.

No 30 Sqn briefly flew the Hawker Tempest

The Russian's timing was ruthless - Berlin's economy was to wither, and the population to starve. Come the winter the need for electricity and heating as well as for food, on top of bad weather, would force an Allied withdrawal. They were proved wrong by what would still be regarded as a major airlift operation even by today's standards. The flying demanded a high level of sustained accuracy and concentration. Aircraft of one type flew in the same direction, at the same height and at a set airspeed, being separated horizontally by only 3 minutes flying time, and vertically by 1,000 feet from a stream of a different type, flying at different airspeed. They were confined strictly within corridors only 20 miles wide.

The total deliveries during the Airlift were 2,325,808 tons, of which No 30 Sqn crews carried

8,729 tons of freight, 25,136 passengers, and 123.5 tons of mail.

The Squadron was re-equipped with Valettas in 1950, flying VIP and Courier flights, and flew the only NATO scheduled flight behind the Iron Curtain to Warsaw. Re-equipped with Beverleys in 1957, it moved to Kenya in November 1959, whence its aircraft ranged over Africa, and flew refugee evacuation and many famine relief operations. In one, it dropped 1,783,000 lbs in 70 sorties, showing a dramatic advance in capability since 1916. In September 1964 the Squadron was moved to Muharraq, in the Gulf, for 3 years before being disbanded

In June 1968 No 30 Sqn was reformed in the UK, and re-equipped with Hercules. Based at Lyneham since 1971, it has participated in emergency aid operations in Nepal, Ethiopia and in many other countries. Hercules crewed by No 30 Sqn have straddled the globe and with the other three Hercules squadrons it was heavily involved in the Falklands conflict, flying many Airbridge flights between Ascension and the Falkland Islands. It also carried out many air-to-air refuelling operations, and provided tanker support for the very last Airbridge in 1989.

No 30 Squadron was heavily involved in Operation Bushel in Ethiopia with crews specialising in the airlanding of relief supplies on dirt strips within the famine areas. The period 1986-90 saw the Squadron's involvement in tasks such as Operation Jubilee, where relief supplies were flown from Belize to flood victims in Jamaica, the airlifting of firemen and Royal Navy divers to Belgium to assist after the Zeebruge ferry disaster, and further disaster relief missions in Nepal as well as to the Caribbean Island of Monserrat in the wake of Hurricane Hugo.

In 1991, a year after its 75th anniversary, No 30 Sqn went to war once more, with Iraq again acting as the cauldron. The Squadron's heavy involvement in Operations Granby and Desert Storm saw all crews flying record-breaking hours, with No 30 Sqn sending the first crew to the Gulf at the start of the Operation, as well as sending the first Hercules crew into the war zone after hostilities broke out on 16th January. The Squadron has played a vital part in ensuring a successful outcome and participated in Operation Provide Comfort, Haven, Jural, Vigour, Grapple.

No 36 Squadron

No 36 Squadron RFC was formed from a detached flight of No 1 Squadron RNAS at Cramlington in Northumberland on 1st February 1916. Under the command of Captain R O Abercrombie and equipped initially with three BE2c aircraft, its operational task was the aerial defence of Newcastle. It was the first RFC Sqn to be specially allotted to home defence duties and its area of responsibility progressively increased so that by May 1916 it had flights detached at Turnhouse and Seaton Carew and was committed to the home defence of the Forth as well as the Tyne and Tees Districts. On the night of 27/28th November 1916 2nd Lt I V Pyott, flying a BE2c, destroyed Zeppelin L34 off the mouth of the Tees. From October 1917, when dominance over the Zeppelin raids had been achieved, the Squadron's role became that of a replacement training unit for pilots and observers waiting to go overseas.

Besides the BE2c aircraft the Squadron also flew the BE12, Bristol Scout, FE2b, FE2d, Bristol Fighter and Sopwith Scout during its period of active operations. Its total World War I casualties amounted to three killed.

No 36 Sqn was disbanded at Usworth on 13th June 1919 but reformed at Donibristle in July 1928 under the command of Sqn Ldr A W Mylne, being equipped with the wooden-constructed version of the Hawker Horsley torpedo bomber. The next two years were spent in training in the torpedo bombing, naval co-operation and general reconnaissance roles, a Blackburn Dart being used to practise the technique of smoke-laying as a cloak for torpedo attacks. In September 1930 the Squadron, having been re-equipped with the all-metal version of the Horsley, moved overseas to Seletar, Singapore. Here the squadron was involved in survey flights in addition to fleet exercises and even bombing sorties against rebels at Tharawaddy.

The outbreak of war in Europe had little impact on No 36 Sqn. However, the Japanese attack on Malaysia saw the squadron flying gallant missions against the Japanese Navy but still being equipped with the obsolete Vildebeest, they were almost wiped out. Following a withdrawal and regroup in

Java they fought to the last aircraft when the were eventually over run and captured.

Having reformed at Tanjore, No 36 Sqn was equipped with Wellington VIIIs in December 1942 and returned to the conflict with a vengeance. Initially flying anti-submarine patrols in the Indian Ocean, the squadron moved to the Mediterranean where it was involved in at least three U-Boat kills. To maximise the amount of time on patrol aircraft from No 36 Sqn operated in detachments around the Mediterranean. The squadron returned to England just prior to the end of the war and flew anti-submarine patrols over the Channel. No 36 Sqn was renumbered No 248 Sqn but was disbanded shortly after.

In 1953 No 36 Sqn was reformed with the Lockheed Neptune with which it flew the maritime reconnaissance role until re-equipped with the Shackleton. In 1957 the squadron was disbanded only to be reformed again in 1958 with the Handley Page Hastings at Colerne.

In January 1965 the Squadron was called upon to play a leading role in the Caribbean and provided a detachment led by Sqn Ldr C Austin whose aircraft became the first RAF aircraft ever to touch down in the Cayman Islands, an occasion which brought out the entire population of Georgetown to form a welcoming party. Returning to the Caribbean in April Squadron Leader Austin then landed a Service aircraft for the first time at Golden Rock, St Kitts and Vigit, St Lucia.

A Handley Page Hastings of No 36 Sqn

Tragedy for No 36 Sqn occurred in July 1965 when a Hastings aircraft, TG577, engaged on a routine parachute training flight crashed near Abingdon killing the crew of six and 35 passengers. No fault was attached in any way to the Captain or his crew

and as a result all Hastings aircraft were grounded for some weeks whilst undergoing modification. December 1965 saw a detachment from the Squadron to the Middle East where its primary task was to provide a shuttle service from Aden to Zambia via Nairobi in support of the RAF units which had recently moved there.

Participation in exercises and training tasks continued to occupy the Squadron. Wg Cdr J D Payling assumed command in December 1966. By the middle of 1967 however, the Squadrons nine and a half year sojourn at Colerne came to an end.

On 1st July 1967 No 36 Sqn officially became part of Lyneham and a few weeks later became the first squadron to be equipped with Hercules C1. Wg Cdr Payling, who had attended a Hercules conversion course in the USA, resumed command of the Squadron on its move to Lyneham. The Squadron settled down to what was to prove an eight-year life at Lyneham in the transport support role and was constantly engaged on a programme of crew training and categorisation, operational tasks, route flying and participation in exercises including a number organised by NATO. In 1967 detachments were made to Muharraq and Bahrain and the squadron assisted in the withdrawal of British Forces from Aden. Aircraft from the Squadron were also used to recover the El Aden Desert Rescue Team from Kufra Oasis.

1968 saw a few unusual tasks which the Squadron carried out including the carriage of freight for the British Transarctic expedition. The collection of a beautifully restored Hawker Hind aircraft presented to the RAF by the Royal Afghan Air Force to commemorate the RAF's Golden Jubilee. Plus a mission of mercy to deliver tarpaulins and weatherproof sheets to the hurricane-stricken city of Glasgow.

During 1970 the war in Jordan saw some crews operating in that country under the auspices of the International Red Cross. This necessitated the crews becoming temporary civilians and enrolling as Red Cross members.

In December the Squadron participated in the evacuation operation from Pakistan during the Indo-Pakistan war and in January 1972 in the withdrawal of personnel from Malta. Later in that year the Hercules force became part of No 46 Group. In December the Squadron participated in Operation Deep Freeze, the US Navy contribution to the US Antarctic Research programme. During the operation the Squadron crew carried the Detachment Commander over the Geographical South Pole and thus achieved the distinction of being the first RAF Hercules to fly over the Pole.

This pattern of participation in civil assistance continued. 1973 was notable for mercy missions to drop food to famine stricken areas of Nepal, Mali, Senegal and other West African countries.

On 1 March 1974 No 36 Sqn took on a further role to its already multifarious tasks, that of the "Special Force". Originally each of the five Lyneham based Hercules Sqs had one crew qualified for Pathfinder duties. These crews were called the Special Force (SF) although each remained with its parent squadron. It was however decided to amalgamate the five crews within No 36 Sqn in order to allow for centralised control and greater standardisation amongst the crews. The five crews were formed into a flight known as 'B' Flight within No 36 Sqn. The task of the Flight at that time was to provide air support for SAS, SBS and 1 Gds Indep Para Coy.

A heavy programme of transport support and participation in exercises continued. Towards the end of July, however, it was officially announced that because of the re-organisation of the Tactical Forces and consequent reduction in Hercules aircraft and crews, No 36 Sqn, together with No 48 Sqn, was to be disbanded. This took place on the 3rd November 1975, with all operational flying having ceased on 24th October.

No 47 Squadron
No 47 Squadron was formed in March 1916 and saw its first action in Salonika against the Bulgarians on the Northern frontier of Greece. In those days the squadron flew as two elements, a fighter and a reconnaissance force. Bristol Scouts, BE12s Vickers Bullets and DH2s were used as fighters and Armstrong Whitworth FK3s and FK8 were used as reconnaissance aircraft.

The end of the Great War did not, however, mean an end to the war for No 47 Sqn. In 1919 it was sent to southern Russia to help support General Denikin's White Russian Forces in their ill-fated attempt to repel the Bolshevik armies. However, the Government was criticised in the House of Commons because Great Britain was taking part in a foreign Civil War, and subsequently No 47 Sqn temporarily became "A" Squadron and became the only unit to fight a war without the inspiration of the Royal Air Force Ensign. Instead the officers and men fought under their very own flag, which is still worn today as a shoulder flash on the flying suits of aircrew. Perhaps of more interest is that No 47 Sqn was the only unit to conduct a campaign in the total absence of whisky - but not without vodka!

Between the wars No 47 Sqn was based in East Africa - notably Khartoum, flying Bristol fighters, Fairey III Fs, Vickers Vincents and Wellesleys. It was from this period of the Squadron's history that the Squadron crest and motto were derived. To gain the confidence of the natives in Khartoum, the local chieftains were gathered to see the river Nile set alight. This was achieved by pouring large quantities of petrol into the river which was then bombed by No 47 Sqn aircraft. One Chief praised the aircraft's ability by saying: "the name of the Nile shall be an omen of your power", hence the Squadron motto, "Nili nomen roboris omen". The crane on this crest is symbolic of the native bird of the Nile and the blue and white background is a representative of the meeting of the Blue and White Nile.

A No 47 Sqn Wellesley over The Sudan in 1934

During World War II No 47 Sqn operated Beauforts and Beaufighters in the Mediterranean and Mosquitos in India and Burma. The Squadron disbanded in the Far East in 1946 and reformed in Palestine, returning almost at once to the UK and Fairford where it operated Halifax transport. In 1948 it moved to Dishforth and then Topcliffe, becoming the first Squadron to operate the Hastings.

The Mosquito was operated in India and Burma

Later that year it took part in the Berlin Airlift. In 1953 No 47 Sqn moved to Abingdon and in 1955 was the eighth unit to receive a Standard. In 1956 it re-equipped with Beverleys, again being the first Squadron to do so and continued to operate these aircraft until they were retired in 1968. The Squadron then returned to Fairford to convert to the Hercules and finally moved to Lyneham in February 1971.

In December 1971, the Squadron made the two, much publicised flights into East Pakistan to evacuate the civilian personnel caught up in the war between East and West Pakistan. Wg Cdr Hannah, the Squadron Commander, was awarded the Air Force Cross for his and the Squadron's part in the evacuation.

In the past, the Squadron has been involved in numerous exercises and deployments in locations such as Germany, Canada, USA, Norway and France and disaster and famine relief in the Sudan, Belize, Nepal, Australia, Italy, Cyprus, Turkey, Bangladesh, and Ethiopia.

In 1982 the Squadron was heavily involved in Operation Corporate, the Falklands Campaign, during which the Squadron was tasked with resupply of Ascension Island. Flights of up to 24 hours were commonplace and for their efforts the Squadron was awarded the Battle Honour South Atlantic 1982. More recently the Squadron has participated in Op Granby, Op Provide Comfort and Op Haven, Op Jural, Op Vigour, Op Grapple and Op Cheshire.

No 47 Squadron is one of two Lyneham squadrons specifically tasked with Transport Support (TS) duties and is engaged in such diverse activities as troop transportation, paratrooping, and resupply duties. In addition, the Squadron has accompanied members of the Royal Family on tours around the world and competed with much success in competitions within NATO as well as supporting the RAF's Red Arrows and Falcons Teams.

Slightly more unusual assignments have been to drop "troops" for the opening sequences of the James Bond Film The Living Daylights and the film Juggernaut. The Squadron also has close links with the community and has officially adopted the Middlefield School for Mentally Handicapped Children at Chippenham.

No 48 Squadron

No 48 Squadron was first formed at Netheravon in April 1916 and had a distinguished career during the First World War. It was equipped with Bristol Fighters and crossed to France in March 1917. By the time of the Armistice the Squadron had destroyed 148 German aircraft, with a further 150 sent out of control.

Following service with the Army of Occupation in Germany, in June 1919 No 48 Sqn was sent to India and in the following year was re-numbered No 5 Sqn. On the 25th November 1935 it was reformed at Bicester only to move to Manston on 16th December 1935, where it was much involved with the work of the Air Navigation School. The Squadron took part in the Hendon Air Display of 1936. It was equipped initially with Fairey Battles and then with Saro Cloud amphibious aircraft, but these were subsequently replaced by Avro Ansons.

On 1st September 1938 No 48 Sqn was transferred to No 16 Group, Coastal Command and moved to Eastchurch. On 25th August 1939, the Squadron moved to Thorney Island and on the outbreak of war commenced its duties of anti-submarine patrolling and convoy escort over the Mid Channel area. Detachments were sent to Detling and Guernsey. It was now fully armed with Ansons. On 4th December 1939 aircraft from the Squadron escorted the King's destroyer on his visit to France and performed the same duty on his return to England on 10th December.

The Squadron's badge was presented by Air Vice-Marshal R L G Marix, DSO, on 22nd February 1940. A detachment was stationed at Bircham Newton from 20th March 1940. The Squadron's first enemy aircraft of the Second World War was shot down on 29th May 1940, by Air Gunner L Dilnutt, who subsequently received the DFM. From the middle of May 1940 action became more intense, the Squadron making many attacks on enemy shipping operating off the Dutch and Belgian

Coasts. On 1st June 1940 an Anson from the flight at Detling was instrumental in saving the lives of 12 men floating in the sea of the North Foreland. For this action the Squadron later received a letter of appreciation from the Admiralty. In July "noisy" patrols were carried out over the Channel Islands with the object of covering the sounds made by our motor-boats landing on the Islands at night.

Later in 1940, detachments of the squadron operated from Hooton Park, the Isle of Islay and Aldergrove from where they flew convoy escort and anti-submarine patrols off the north of Ireland and to the north and west of Scotland. Following a move north to Stornoway, and later Skitten, their aircraft hunted and attacked with considerable success. Their effectiveness against enemy shipping was enhanced and convoys benefited by being escorted further. From December 1942 the squadron's final phase of its maritime life began with a move to Gibraltar, where it enjoyed notable success against U-boats, sinking two and sharing in the sinking of a third.

In March 1948 No 48 Sqn underwent its final change of role when it returned to Down Ampney in England and converted to a transport squadron. The new roles were "trooping", dropping supplies, troops and leaflets over occupied Europe, and casualty evacuation. Its major operations were the Normandy invasion, the 1st Airborne Division's assault on Arnhem and the Allied crossing of the Rhine, dropping troops and towing gliders. At the end of the war in Europe the squadron was ordered to the Far East, where its arrival coincided with the Japanese surrender. The squadron was disbanded on 16th January 1946.

In February 1946 No 215 Sqn was renumbered No 48 Sqn and remained based in Singapore for the next 25 years. The Squadrons primary role was the maintaining of scheduled trooping and freighting tasks which included supporting the Christmas Island base from 1960-64. In addition the Squadron retained a capability for the assisting in the relief of the frequent disasters and famines throughout the Far East. The role of the Squadron assumed more importance and was predominant during the Communist insurgence in Malaya and the Indonesian confrontation, when air supply of isolated army and police strongpoints was vital.

In July 1963 No 48 Sqn sent a detachment to Kuching in support of the Borneo operations, dropping supplies in poor weather and mountainous terrain. On one occasion one of its aircraft was damaged by ground fire from Indonesian soldiers and in May 1964 fighter escorts were provided when the Squadron had to drop supplies near the border. After May 1964 the detachment was provided by No 48 Sqn together with another squadron on an alternating basis once a quarter. After the end of the Borneo Confrontation in August 1966 the Squadron continued for a time to operate in the more usual transport roles, route flying (principally to Hong Kong), route training (throughout the Far East) and the normal training programme. Added to these duties was one less than usual role, dropping supplies to jungle stations along the northern border of Malaya.

A No 48 Sqn Hercules overflies the Malayan jungle

In April 1967 the Squadron was disbanded, only to be re-formed in October the same year with an establishment of 12 Hercules. The tasks were, once again, principally route flying and exercising in the support role. In May 1968 the Squadron made its first round the world trip when one of its aircraft flew back to the United Kingdom and then returned to the Far East by the westabout route, a flight of some 21,000 nautical miles. In September 1971 the Squadron moved to Lyneham, but despite the change in theatre its world-wide commitments continued. Some examples of the Squadron's work were that in December 1972 one of its aircraft participated in Operation Deep Freeze in Antarctica. In March 1973 it took part Khana Cascade, the airlift of food and supplies to the remoter parts of Nepal. In the summer of 1974 it helped in the evacuation of service personnel and civilians from Cyprus. During Christmas in 1974 one of its aircraft took supplies into Darwin after the destruction of the city by a cyclone and brought a number of refugees out. In 1975 it had an aircraft on standby to take part in the evacuation of Saigon. In October 1975 it supported the Harrier detachment to Belize.

In January 1976 No 48 Sqn was once again disbanded.

The farewell march past for No 48 Sqn at Changi in 1971 before returning to the UK

No 57 (Reserve) Squadron

No 57 Squadron, RFC was formed at Copmanthorpe, Yorkshire, on 8th June 1916 where it was equipped with FE2ds. At the end of the year the Squadron moved to France where it flew reconnaissance and offensive patrols as part of the 9th Wing. It was re-equipped with DH4s in May 1917 and changed its role to long distance high altitude bombing and photo-reconnaissance.

During the period 1916 to 1918 a total of 300 tons of bombs were dropped, 196 successful reconnaissance mission were flown, during which 22,000

photographs were taken, and a total of 166 enemy aircraft were destroyed. While these totals were remarkable they were achieved at a great cost - at one point the entire flying personnel were casualties of enemy action. Despite this the Squadron remained in action with replacement crews. It was from this particular incident that the Squadron badge was conceived - a Phoenix rising from the flames and the motto Corpus Non Animum Muto or "the body changes but not the spirit".

At the end of the War the Squadron was employed in communications, flying for the Armistice Commission, before being disbanded in December 1919.

The Squadron re-formed at Netheravon in October 1931 with Hawker Harts and moved to Upper Heyford the following September. No 57 Sqn took a leading part in the Hendon Air Displays in 1934 and 1935 and led the light bomber formation in the flypast at Duxford in honour of King George V's Silver Jubilee. In 1936 the Harts were exchanged for Hinds which in turn were exchanged for the Bristol Blenheim in 1938.

The Squadron flew to France as part of the Air Component of the British Expeditionary Force shortly after the beginning of the WWII. During May 1940 it suffered heavy casualties to the extent that during 10 days of operations it had been all but eliminated as an effective unit. The remnants were evacuated to England where new aircraft and crews enabled the Squadron to be back in action on 11th June. Following a short spell with No 2 Group at Wyton the Squadron carried out anti-shipping sweeps over the North Sea with Coastal Command from bases in Scotland.

In November 1940 No 57 Sqn returned to Wyton and converted to Wellingtons which it operated for the next two years during the Bomber Command offensive against Germany from Feltwell and Methwold. In September of 1942 the Squadron moved to Scampton where it converted to the Lancaster. Within six weeks the Squadron was fully operational and joined the Lancaster Main Bomber Force in many vital raids throughout Germany and Italy. The Squadron flew its last wartime mission on 25th April 1945.

In August the Squadron became the first unit to operate the Lincoln which it flew on service trials before being disbanded on 25th November 1945. The following day the Lincoln Flight of No 103 Sqn was redesignated No 57 Sqn.

Following a number of years at Waddington No 57 Sqn was detached to Tengah for strikes against the Malayan Terrorists. In May 1951 the Lincolns were temporarily replaced with the Boeing Washington (RAF operated B-29s) before the arrival of the first British Jet bomber - the English Electric Canberra. These it operated until disbanded in December 1957.

On 1st January 1959 No 57 Squadron was reformed with the Victor as part of Britain's V Bomber Force. Detachments were flown to Singapore during the Indonesian Confrontation. The Squadron proved to be very successful in winning trophies at the bombing and navigation competitions. On 20th July 1962 HRH Princess Marina presented the Squadron with its Standard.

In January 1966 the Squadron moved to Marham where it was re-equipped with the Victor K.1 tanker. The Squadron assisted in expanding the development of air to air refuelling by pioneering night refuelling as well as lengthy deployments. In 1969 the Squadron was the first to be awarded the Sir Alan Cobham Trophy for the most efficient tanker unit.

In 1957 the Squadrons capabilities were improved with the introduction the the Victor K.2 and these continued to be flown in support of the Javelins and Lightnings, later the Phantoms and Tornados, which provided the UK air defence against the regularly probing Soviet aircraft.

No 57 Sqn had many close encounters with the Hercules when operating the Victor K.2

In 1982 No 57 Sqn proved the vital role of air to air refuelling during a modern conflict following the invasion of the Falkland Islands by Argentina. Due to the distances involved, within a short time of the Task Force steaming south from Ascension every aircraft flying south required air to air refuelling to be able complete its mission. These ranged from other Victors in the MRR role, Harriers and Sea Harriers to strengthen the carriers compliment, Nimrods on MRR and anti-shipping roles, Vulcans on the "Black Buck" raids as well as the Hercules. Even when the conflict finished a No 57 Sqn detachment remained at Ascension to support the Air Bridge until June 1985. On 30th June 1986 No 57 Sqn was disbanded at RAF Marham.

On 12th October 1992 the Squadron was reformed at RAF Lyneham from the re-numbered No 242 OCU as No 57 (Reserve) Sqn and currently provides the role of the Hercules Conversion Unit.

No 70 Squadron

No 70 Squadron RFC was formed at Farnborough on 22nd April 1916 with Sopwith Strutters before moving to France, where it was engaged on the Western Front in bombing, reconnaissance, air fighting and escort duties. During this period one of the Squadron Commanding Officers was Major A W Tedder, later to be Marshal of the Royal Air Force Lord Tedder. In July 1917 the Squadron re-equipped with Sopwith Camels, the first Squadron to do so, and these remained until it was disbanded in January 1920.

In February 1921, No 58 Sqn based at Heliopolis in Egypt with Handley Page O/400s and Vickers Vimys, was renumbered No 70 Sqn. The following year it moved to Iraq and remained there until 1938. In August 1929 the Squadron moved to Halwan in Egypt, and was equipped with Valentines, in the following year these were replaced with Wellington Bombers.

During the war the Squadron's bases depended on the fortunes of the allied desert armies and, in December 1943, No 70 Sqn moved to Italy with the invading army where it remained until the end of the war. Towards the end of the conflict the Squadron converted to Liberators. In October 1945 the Squadron moved back to the Middle East and in March the following year disbanded at Shallufa in

Egypt. Two weeks later it reappeared when No 178 Sqn, equipped with Lancasters, became No 70 Sqn. It was disbanded again a year later but was revived once more after 13 months when No 125 Sqn, based at Kabrit in Egypt with Dakotas, was renumbered No 70 Sqn - a Phoenix rising from the ashes.

In 1950 the Squadron received Vickers Valettas and was busily engaged in the Suez Canal Zone. In 1955 the Squadron received its Standard at Fayid in Egypt from Air Vice Marshal R Hazelton-Nicholl, a former Squadron Commanding Officer. During that year the move was made to Cyprus and the first Hastings transport joined the Squadron at Nicosia. During the Suez crisis in 1956 the Squadron dropped paratroops as part of the assault on El Gamil airfield. In 1967 the Hastings were replaced by Argosys, becoming in 1970 a two-type Squadron with the introduction of the Hercules. Both aircraft types flew in the medium range transport role and were heavily involved in the support of our force in Oman.

An Argosy C.1 of No 70 Sqn when it formed part of the RAF Near East

The Squadron played major roles in the evacuations from West Pakistan in 1971, the UK Cairo airlift and finally in 1974, the Cyprus airlift of evacuees from Kingsfield airstrip during the Greek-Turkish conflict and the British Troop reinforcement of the Sovereign Base Areas. Following our rundown of forces in the Near and Middle East, the Squadron moved from Akrotiri in January 1975 to its present location at Lyneham, having completed 58 years in overseas theatres.

No 70 Sqn was once again in action overseas in 1980. The Hercules carried out many low level sorties in Operation Agila as part of the controlling force in Rhodesia during the transition to

A No 70 Sqn Hercules operating out of Firq airstrip in Oman during February 1971

independence. Within 12 months a Squadron detachment was sent abroad again to Nepal as part of the famine relief operation, Khana Cascade II.

1982 saw the Squadron enter the war in the South Atlantic. Responsible for long sorties from Ascension Island to the Falkland Islands and the Naval Task Force, the Squadron flew many hours and learned a new skill of air-to-air refuelling. No 70 Sqn also gained the World Record sortie duration for a C-130 of 28 hours and 3 minutes. For these active service operations, No 70 Sqn received the South Atlantic Campaign battle honour. Subsequently, in 1984, a new standard was presented to No 70 Sqn by Her Royal Highness The Princess Anne.

November 1984 signalled the start of a new task for the Squadron: Operation Bushell. Famine relief missions in Ethiopia continued throughout 1985 and as a result many thousands of lives were saved. As 1986 heralded the significant milestone of Seventy Years of Seventy Squadron, its members past and present were able to look back on its history with justifiable pride. 1989 saw the arrival of a new OC, Wg Cdr C J Morris. August 1990 signalled a new operation for the Squadron - Granby, with detachments to Akrotiri and Arabic states. Whilst February 1991 saw Operation Desert Storm to its conclusion, over the horizon dawned the relief operation for the Kurds - Provide Comfort. For their performances during Operation Provide Comfort Wg Cdr Morris was awarded the OBE and the MBE and Flt Lt Young was mentioned in dispatches. The Sqn participated in Op Haven, Jural, Vigour and Grapple.

The Squadron celebrated its 75th anniversary later in the year. In October 1991 the now Gp Capt Morris was succeeded by Wg Cdr C B Le Bas.

No 70 Sqn badge contains a winged lion which is representative of the Assyrian Lion of Iraq where the Squadron was based for so many years, and perpetuates the memory of the Napier Lion engine that powered the Squadrons in the 1920s. The motto "USQUAM" translates as ANYWHERE.

No 242 OCU

No 242 OCU was formed at RAF Dishforth in 1951 by the amalgamation of No 240 OCU from North Luffenham operating Dakotas and No 241 OCU at Dishforth operating Hastings. While based at Dishforth, the OCU also trained Valetta and Beverley aircrews. In 1962 the OCU moved to RAF Thorney Island taking its Hastings and Beverley aircraft, which were joined the following year by the Argosy from RAF Benson. Training on the Hastings ceased after 117 Course and on the Beverley after 41 Course in early 1967 prior to the commencement of Hercules training. Early in 1969, Argosy training at the OCU ended with No 32 Course and in 1970 the Andover training unit moved in from RAF Abingdon to become part of the OCU. Andover training ceased abruptly in 1975 during No 36 Course and No 242 OCU was rendered homeless by the impending closure of Thorney Island.

The Vickers Valetta aircrew were trained by No 242 OCU

The Ground Training Squadron and Conversion Squadron of No 242 OCU moved to RAF Lyneham and together with Training Squadron, Simulator Squadron and Support Training Squadron which were already resident at Lyneham, thus 242 OCU was complete at one location by November 1975.

Then, No 242 OCU was responsible for the conversion to type of all RAF Hercules aircrew, the periodic refresher training and categorisation of Hercules squadron aircrews, all RAF Hercules simulator training and transport training. The Air-to-Air Refuelling (AAR) Cell was formed on No 242 OCU during 1982 to train RAF Hercules crews in AAR techniques. Additionally, training is given to crew members from many other air forces which operate a variety of Lockheed C-130 models. The OCU participated in Operation Corporate and Operation Granby.

As part of the re-organisation of the RAF, No 242 OCU was renumbered No 57(R) Sqn on 1st July 1992.

United Kingdom Mobile Air Movements Squadron

Although it does not have any aircraft the United Kingdom Mobile Air Movements Squadron, better known as UKMAMS, is synonymous with the tactical air transport fleet of the Royal Air Force and is also based at Lyneham. The present passenger terminal was opened in 1961 but the history of air movements at this Wiltshire base goes back to 1943 with the arrival of the York aircraft. Since then, Lyneham has remained the biggest RAF transport station, although it was not until early in 1974 that UKMAMS moved from Abingdon to amalgamate with Lyneham's Air Movements Squadron.

Today UKMAMS has two main tasks. Firstly, it is responsible for all passengers and freight handling at Lyneham - this includes the loading and unloading of the huge volume of air cargo which passes through the station every month to or from countries throughout the world, either on the Hercules aircraft based here, or those aircraft of foreign or Commonwealth air forces that regularly call here. The four base shifts handle about 1,500 tons of cargo and approximately 5,000 passengers each month, working an around-the-clock shift system to cover every minute of the day. The Air Cargo Section is also responsible for the control of aircraft pallets and nets for the RAF throughout the world and they closely monitor their whereabouts and serviceability.

Foreign visitors have become so frequent at Lyneham that there now exists a small but full-time Foreign Aircraft Section, dedicated totally to the handling and turn round of visitors from places as far and wide as South America and New Zealand, although the majority come from numerous Middle Eastern Countries.

The second UKMAMS task is to provide mobile teams capable of deploying anywhere in the world, often at short notice, to locations where there is no military presence or organisation capable of dealing with air movements activities. The teams, each consisting of six personnel, have a unique opportunity of seeing many parts of the world which are normally beyond the reach of most Service personnel. Teams are specially trained for this mobile role at Lyneham and have to be capable of operating in field conditions for extended periods. Detachments vary in length from 1 or 2 days to 3 months and, on average, teams spend three quarters of the year away from base, each man recording over 300 flying hours annually.

The Mobile teams handle approximately 5000 tons of cargo and 9000 passengers each month. To support the teams, UKMAMS is equipped with specialist air portable vehicles, tentage and radios. The squadron also has its own operations room and training cell, as well as a team of technicians and engineers who are an integral part of this organisation.

A UKMAMS team at a desert strip in Kuwait during the Gulf War

UKMAMS was first given squadron status on 1st May 1966 and in 1973 it received its official badge bearing its proud motto "Swift to Move". In 1985 the Squadron badge was dedicated in the floor of the RAF Church, St Clements Danes, London.

No 4626 (County of Wiltshire) Aeromedical Squadron, R Auxiliary AF

No 4626 (County of Wiltshire) Aeromedical Squadron was formed at RAF Wroughton in September 1983. As the numbers steadily increased the Squadron was forced to move to RAF Hullavington in April 1986, and more recently in March 1993, the Squadron moved to it's present base at RAF Lyneham.

Over the past 10 years members have flown some three million miles undertaking peacetime aeromedical evacuation duties from almost all parts of the world including Denmark, Norway, Cyprus, Turkey, Hong Kong, Nairobi, Germany, Ascension Island, the Falkland Islands, USA, Canada, Northern Ireland and the Shetland Isles.

After the mounting tension and speculation, No 4626 Aeromed Sqn was mobilised in January 1991 for active service during the build up for the Gulf War. The Squadron was deployed to Saudi Arabia within 10 days and within 48 hours of arriving in theatre its personnel were at their forward operating bases and had witnessed the first Scud missile attacks.

This meant that a unit of the RAuxAF was in a combat zone under enemy fire for the first time since the Second World War. No 4626 set up or took over facilities at Riyadh, Al Jubayl, Dharhan and Muharraq in Bahrain. All aeromedical flights carried teams drawn from the Squadron.

On returning from the Gulf in March 1991, the Squadron was awarded the Robins Trophy for operational efficiency.

No 47 Air Despatch Squadron (Royal Logistics Corps)

As with UKMAMS, No 47 Air Despatch Squadron has no aircraft but is synonymous with current RAF Hercules operations. It is also unique in that although part of the Hercules operation it is not an RAF unit but part of the newly formed Royal Logistics Corps (RLC) of the Army. Prior to that it was part of the Royal Corps of Transport (RCT).

The history of air transport can be traced back to the First World War, to air supply operations in Mesopotamia, starting during the siege of Kut-el-Amara in 1916 and later on the Western Front, where, within the limits imposed by the type of aircraft and equipment, it could be considered a successful innovation.

Nevertheless, in common with many other technological advances, British development of the concept stopped in 1918. It was not until the Second

World War and the development of transport aircraft that this method of resupplying troops who could not be supplied by surface means became significant. In 1942 there was no equipment designed for dropping supplies: no parachutes, no containers and no roller conveyors; there were no units or men trained in the required specialist techniques. There were, however, aircraft - the ubiquitous Dakotas - and these were available in large numbers. In war, need is a great spur, thus organisation, equipments and techniques of air supply were developed with unprecedented speed.

Members of No 47 AD in front of an RAF Dakota

By 1943, in Burma, it had been proved that an army in the field need not be dependent upon its ground lines of communications, nor need it hold large stocks of supplies. At the time when supply by air was in greatest demand by the XIVth Army in Burma over 2,500 tons were transported by air daily. Of the total tonnages lifted approximately 60 per cent was dropped by parachute. The responsibility for packing, installing and despatching loads from aircraft was assumed by the Royal Army Service Corps (predecessors of the Royal Corps of Transport) and Royal Indian Army Service Corps Despatch Units.

This began a close association between the Army and the Royal Air Force which continues to this day. Since 1942 Air Despatch units have lived and worked closely with the Royal Air Force in all parts of the world in support of ground forces, airborne forces, special forces and other services and on various disaster relief operations. The development of an Air Despatch organisation in Britain was very much slower than in the Far East. The problems to

be faced in north-west Europe differed from those in the Far East in several respects. With the exception of airborne operations, supply and maintenance by air were planned as emergency measures rather than as a normal system. For this reason the Air Despatch Group - formed largely to resupply the First Airborne Division and resistance groups within Europe - was only used spasmodically and was rarely stretched to its full capacity. In addition, the enemy opposition from air and ground was very much heavier in north-west Europe and this had considerable influence on the technique for dropping, which was designed to eject the whole load in one pass over the dropping zone.

The early operations of the Air Despatch Group, including D-Day, Falaise Gap and the Relief of Paris, were a prelude to the Arnhem operation. Nine hundred personnel of all ranks of the Group flew on 600 sorties during attempts to resupply the Airborne Division. 264 were shot down, of whom 116 were eventually missing or killed. Over 60 aircraft were destroyed by the enemy. As a result of their part in the operation the Air Despatch units were awarded the right to wear a formation sign of their own. It is now a familiar yellow Dakota on a blue background which is worn with pride by Air despatchers wherever they are serving. A reminder of these operations was provided in 1974 when a window was installed in All Saints Church, Down Ampney in Gloucestershire with the following inscription. "In memory of the men and women of the Royal Air Force, the First and Sixth Airborne Divisions and the Air Despatch Group, RASC, who took part in operations from Down Ampney 1944-45". It was dedicated on 9th June 1974 by the Bishop of Gloucester.

In post-war years air supply has been called upon to meet many military and civil contingencies. The Air Despatch Group played an auspicious part in the successful campaign against communist terrorists in the Malayan emergency which started in 1948, providing the vital lifeline without which patrols could not have penetrated to the jungle hideouts of the insurgents. As the campaign progressed Army and Police Forts were established in deep jungle which involved air dropping all the building and defence materials. Units were not only dependent on the air supply for their ammunition and the rations but also for those things that could make life in the jungle more tolerable. Techniques were developed to give the units what they needed from eggs to live chickens and goats, barbed wire to Tiger beer and medical supplies to Ghurka rum. There were even instances when champagne, a birthday cake and bottled oysters were included in supply drops!

A particularly important part was played in the campaign by the Valetta aircraft and an especially close association developed between 55 Air Despatch Company, RASC, and No 52 Squadron RAF who received a ceremonial kris from the Prime Minister of Malaya in recognition of their services. It is noteworthy that 35 members of 55 Company lost their lives as a direct result of operations: the highest number of casualties suffered by any unit throughout the emergency.

Since the war, too, Air Despatchers have been engaged in supporting operations in East Africa, Cyprus and Borneo - as well as in Berlin Airlift. In 1973, a famine relief operation was mounted in Nepal. Some of the 2,000 tons of desperately needed grain was delivered to the starving population in the remote and inaccessible areas of the Himalayan foothills. It was a race against time before the monsoon would stop operations.

On 30 June 1976, as a result of the 1975 Defence Review, the last Air Despatch Regimental Headquarters was disbanded. The ability to supply a force by airdrop continues, albeit on a reduced scale. Today 47 Air Despatch Squadron Royal Logistics Corps, based with the Royal Air Force Hercules fleet maintains the well founded and close operation between the Army and the Royal Air Force and maintains the expertise to prepare and despatch a wide variety of loads ranging from a harness pack - suitable for a small patrol - to the vehicle mounted Medium Stressed Platform (MSP). The Squadron works not only with the Royal Air Force but also with the members of the Royal Navy, Royal Marines and members of various civilian expeditions and similar organisations.

No 47 Air Despatch provided a valuable contribution to Operation Corporate, Operation Granby, Operation Provide Comfort, Operation Haven and Operation Vigour.

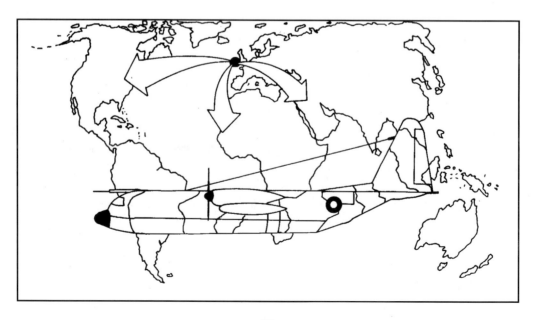

Lockheed has been delivering the C130K model in a natural metal finish to MCE from 1966 onwards for painting.

The first paint scheme was a two tone gloss brown, with a black underside and a white 'cap' above the flight deck. This line up was at Lyneham on 26 July 1972.

The next paint scheme was similar to the first but in matt finish without the white 'cap'.

From 1979 the paint scheme was dark green, medium grey and light grey underbelly.

By 1988 the camouflage had been changed to green and grey, including the underbelly. Both schemes can be seen in this line-up at Lyneham in 1988.

Some aircraft had black underseal for strip operation from 1986 but in 1987 a trial was carried out on XV196 in the matt pink alkali-removable finish (ARTF). This scheme was utilised during the Gulf conflict.

XV 215 was painted in white ARTF for trial purposes in 1993.

XV 211 with was painted in medium sea grey for the same trial.

A C1K with a pod on each wing (foreground) and the W2 (background).

A C3P with a stand under its number one engine (foreground) and a C1P beside it.

Airwork civilian staff are seen here during a modification programme.

Electrical technician from BLSS about to fit a new number one fuel quantity gauge. Note the test equipment.

47AD squadron RLC personnel are preparing the one ton loads. From L to R can be seen the different stages of preparation.

XV217 on an unprepared strip during an exercise.

XV217 on SAR duties over the sea.

ALSS team during a propeller change with the use of a crane. Note the safety hard hats worn by the team.

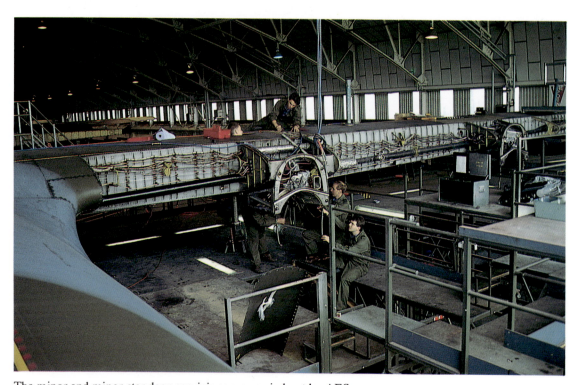

The minor and minor star deep servicings are carried out by AES.

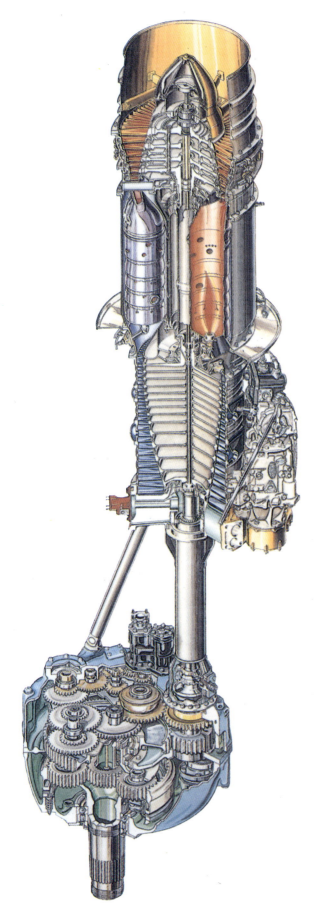

ALLISON TURBO - PROP ENGINE 501 - D22A T56 - A - 15

This is a complete engine, propeller and the nacelle on a stand, commonly known as a Quick Engine Change (QEC) kit.

Front instrument panel. Front left - (Captain), Centre - (Engine instruments). Right - (Co-pilots). The four throttles (left) and the four condition levers on the centre console can be seen.

The same instrument panel and also the engineer's overhead panel illuminated for night flying, but in the Link-Miles simulator.

The crew monitoring the engine start. Note the Captain's left hand on the start button and the right hand on the condition lever.

The Flight Engineer operates 90% of the Engineer's Overhead panel.

The Navigator's instrument panel.

A 'fuel bowser' is being driven out of XV221 at Bahrain during the Gulf conflict.

Rear view showing the cargo door locked up and the ramp lowered and resting on the support. The interior shows the aircraft withuot any fanciful trimmings.

The PUMA helicopter (partly dismantled) is being loaded using extra support between the ramp and the concrete floor.

When dense freight like this ammunition are loaded onto the aircraft, only a third of its cubic capacity (volume) is used up.

A typical para sortie exiting from the side doors.

This picture of the Fifth airborne brigade shows the speed with which 64 paratroopers are despatched.

The MSP loads are prepared in the hangar at South Cerney before onward transportation by road to Lyneham.

Two MSP loads are despatched by the Automatic Extraction (AE) method. This allows the co-pilot to select the switches which then allows the extractor parachutes to pull the first load out of the aircraft safely before the second one.

This "Khe Sanh" approach allows the Hercules to fly at medium altitude to an airfield and descend at a steep angle for a tactical landing to avoid ground fire. It is now used to ferry humanitarian supplies of food and medical aid to Sarajevo in Bosnia.

This planform shows the routing of the air to air refuelling pipe.

Seen here are five Hercules in a formation. A C1P leads two C3P's a C1K (with its hose trailed) and finally another C3P on the 75 Anniversary of the RAF.

Part of a formation waiting at the holding point prior to lining up on the runway.

The Flight Engineer's direct view of a large formation of Hercules.

The crew of the above formation.

Two C1P's and a C3P are seen as a formation near Swindon.

The Halcones aerobatics team of the Chilean Air Force formates with a C3P over Wiltshire.

A C1K refuels a C1P over the sea.

Victor to Hercules air-to-air refuelling is difficult, because the former's minimum airspeed is the Hercules 'maximum' airspeed.

The Hercules Tanker's vertical and horizontal yellow line markings under the fuselage are reference guides for the receiver aircraft. This enables the Captain to align the probe with the basket before final coupling.

The 'basket' is only three ft. away. The relative speed would be about 5 knots, however both aircraft would be flying about 240 knots.

The W2 has a few nicknames. One of them is 'Snoopy', always snooping for clouds.

An assortment of clouds at Mount Pleasant Airfield, Falkland Islands.

Many landing zones (LZ) were constructed by the Army engineers in Kuwait and in some parts of the Arabian Peninsular near Iraq. Seen here is a C1P rolling down the unprepared strip.

The same aircraft taking off.

On sunny days, during the Gulf conflict, the 'shadow' of the Hercules aircraft was a constant companion!

Immediately after the 'cease fire', the RAF Hercules was the first fixed wing aircraft to land at the 'damaged' Kuwait International Airport.

During conflicts and wars it is customary to paint 'unofficial' works of art on the aircraft. During the Gulf conflict this was no exception.

"Operation Bushel" in Ethiopia alleviated the sufferings of the famine victims. Note that some of the loads are landing upside down.

"Provide Comfort" operations followed after the Gulf conflict. Food, medical and other supplies were taken to the Kurdish people in Northern Iraq.

C3P XV199 over the pan at RAF Chivenor, North Devon.

C1P XV206 on a low level sortie near Lyneham. This was the first Hercules to be locked on by hostile radar in August 1992 in Bosnia.

XV292 painted in the 25th Anniversary scheme in 1992 This aircraft attracted many people at the airshows throughout 1992. Badges - Left to Right; 242 OCU, 70, 48, 47, 36, 30 AND 24 Sqns. The extreme right large badge is the RAF Lyneham Station Badge.

The four out of five aircrew who brought the first C130K Hercules XV177 to the UK pose in front of the Air Terminal building to mark the achievement of 1,000,000 hours by the Hercules fleet.

XV 292 over Lyneham.

XV 292 with engines running shows off its colour scheme on a frosty autumn morning in 1992.

Crew of 47 sqn. seen in front of the Air Terminal at Sarajevo, Bosnia. The ' Khe Sanh' approach onto this airfield made it possible to deliver the urgent medical and food supplies.

Crew from all the flying Sqns. flew into Zaghreb in Croatia. The freight was then transferred to another Hercules to be flown by crews of 47 Sqn. into Sarajevo.

FUEL TANK (schematic)

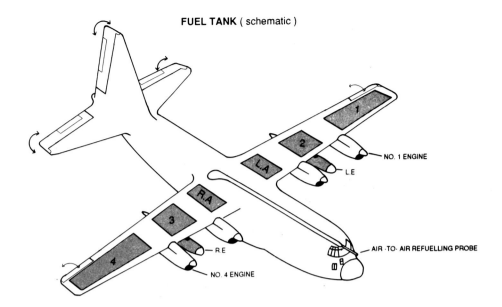

FUEL TANKS
1   = Wing Tank
2   = Wing Tank
L.A = Left Auxiliary
L.E = Left External
R.A = Right Auxiliary
R.E = Right External
3   = Wing Tank
4   = Wing Tank

NO. 1 ENGINE

L.E

AIR·TO·AIR REFUELLING PROBE

R.E

NO. 4 ENGINE

RUDDER CONTROL SYSTEM

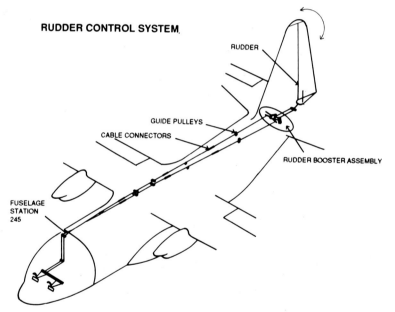

RUDDER

GUIDE PULLEYS

CABLE CONNECTORS

RUDDER BOOSTER ASSEMBLY

FUSELAGE
STATION
245

LARGE LOADS? NO PROBLEM!

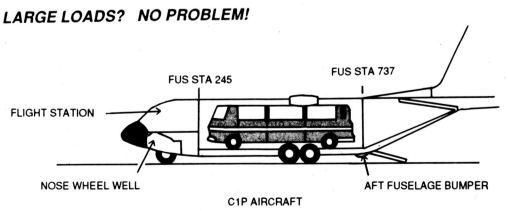

FUS STA 245

FUS STA 737

FLIGHT STATION

NOSE WHEEL WELL

AFT FUSELAGE BUMPER

C1P AIRCRAFT

163

AXIAL-FLOW COMPRESSOR PURE JET/TYPICAL TURBOPROP

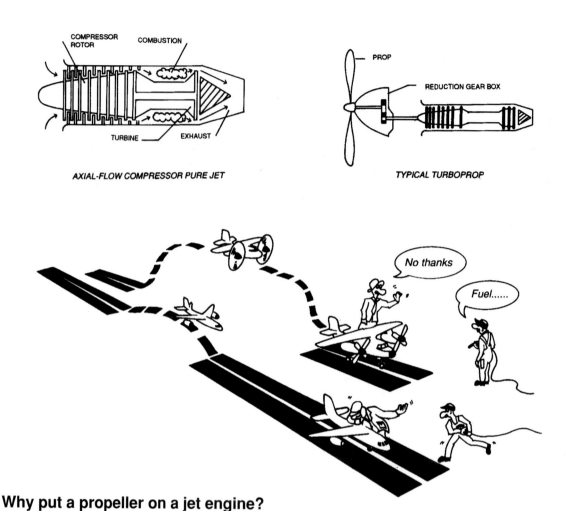

AXIAL-FLOW COMPRESSOR PURE JET

TYPICAL TURBOPROP

Why put a propeller on a jet engine?

At all subsonic speed the turboprop will produce more thrust than a pure jet engine of the same size, giving the following advantages:

1. The aircraft requires only a short runway for take off and landing.
2. The ability of the propeller to provide reverse thrust for braking efficiency.
3. The propulsive efficiency is greater at take off hence it gives a high initial take off thrust.
4. Econonmic at subsonic cruising speed.
5. Optimum range to payload relationship.

The pure jet engine of the same size as the turboprop with its large diameter propeller needs its turbine to accelerate the hot gas at a greater velocity. This causes a high 'energy loss' in the high velocity stream. However in the Hercules the propeller blades absorb the turbine energy, hence only a small amount of 'energy loss'.

AIR BRIDGE

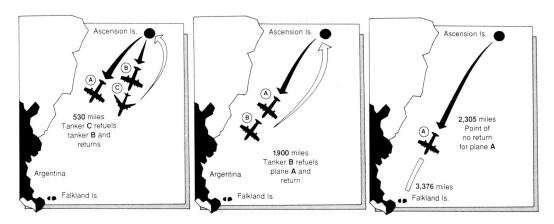

In 1984 each flight for the freighter from Ascension Island to the Falkland Islands required the services of two tankers.

A = Hercules freighter (C1P)
B = Hercules tanker (C1K)
C = Victor Jet tanker (K2)

C refuelled **B** about 530 miles south - east and returned to *Ascension*. **A** and **B** the flew as a formation and about 1950 miles **B** refuelled **A** and returned to Ascension. **A** then proceeded to *RAF Stanley* in the *Falkland Islands*.

EMERGENCY EXITS (SOS)

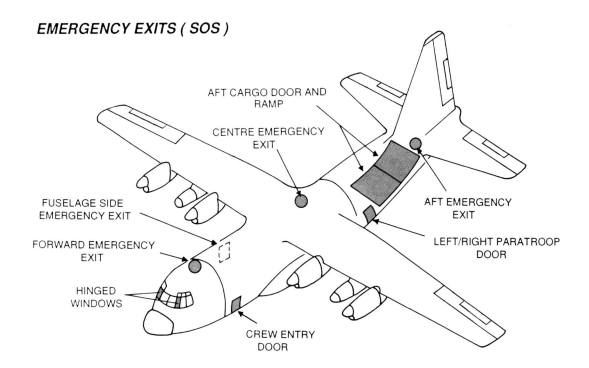

OVERHEAD PANEL

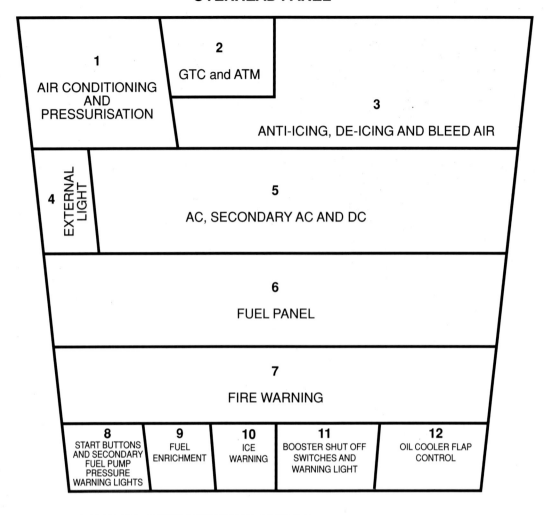

1 AIR CONDITIONING AND PRESSURISATION	**2** GTC and ATM				
	3 ANTI-ICING, DE-ICING AND BLEED AIR				
4 EXTERNAL LIGHT	**5** AC, SECONDARY AC AND DC				
6 FUEL PANEL					
7 FIRE WARNING					
8 START BUTTONS AND SECONDARY FUEL PUMP PRESSURE WARNING LIGHTS	**9** FUEL ENRICHMENT	**10** ICE WARNING	**11** BOOSTER SHUT OFF SWITCHES AND WARNING LIGHT	**12** OIL COOLER FLAP CONTROL	

ENGINE STARTING SYSTEM COMPONENT LOCATIONS

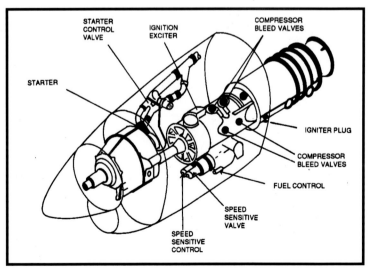

Engineer's overhead panel contain's over 200 gauges, warning lights, switches and controls. *(Refer to photograph in the colour section)*

Refer page 25 - Engine start sequence

FRONT INSTRUMENT PANEL

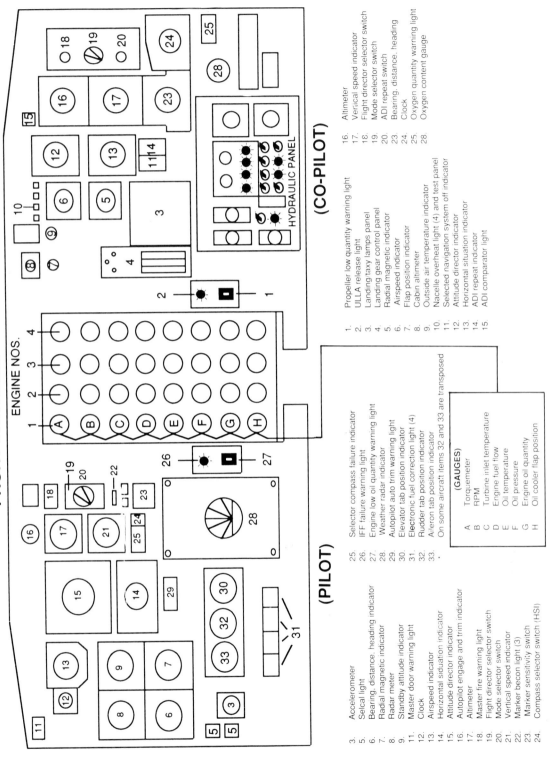

ENGINE NOS.

(PILOT)

(CO-PILOT)

HYDRAULIC PANEL

1. Propeller low quantity warning light
2. ULLA release light
3. Landing/taxy lamps panel
4. Landing gear control panel
5. Radial magnetic indicator
6. Airspeed indicator
7. Flap position indicator
8. Cabin altimeter
9. Outside air temperature indicator
10. Nacelle overheat light (4) and test panel
11. Selected navigation system off indicator
12. Attitude director indicator
13. Horizontal situation indicator
14. ADI repeat indicator
15. ADI comparator light
16. Altimeter
17. Vertical speed indicator
18. Flight director selector switch
19. Mode selector switch
20. ADI repeat switch
23. Bearing, distance, heading
24. Clock
25. Oxygen quantity warning light
28. Oxygen content gauge

3. Accelerometer
5. Selcal light
6. Bearing, distance, heading indicator
7. Radial magnetic indicator
8. Radar meter
9. Standby attitude indicator
11. Master door warning light
12. Clock
13. Airspeed indicator
14. Horizontal situation indicator
15. Attitude director indicator
16. Autopilot engage and trim indicator
17. Altimeter
18. Master fire warning light
19. Flight director selector switch
20. Mode selector switch
21. Vertical speed indicator
22. Marker beacon light (3)
23. Marker sensitivity switch
24. Compass selector switch (HSI)

25. Selector compass failure indicator
26. IFF failure warning light
27. Engine low oil quantity warning light
28. Weather radar indicator
29. Autopilot auto trim warning light
30. Elevator tab position indicator
31. Electronic fuel correction light (4)
32. Rudder tab position indicator
33. Aileron tab position indicator
* On some aircraft items 32 and 33 are transposed

(GAUGES)

A. Torquemeter
B. RPM
C. Turbine inlet temperature
D. Engine fuel flow
E. Oil temperature
F. Oil pressure
G. Engine oil quantity
H. Oil cooler flap position

CIK (Tanker) Navigator's panel

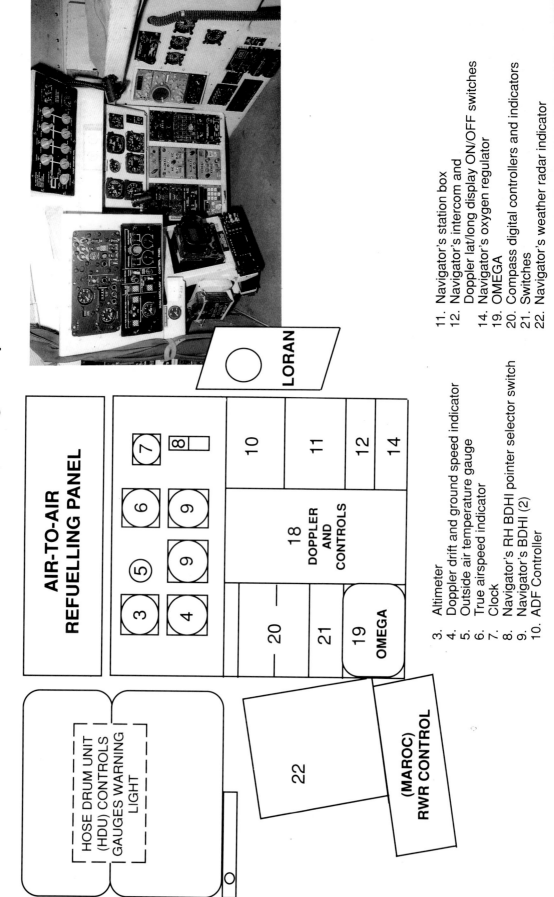

AIR-TO-AIR REFUELLING PANEL

3, 5, 6, 7, 4, 9, 9, 8

20, 21, 19 OMEGA

18 DOPPLER AND CONTROLS

10, 11, 12, 14

LORAN

HOSE DRUM UNIT (HDU) CONTROLS GAUGES WARNING LIGHT

22

(MAROC) RWR CONTROL

3. Altimeter
4. Doppler drift and ground speed indicator
5. Outside air temperature gauge
6. True airspeed indicator
7. Clock
8. Navigator's RH BDHI pointer selector switch
9. Navigator's BDHI (2)
10. ADF Controller

11. Navigator's station box
12. Navigator's intercom and Doppler lat/long display ON/OFF switches
14. Navigator's oxygen regulator
19. OMEGA
20. Compass digital controllers and indicators
21. Switches
22. Navigator's weather radar indicator

ACKNOWLEDGEMENTS

The author would like to thank the following people for their invaluable help namely: Sqn Ldr Singleton (AHB), Flt Lt Ted Querzani (CRO), Wg Cdr M Stringer, Wg Cdr A Main, Flt Lt Davie (Educ.), Flt Lt C Kemp (RAF Retd.), Cpl J. Osborough, Sgt, Steve Ware, Simon French, Lorretta Flack, Typing pool staff, JATE, 47 Sqn., 30 Sqn., Richard Lian

A book of this nature will be dull reading without the following contributions in bringing to life some of the pertinent events in Chapters five and six.

Sqn Ldr Piper (HGTS)	-	Khana Cascade
Flt Lt C Kemp (RAF Retd.)	-	Nicaragua, foiled hijack!
Wg Cdr C Le Bas	-	Operation Titan
Sqn Ldr H Burgoyne	-	First operational AAR over the South Atlantic.
Flt Lt T Sharp	-	Free Kuwait.
M Eng A Kitson	-	WMk2
Via Maj MW Titus (CAF)	-	Preparation of MSP Load
MALM B Birkin-Hewitt	-	Tea for who! MSP drop sortie.
WO2 B Lawson (47 AD)	-	Preparation of 16 x 1 Ton loads
Cpl D Marsh (47 AD)	-	Manual 16x1 Ton drop sortie
MALM D Whiting and MALM R Caddick	-	Para drop sortie
MALM MJ Clabby	-	Stores drop sortie, South Georgia.
Sqn Ldr Mackintosh, Sqn Ldr Evans	-	Crew duties : Captain, Co-pilot and Navigator.
M Eng R Millward	-	Crew duties : Flight Engineer
M Eng P Knotter	-	Crew duties: SKE
Sgt S Miles	-	Crew duties : ALM
F Sgt E Botham	-	Crew duties : AGE

PHOTOGRAPHS SUPPLIED BY: PAGE NUMBER

© CROWN COPYRIGHT MOD/1993. Reproduced with the permission of the Controller HMSO	9,10,12,13,47,54,55,59,60,61,77BL, 79R 82R,8BL,84TL,85,97,136,153T,159T
Marshall Aerospace	12T,27B,37,38,39,4DT
Lockheed	11R
Link-Miles (Simulator)	140
Allison Gas Turbines	139
Jeremy Flack/Aviation Photographs International	8,14,15,22,23TL,32T,32BR,40B,46,6566L,67,69L,71, 74,75,76TR,77TL,77R,89TR,93,94R,95,96, 105,106,109,114,125,132,133B,134B,144B,145,146B, 147B,148, 149,150T,151B,157B,
Cpl JA Osborough	17R,18L,19,20R,24,78BL,89TL,90BL, 94L,139L,144T,156,162.

Mr A Balch	131,133T,134T,150B,152T,159B.	Sgt R Hick	153B
Flt Lt D Fry	90TL,90TR,92,154,155T	Cpl Macready 395 AD Tp Rct	84BR
Cpl G Iverson	108BL,112,158	Mr P Ridgwell	147T,160B
FS J Orr	78TL,82T	Flt Lt N Young	157T
MALM MJ Clabby	69R,83TL	M Eng A Kitson	44
Flt Lt H Roberts	66R,151R	Mr J Kent (MET) Farnborough	45
Flt Lt J Rowlands	1R,64,120	Sgt A Chestnut	56T
Sqn Ldr H Burgoyne	58,173	Ex-M Eng B Gardener	123
MALM B Desmond	43B,152B	Flt Lt P Keeble	126R
Wg Cdr C Le Bas	57L,62T	24 Sqn	115
Sgt M Lee	70, 76TL	30 Sqn	53R,86,117,118,127
Cpl P Rowlands	111L	47 Sqn	32TR,57R,68,84TR,91B,122
M Eng J Crossland	76BR	70 Sqn	11L,126L
Flt Lt M White	155B	47 AD Sqn RLC	129
SAC A Hobson	143	29 Regt RLC	146T
Sqn Ldr P Oborn	78R	80 PC	113
Sgt Elmo	83BR	The rest by the author	
Flt Lt T Smith	83TR		

A further thanks to: Paul, Georgette, Vanessa, Karen of RAF Lyneham (Photographic Section) and Glen, Steve and Tony of RAF Chivenor (Photographic Section)

Ray Chaplin (Ex ALM)
Cpl "Ronnie" Corbett
MALM Roy Caddick
Sgt Max Chapman
Flt Lt Dave Cox
MALM Pete Colven
Flt Lt Mark Chattaway
Flt Lt Danny Coulson
Sgt Andy(Hazel) Chestnut
Cpl "Scoops" Cooper
JT Dave Cox
Sgt Mick Clark
Ian Catchpole
MALM M J Clabby
Simon Cox
Simon Coy
Pat and Chas
Cpl Tiny Draper
Eddie Drayton (Ex Gnd Eng)
Cpl Paul Douse
Cpl Shuggie Dickson
Cpl Ian Dewar
Mark Drewett
Cpl Karen Driver
Rick Downing
Andy Dewitt
Cpl Del Davey
Cpl Clive Duffield
SAC Mark Doodsun
Mick Daykin
Aaron Dneman
D J Dyer
Graham Durose
Cpl Archie Deacon
Mr & Mrs B J Dolby
SAC Paul Dersley
Cpl D Daile
Mr & Mrs R T Dickenson
Cpl Anthony Davies
Cpl Peter Deakin
J/T "Danny" Daniel
Andrew "Taff" Davies
Rick Dangerous

MEng Dave Dodd
Sgt C A Drew
Flt Lt John Duffin
Flt Lt D Dixon
Steve Drurey
Roger Dickinson
Mr B D Davies
Sqn Ldr A M J Davy
Flt Lt Martin Davis
Cpl Anthony Davies
Cpl Peter Deakin
JT "Danny" Daniel
JT Tyrone Driscoll
Cpl Glenn Dunwell
Cpl John Darling
MALM Bert Desmond
Flt Lt John Duffin
Sgt Miles Davey
FS Pete Durkin
Flt Lt Keith Daulby
SAC Mark Davies
D C Dearne
Biffa Davison
John Davison
SAC Matt Davies
SAC "Squeaky" Elston
Eddy
Sheila Edwards
Pete Escott
Cpl Mark Edwards
SAC "Richie" Elliott
Cpl Mike Edwards
Ian Ellison
Aaron Eastmond
Shads Edwards
Mr & Mrs Ellis
Mrs W Evans
Miss V A Ellis
Tony Eley
Mr D W Elmore
SAC Tails Evans
F/Sgt M T Ellwood
C/T Dave Everly

Cpl Gareth Edwards
Cpl Steve Evans
Fg Off Everett
Flt Lt Howard EDE
MEng L Evans
Russ Evans
Debbie Evans
Sgt Martin Edwards
Wg. Car Colin Eames
Mick Fry OTB
Graham Fitzgerald
Murrie Franks
Richard Franklin
Cpl Pat Foster
SAC Paul A Felton
Cpl Mick Foster
Simon Footer
P L Foster
Colin Field
Cpl P J Fraser
Cpl Keith Fairbairn
Frankie
Paul Fearn
SAC Flaherty
SAC Charlie Foulds
Cpl Jeff Files
P I Foster
Cpl Neil Fouch
SACW Jo Featherstone
MEng Fergi Ferguson
Ian Ferguson
SAC Steve Flack
Cpl Fuzzy Fursdon
Mr I C Gowers
Chris Gregory
Brian Gardener (ExMEng)
Gus Gooch
N C Greenwood
Griff Griffiths
Flt Lt Andy Gannon
SAC Paul Grainee
Simon Gill
Dougals Geater

G's Gardiner
Chris Godfrey
Lee Grist
Steve Graham
SAC "Bungle" Gates
SAC Julian Godden
Gazza
Gordon Gerrard
SAC Steven Goodenough
Cpl Martin Glenn
JT Stu Gilpin
Sgt Steve Gazzard
SAC Stuart Grange
SAC Mark Greges
Cpl Simon Golby
SAC Mark Trotters
Granados
Cpl Andy Glover
CT Davey Gingell
Cpl Chaz Gelder
SAC Iain Grigg
Nick Grace
Colin Goodwin
Mick & Sheree Gwilt
Pat Granger-Brown
SAC Goad
Mr K Greaves
SAC N Goy
Cpl Simon Golby
Cpl Andy Glover
Fg Off Mark Grigg
Sgt Tony Griffiths
MALM Graham Gudgin
MAC Glenton
"Gibbo"
FS Derek Gray
Flt Lt Alex Gibbon
Fg Off Mark Grigg
Sgt Paul Griffiths
JT M Grimstead
Peter F Griffiths
Simon Griffiths
SAC Mark Greggs

I. C Gowers
Geoff Hallett (Ex FS)
Simon James Hurford
JR Hartley
Sgt John Haslope
Peter John Holmes
Bruan Harry
SAC Lynn Hagland
SAC "PV" Hewitt
SAC Steve Hughes
Pete Hoyle
Sgt Geoff Haines
Darren Hughes
SAC Zak Hussain
G Homer
Jim Hunter
Matt Helm
Herbie Habberfield
Graham Hunter
Sgt Jamie Honeyset
SAC Reg Hollis
SACW Kylie Hesketh
SAC Dave Homer
Harry Howick
Mick Hart
Mike Hurst
Sgt Rob Hick
Rob Harris
Darren Hunt
Karen Holness
Jason Hazelden
Jeff Hill
Dick Hart
G Harmer
Graham Hallett
Cpl Brian Howard
Cpl Phill Henstridge
Mr M Headley (ExRAF)
JT Hanniball Hanson
Sgt Ginee Hodgkins
CT Keith Hutchins
Cpl Jiz Hampson
Sgt Guy Hilton

JT Trev Hammond
Cpl John Haddow
Cpl Ian Harwood
Duncan Hollamby
CT Ken Hodgson
SAC Dave Hartsmorne
SAC Jase Hazell
Mark Hartley
Tim Hebborn
JT S J Holden
Mr & Mrs Hill
Sgt "Trunky" Hunn
SAC J J Hatton
SAC Jim Holt
Sqn Ldr Alex Hurley
Paul Harris
Flt Lt Andy Hoaen
SAC Bingo Hawkard
MEng Mark Hamill
SAC Jez Holland
Carl Howcroft
Flt Lt Henry Howard
Flt Lt Jenny Hymans
FS Chris Hall
Arthur Huskie
Flt Lt Phil Hawkins
Flt Lt S I Harbron
Fg Off P C Haynes
Mr J Houghton
SAC James Hunter
Cpl Paul Haywood
Cpl Simes Handley
Billy Hill
Gerry Hudson
(Squipper)
Flt Lt Al Hill
FS Ian Hamilton
Cpl Brendan Hall
Sgt Mark Handley
JT Tim Harvey
Cpl Keith Hughes
Cpl Kev Hardy
Sgt Hunn (Trunky)

Cpl Ian Harwood
CT Ken Hodgson
SAC Dave Hartshorne
SAC Jase Hazell
Torsten Hossle
Babs Harris
Scott Innes
Joe Ion
Cpl Steve Ireland
FS Keith Irving
Sqn Ldr R P Illett
Issy
Merv Johns (Ex Gnd Eng)
JJ (MT)
Steve Joy
Andy Jones
SAC Chris Jones
Dom July
Cpl Lee Jakeman
Trev Jones
SAC "Buzz" Jordan
Nick Johnson
Jevo
Kris "Crash Dummy"
Johnson
Arnold Jones
S P Jones
Vic James
SAC's Janet & Andy Jones
SAC Pete Jones
JT Tony Jones
SACW "Larry" Jackson
Phil Jones
SAC (BJ) Jordan
Mr & Mrs D Jefferson
Mr & Mrs B Jenings
WO Mel Jordan
Casey Jones
Cpl Chris Jones
Cpl Adrian Jones
SAC Brian Johnston
Jake Jacobs
Kevin & Michelle Jones

SP Jones
C/T Hugh Jupp
Sgt M W Jones
Steve Jones
FS Pete Jones
Flt Lt Simon Johnson
Flt Lt Jillett
Phil Jones
SAC B J Jordan
Jacko Jackson
FS Doug Johnson
FS Bob Jones
MALM Howard O Jones
Sgt K W C Jaggard (Ret'd)
Ian Johnson
Craig Jenkins
Sgt Taff Kelly
Cpl Gary Kendall
SACW Sonya Kewley
Mike Knight
Mike Kay
Cpl Dave Kinloch
Brian Kewley
Sgt Rog Kemp
CT Al Kay
JT Paul Kennedy
Keightley Viv & Joanne
Pete Knight
SAC Rod Kemsley
Graham & Debbie Knotts
SAC S G Kelly
Flt Lt Chris Kemp (RAF Retd)
Flt Lt Peter Keeble
Flt Lt Bob Kevan
Sgt Gordon King
SAC Bob Kilgour
Flt Lt B Kennish
Flt Lt Arthur Kingdom
Flt Lt B Kennish
SAC Mark Kift
Cpl S J Kirby
SAC Dean Kilgour
Gp Capt King

CT Mike Libby
Sgt (W) Sue Landsdell
CT Lewin
Tony Loveridge
Kev Leeks
Cpl Mark Lishman
Sgt Kev Laing
Dave Lewis (Coachpool)
Cpl "Gripper" Lever
Cpl Dave Littlewood
Martin "Shadow" Lacey
Stefon Leonard
FS Looen (Loo)
Sgt Ed Lockley
MWB Logan
Mr & Mrs Lee
Mark Lee
Mr & Mrs T Luff
Di Llewellyn
Mr & Mrs A Locke
SAC T Loweth
Miss J S Lamb
SAC Dave Lound
Cpl Dave Lawson
Cpl Andy Loasby
Ray Lloyd
Cpl Dain Lewis
Sgt Bob Leggett
Cpl Andy Leishman
Sgt Percy Lucas
Chris Lewis
SAC Steve LLoyd Brennan
Wg Cdr Chris Le Bas
FS Dave Lennie
Fg Off Andy Luggar
Sgt Steve Lane
Ray Lloyd
Dave Lewis
Marcus Lee
Sqn Ldr Lecount E W
Cpl Dain Lewis
Steve Lydon
Doc Livingston

MEng Thomas Lee
Sgt Tim Lambert
Sacto Lyndon
Fg Off Paul Lloyd
Dave Lawrence
John Lawrence
Lockley
Ian Leckenby
J/T Rick Lock
Mike Lowes
Cpl Dave Lawson
Cpl Andy Loasby
Mr Don McNab
Phil 'Soapy' Marles
Cpl G J Murray
Loraine Marasinska
SAC Neil McKenzie
Paul Mitchell
Steve Macia
Cpl John Magill
Bob Mathieson
Dave Morgan
Gerry Mooney
Steve Morse
Sqn Ldr Paul Melling
Graham Miles
Sparky Mills
Flt Lt Geoff Maple
Duncan Metcalfe
Nige Malyon
SAC P R Marles
Mrs Carole Moore
Sgt Matt Marmoy
Sgt Steve Moore
Moggy Morgan
Dean Mayfield
Jason Marsden
S H Marsh
H J Mills
Wayne McAvoy
Mary Merchant
SAC Daryl Mayhew
Cpl M J Marsh

Richard Morris
Mr & Mrs Moore
Julie Maxwell
SACW Louise Morris
SAC Mac
SAC J K Miller
Mrs S Muggleton
Mr & Mrs Moody
Mrs L McKay
Mr D K Morgan MBE
Paul McDermott
Chf Tech Eric MacArthur
Sgt Martin Matthews
Cpl Ian McKay
Chf Tech Dave McGurk
Sgt Paul Matthews
M J Magee
Cpl Steve McCourt
Flt Lt Andy Miller
Flt Lt Graham Macaulay
Axel McDonald
Dex Mann
Steve Miles
FS Graham Morgan
Flt Lt John Maynard
Flt Lt Richard Mavor
Steve Masters
Sqn Ldr Malcolm Maultby
Flt Lt Tony Mortimer
George Muir
Martin Matthews
Flt Lt Paul McEwan
Gordon Morris
Sgt Carl Melen
Wg Cdr A Morris
Sgt Andy MacKay
Flt Lt Russell Muir
Sgt Bob Mason
Flt Lt Guy McCann- Moon
Flt Lt Colin McLea
MALM Mike Magee
MALM Bob Mahoney
Dalene McLaren

Cpl Gary Mills
Dave Merrison
SAC Phil Moulson
Chf Tech Pete Mitchell
Jnr Tech Spud Murphy
SAC Nige Milham
Sgt Ray Morgan
SAC Toby Masters
Tony Murray
Lynda Murray
Chf Tech Peter McGunigle
Chf Tech Steve Mills
Cpl George McNee
SAC Paul Mathias
KC Miller (DFS)
Cpl Barrie Norman
R A Nicholson
S Naxlor
Darren Neal
Dickie Nurse
Cpl Arthur Negus
P R Nightingale
Anna & Donald Nicholson
Paul Nolan
SAC Jim Northfield
Mick Nock
Dave Nicholls
SAC 'Rhino' Neal
Jnr Tech K W Neale
Gordon Nicoll
SAC Colin Nicolson
Bob Northover
Nick Nicholls
FS Osborn
Andy O'Sullivan
FS Jane O'Donoghue
Dave Overhill
Cpl 'Mad' Phil Ovenden
Tracy Osborough
Shaun O'Rourke (Ex RAF)
Jon O'Rourke
Pete Offin
Cpl Ian Orr

SAC 'Tintin' Old
Cpl Wookie Oxford
Paul Oborn
FS John Orr
SAC Steve Oxford
Fg Off M Oxford (Ex 24)
Trevor Pogue (30 & 70 Sqn)
Sgt J Patel
Pickels
Ian Pritchard
SACW Helen Pocock
MC Phillips
N Park
SAC Nath Prior
Mich Powell
SAC Al Pratt
Flt Lt Bob Plant
Cpl Viv Neary-Phillips
Cpl Mal Paton
Sgt John Pert
Fg Off Richard Prime
FS Polly Parkin
Plums
Fred Pidgeon
SAC (Snebber) Prentice
Sgt Andy Pickard
Jnr Tech Kev Pattenden
SAC 'Si' Parker
Harry Palmer
Cpl Pollard
D L Pollard
Ray Prince
Nige Pryor
A S Perry
G Priest
Cpl Andy Peacock
FS Al Ponting
SAC Sean Perkins
SAC Ross Priday
Fg Off D E Payne
Sgt S B Pardoe
Jerry Parnell
SAC Jim Potter

Mr Rej Peter (Ex RAF)
Cpl Paul Peacock
SACW Jo Parker
Mr & Mrs T J Parker
Jnr Tech Percy Percival
Jonpot
Cpl Noel Phillips
SAC O Peltier
Mr & Mrs D Parnall
SAC B A Parkinson
Jerry Parnell
Cpl Chris Perry
Judge Pickles
Dean Pringuer
Flt Lt Rich Parice
MALM Dave Porter
SAC B A Parkinson
Cpl Polly Parrott
SAC Trev Power
Ian Parker
SAC Rob Parnell
Chf Tech 'Mac' Pile
Tony Packman
Sgt Den Pritchard
Cpl 'Sid'Pinwill
Roger Payne
Philpot
F. S. Gary Plaistow
JT (W) Clare Phillips
Angie Powel
Phil Prat
Sqn Ldr Piper (HGTS)
Veenod Peerthy
Sgt. T. Patel
CT Ron Plant
Flt Lt Ted Querzani
Flt Lt Lynn Rogers (24 Sqn)
Cpl Ian Robinson
Sqn Ldr Tom Rounds
Flt Lt Huw Roberts (RAF Retd)
Rob Rogerson
Jim Rodger
Cpl Ian Rowlands

Cpl J W Riddell
Sgt C A Robinson
Cpl Bobbie Roberts
FS Ray Ralph
Dave Ronald
Garry Rees
Irene Richens
Dave Rees (Coach Pool)
Sgt Dave Rees
Cpl M K Reid
Mick Ranson
Rim Roberts
Robby
C V Rice
Yvonne Rowe
WO Alex Rennie
Cpl Steve Reynolds
Cpl Andy Read
Flt Lt Riddell AES
Mr & Mrs T S Ross
Dave Roach
Mr & Mrs D Rowlands
Ginger Rees
Cpl & SACW S Rodgers
Mr A G Russell
SAC Carl Robinson
SAC 'Griff' Ritchie
Jnr Tech Nich Rowell
Cpl Derek Robb
Flt Lt Rowsell
J W Ranscombe
Sgt Mike Rodwell
Sgt Tiny Russell
Sgt Doc Rippin
Sgt Dave Russell
WO D G Rossant BEM
Flt Lt Andy Roberts
John Rowland
Sgt Dave Reese
Sqn Ldr Steve Rixson
Fg Off Darryn Rawlins
Flt Lt Terry Randells
Ros Robinson

Jnr Tech Nich Rowell
SAC Karl Robinson
Sgt Oz Reardon
Flt Lt Laurie Ramage
Flt Lt B A Robertson
Reidy (SE Fitt)
Sqn Ldr Bill Ragg
John Risdale
Gordon Rowley
Andy Reynolds
Graham Ramsay
Ken Reid
Grd Eng Chris Stratford
Mr J C Skelton
SAC Stoodley
Cpl Stanbury
FS Speedy Soane
Sukjit Singh (Suki) Ex RAF
Andrea Stansfield
Eddy Scott
Fg Off Andy State
FS Keith Smith
Jon Smith
John Shearing
SAC Stephen Smith
SAC Stu Slee
Cpl A L Stacey
Spanners
Bernard Shaw
AL Smith
Diana Sloper
Paul Stainer
Ray Sturgess
SAC 'Ted'Steadman
Cpl "Stan" Stanyard
SAC Rob Sterland
Martin Stratford
Stano
Mal Smith
Kev Straker
Steve Stevens-Wade
Ken Stroud
Dave Seymour

Keith Simkiss
C G Starr
D R Sage
D A Shortland
M A Shearn
Cpl Tony Seager
Sid Skull
FS David Stoddart
E J Single
Sgt "Elmo" Simpson
Cpl K Smifff
Cpl Ian Savage
SAC Benny Smith
Brian Shingler
Warwick Spencer
Rick Sorrill
Mark Snelson
Chris Smith
CT Tony Stalker
SAC Jez Stevens
SAC "Mr Singe"
Speedy
John Sillivan
Pete Sensecall
Mr & Mrs Sharp
Mr & Mrs Sobey
Martyn Sobey
Mr & Mrs Smith
Mr & Mrs G Smith
Mr & Mrs P Seymor
Mr & Mrs R Smallridge
Bob & Carroll Stanley
Cpl M A Salmon
SACW Sarah Scott
SAC D J Sheppard
Cpl Andy Smart
C G Stark
D R Sage
D A Shortland
M A Shearn
Sgt John Schofield
CT Bob Savage
Fg Off A J Sutherland

Brian Shingler
Rick Sorrill
Mark Nelson
Chris Smith
FS Pam Skelton
Sgt Lisa Stainton
Flt Lt Craig Strickland
Flt Lt Phil Spink
Flt Lt Nick Stein
Sgt Dave Sharp
Brian Spurway
Cpl R J Setchfield
Tiny Spires
Flt Lt Bob Stamp
Flt Lt Doug Scott
Flt Lt Mike Steer
Flt Lt R E Snowdon
SAC M R Singe
SAC Tim Scoble
Mr M J Scoble
Jim Spowart
Vikki Shields
Sgt Ken Sabir
CT Pete Stockman
Cpl G Schelshorn
Flt Lt Dave Saunders
Sgt Rog Shaw
SAC "MANG" Smith
Rachel Sedgwick
Sgt Flo Shouls
Sgt Neil Simpson
Fg Off Richie Skene
Sgt Chris Smith
MALM John Seaton
Sgt Bob Shilling
Doug Stone
Cpl Paul Storer
Cpl Ian Savage
SAC Benny Smith
SAC Craig Sewell
DP Smith (DFS)
Strooky
John Sutton

J. C. Skelton
SAC Dave Thurlon
Rev (Flt Lt) Jan Taylor
SAC Matt Thompson
Marty Thorp
Eric Tetlod
Cpl Bruce Townsend
Tucker Thompson
SAC Joes Tatley
Robert Truelove (Coachpool)
Stuart A Turner
SAC Paul Tomlinson
Mike Taylor
SAC P umman
Cpl Steve Thomas
Cpl "Tommo" Thompson
Flt Lt Jamie Telfer
Flt Lt Thompson
JT Mick Talbot
Fg Off Jerry Tyzack
Flt Lt Donald Turnbull
Kev Tame
JT Martin Treen
SAC Simon C Todd
SAC Simon Taylor
Tom Thomas
Andy Torrance
CPL P.C. Tippett
Cpl Upton
MALM Satn Unwin
Stu Vince
Spencer Ian Newby
Voss
MEng Gary Vince
Flt Lt Andy
Valentine
Fg Off Tim Vaughan
Cpl Chris Vaughan
Geoff "Oily" Ward
Dave "Woody" Wood
Sgt M R Williams
SAC Walker
Cpl Eddie Wren

Alex "Wurzel" Williams
Mrs Sheena West
Norman Whitworth
Paul Woodman
Cpl Dava Winberg
Cpl Pete Webber
SAC Geoff Williams
Ian Wilkinson
Richie Watkins
Ed WaySgt Dale Walker
Elwyn (Chalkey) White
Ray Wallace
SACW M E Williams RAuxAF
N K Watts
Mark Watts
FS Dave Williams
Wg Cdr Bill Baird
Sgt Danis Wilson
Phil Wright
SAC Dominic Wilson
SAC Phill Williams
Wg Cdr T L Woods
Nigel Whitaker
Simon Williams
Sgt Ken Wymer
Mark White
Bill Worthington
Rick Walker
Terry Wilkinson
Keith Walker
Sgt Steve Withan
Cpl Dan Walmsley
Sgt Dave Williams
SAC Sion Wride
Sharn Wood
Mr & Mrs Wiggins
Cpl & SACW S P Wicks
Cpl M A Ware
SAC & SACW D Williams
Mr & Mrs D Williams
FS Rog Winter
SAC Pete Williams
Sgt Graham Wakeling

Simon Ward
Cpl Mick Wheeler
SAC Paul Wooley
Cpl "Woody" Woodbridge
Cpl Mark Webster
Flt Lt D Warby
CT Mick Wilkinson
MALM Dave Whiting
Simon Ward
Ian White
Sgt R J Weston
Flt Lt John Wood
Sgt Stu Wright
Flt Lt Catherine Wooll
Sgt L J Weston
Flt Lt Mark Walton
Flt Lt Martin Woolley
Sqn Ldr W J H Wickson MBE (Ret'd)
SAC Paul Woolley
Cpl "Woody" Woodbridge
Flt Lt Martin Woolley
Sgt Jim Whitworth
Sgt Paul Wise
Flt Lt Sam Wright (RAF Ret'd)
Fg Off Duncan Wright
Cpl Neil Watson
Sgt Richie Williams
Gary Whinfrey
Ian Wickson
Harry Wright
SAC Pete Williams
Sgt Graham Wakeling
Cel. Dee Walters
Austin Waterworth
Sgt. M. E. Williams
Bones and Beverley Wilkinson
Geordie Young
Colin York
Sid "Picard" Young
Gaye Young
Flt Lt Nick Young

The largest radio control Hercules model was built by the Model Hercules group (*below*) from Warrington.

Paul Fetherstone
Clive Goodier
Phil Holt
Andrew Johnson
Dave Johnson
John Mepham
Dave Phillipson
Jack Wilkinson

LAST OF THE MANY...:

Steve Armson
Barrie Anderson
Colin Amphlett
D S Brace
D M Brown
Kyle Barclay
Jim Crow
Tony Cross
Brian Clayton
John A Colyer
Flt Lt Etches
Barry Fitz-John
Alex Grun
Roy Gibbs
Ade Holmes
Fred Heath
Graham Lavers
C J Mills

Thomas McKay
D H Nicholas
Mark Noble
Chrys Petruse
Arthur Pound
Len Stairs
Bob Smith
Ron Turner
Mike Underdown
Robin Whitington
Sqn Ldr Mike Morison
Richard C Bailey

SUBSCRIBERS
47 AD SQN RLC

Maj Carlisle
Sgt Dave Attwood
Jon Atherton
Day Andrews
Taff 'Ako' Aktins
L/Cpl Paul Burgess
Brad
Jack Barnett
Herbi Boultin
Buey Buchanan
Butch Buchicchio
John Burton
Bob Crowther
Ginge Colligan
Al Cone
Cpl Nobby Clarke
Pte Jamie Douglas
Daygo
Taff Digger
Craig Donald
Tim Dowson
Keith Dowty
L/Cpl Ian Ellis
Tim Edwards
Jock Ewen
Cpl Si Fox
L/Cpl Dougie Ford
Pte Taff Frazier

Pte Taff Fry
Franky Fryer
Flowers
Chris Fielder
Andy Fletch
Cpl Jim Glass "TW"
L/Cpl Scott Goode
Dickie Gittins
Pte Taff Head
Cpl 'Melon' Hook
Billy Hughes
Bob Hayward
George Hilliar
Martin Holdstock
Bob Hoskin
Si Ireland
L/Cpl Phil Jones
L/Cpl 'Geordie' Johnstone Jnr
Dave Jelly
J Ned Kelly
Cpl 'Taff' Lock
Jock Livingstone
Eddi Lawson
WO2 B Lawson (MAD)
Dave Laurence
Kev Lockley
Barney Lane
Pte Andy Murray
Dave Miles
Cpl Dave McEntee
L/Cpl 'Megs' Megilley
Chris McMillan
Geordie Murph
Cpl Stan Norcross
Anni Oatley
L/Cpl Craig
Patterson
Capt Shindi Poonia
Paul
L/Cpl Mat Rush
Dario Rondelli
Rocky Rockall
Steve Ritson

Eddi Scobi
Sqt. Somerford
Massive Steve
Jock Turley
Graham Tolson
A Townsend (Andy T)
Cpl Henry Wilkes
Pte 'Westy' Westlake
Martin Whitbread
Woody
Phil Williams

29 Regt RLC
Lt Col R G C Campbell RLC
WO1 (SSM) R Bonnair RLC
SSgt C A Fisher
Capt S D Glynn RLC
WO2 (RQMS) D J Griffin
WO2 (SQMS) T G James AGC
WO1 (RSM) V E Maham BEM RLC
Maj I S Ormerod RLC
WO1 D J Pearce RLC
WO 2 M Sennett
Maj M W Titus CAF

50 MC Sqn RLC
Lt N C Allison RLC
Capt B C Anderson RLC
Lt S J Sailor RLC
Maj T E D Seales RLC

PAST AD SQN MEMBERSƒƒD
C Arkless (Ex 55 AD)
R L (Bob) Austin (EX Sgt 47 AD)
R L Bland (55 Coy (AD) RASC)
Major A K J Batty MBE (Ex 47 AD Coy RASC)
Mick Broad (Ex 47 AD)
R Dobry (Ext 47 AD)
R E Furness (Ex L/Cpl 47 AD)
D A Kilgour (Ex 47 AD)
Ken Law (Ex 47, 55, 52 AD)
Rod Matthews (Ex 47 AD JATE)
Capt W J Campbell